WHAT WERE SOME OF THE OCCUPATIONS OF AMERICAN JEWS DURING THE COLONIAL PERIOD?

WHAT WAS SO FUNNY ABOUT THE MARX BROTHERS?

WHEN WERE AMERICAN JEWS IMPORTANT IN THE SPORT OF BOXING?

HOW DID THE DAUGHTERS OF JEWISH IMMIGRANTS ADVANCE IN THE WORKING WORLD?

WHAT JEWISH-AMERICAN WOMAN BECAME PRIME MINISTER OF ISRAEL?

ARE DEPARTMENT STORES JEWISH?

The answers to these and other questions can be found in this intriguing, immensely readable book on Jewish life in America. From the establishment of temples to the creating of department stores, and from Harry Houdini to Steven Spielberg, *Everything You Need to Know About America's Jews and Their History* expands our knowledge of the Jewish-American experience even as it engages and entertains us.

EVERYTHING YOU NEED TO KNOW ABOUT AMERICA'S JEWS AND THEIR HISTORY

ROY A. ROSENBERG served for more than twenty years as rabbi of the Temple of Universal Judaism in New York City. A regular contributor to academic and popular periodicals, he is the author of four previous books, including *The Concise Guide to Judaism* (Meridian). He lives in Brooklyn, New York.

EVERYTHING YOU NEED TO KNOW ABOUT AMERICA'S JEWS AND THEIR HISTORY

Roy A. Rosenberg

A PLUME BOOK

PLUME
Published by the Penguin Group
Penguin Putnam Inc., 375 Hudson Street, New York, New York 10014, U.S.A.
Penguin Books Ltd, 27 Wrights Lane, London W8 5TZ, England
Penguin Books Australia Ltd, Ringwood, Victoria, Australia
Penguin Books Canada Ltd, 10 Alcorn Avenue, Toronto, Ontario, Canada M4V 3B2
Penguin Books (N.Z.) Ltd, 182–190 Wairau Road, Auckland 10, New Zealand

Penguin Books Ltd, Registered Offices:
Harmondsworth, Middlesex, England

First published by Plume, an imprint of Dutton Signet, a
member of Penguin Putnam Inc.

First Printing, October, 1997
1 3 5 7 9 10 8 6 4 2

Copyright © Roy Rosenberg, 1997
All rights reserved

LIBRARY OF CONGRESS CATALOGING IN PUBLICATION DATA: IS AVAILABLE

ISBN: 0-452-27628-4

Printed in the United States of America
Set in New Baskerville

Designed by Steven N. Stathakis

BOOKS ARE AVAILABLE AT QUANTITY DISCOUNTS WHEN USED TO PROMOTE PRODUCTS
OR SERVICES. FOR INFORMATION PLEASE WRITE TO PREMIUM MARKETING DIVISION,
PENGUIN PUTNAM INC., 375 HUDSON STREET, NEW YORK, NEW YORK 10014.

For my grandchildren

Daniel Aron Pollack
August David Rosenberg
Jason Gabriel Pollack

and others who may yet be born
to enrich this blessed land

Thanks to Deb Brody, editor,
and Faith Hamlin, literary agent,
for their help in accomplishing the
publication of this addition to
"everything you need to know"

Contents

Introduction   1

1. From the First Settlement to the Civil War   7

2. From the Civil War to the Second World War   43

3. From the Second World War to the Present   177

4. Some Aspects of Jewish-American Life   212

Sources   247

Index   251

Introduction

"Are the Jews a race or a religion?," or perhaps, "Are the Jews a nationality or a religion?" This is a question that has often been asked by both Jews and others over the course of the past two centuries, if not earlier. Of course, the Jews are not a "race," as that word is understood by anthropologists. And Jews are not a "nationality," when that word is used to imply, as it very often does, citizenship in a particular nation-state. But if the question is worded more accurately, to ask "Are Jews an ethnic community or a religion?," it becomes a very worthy question indeed. In today's world it is a question that need not be asked about very many groups other than the Jews. (The Sikhs, who stem from India and Pakistan, are another group about whom this question might be raised.) In the ancient Near East, however, from whence the Jews originally came, this question did not need to be asked, for each ethnic community, like the Jews, worshiped its own deity (or deities).

It is only the Jews, out of all the ethnicities that made up the ancient Near East, that have preserved their primeval attachment to their God and have not merged into the transethnic religions, Christianity and Islam, that arose in that part of the world, even though these religions worship the same God as the Jews. The Jews, therefore, remain an ethnic community with their own distinct religion, just as they were in ancient times. The other ethnicities of ancient days, such as the Egyptians, severed their tie to a distinctive ethnic religion when they became either Christian (the Copts) or Muslim (the great mass of Egyptians).

The Jews, as is well known, retained their distinctive religion even while spreading across most of the world. While part of the Jewish diaspora during the first and second centuries A.D. is attributable to forcible expulsions by the Romans from the Judean homeland, a large Jewish community had remained in Babylonia and Persia from about 600 B.C. Jews flocked to the great Hellenistic centers, such as Alexandria in Egypt and Antioch in Syria, as soon as they were developed by the Ptolemaic and Seleucid rulers, the successors to Alexander the Great. Over the centuries Jews settled in large numbers in Asia Minor, in Spain, Italy, the Rhineland, North Africa, Yemen, France, the German principalities, and Eastern Europe. (Jews early on had settled in England, but the community was expelled in 1290; no Jew was legally entitled to reside in England until the 1660s.) While it is wrong to think of the Jews in these regions as suffering unrelenting torment and persecution, they were deprived of many of the minimal civil and human rights enjoyed by others in the population (Christians in Europe and Ethiopia, Muslims in North Africa and Asia). They were often subject to arbitrary taxation, confinement to certain areas of residence, and, on occasion, murder, pillage, and expulsion.

The Jewries of these various lands were looked upon by both Jews and non-Jews as distinct ethnic communities, separate from the majority populations in whose midst they dwelled not only in terms of religious faith but in other ways as well. Some of these Jewish communities spoke and wrote their own distinctive languages. The Jews of Muslim Spain spoke Arabic, like their neighbors, but they wrote it using Hebrew alphabetic characters rather than Arabic cursive script. When Christian forces reconquered Spain, the Jews adopted the Spanish language, but intermixed therein were many Hebrew words. This language, which came to be known as Ladino, was also written in Hebrew alphabetic characters. The Jews of Germany spoke their own German dialect, preserving many Hebrew words, the whole written in Hebrew characters.

The Jews of Eastern Europe, most of whom stemmed from immigrants from Germany, brought this language with them. It is known as Yiddish ("Jewish") and boasts a rich literature. It is still preserved by many Jews of East European ancestry who settled in North and South America (and even in Israel, where the official language is the classic Jewish tongue, Hebrew). The Jews who lived in Christian countries differed from the majority populations in their daily diet, primarily because of the laws of *kashrut* ("fitness") found in the Hebrew Scriptures and later rabbinic regulations. Jews had their own educational system, and a system of self-government in the lands in which they lived. They were ordinarily subject to rabbinic law within their own communities, and had no recourse to the judicial system of the majority population unless someone from the majority population was involved in the point at issue. This way of life seems foreign to contemporary Americans, but it was the accepted way of life for both Jews and non-Jews over many centuries.

In the realm of religion, the only form of Judaism that existed until about two hundred years ago was what we today call "Orthodox." Within the religiocultural fellowship two major streams were recognized: that of Sepharad, the Jews of Spain and Portugal who later spread throughout the Mediterranean world, and that of Ashkenaz, the Jews of Northern Europe. These two groups differ in having slight variations in their pronunciation of Hebrew, in some of the forms of liturgical prayer and dietary regulations, and in some of the foods that might be eaten at celebrations of various holy days. Polygamy was prohibited among Ashkenazic Jews by rabbinical edict about 1000 A.D., but no such prohibition was ever imposed by religious authority upon Sephardic Jews. (It is, of course, forbidden by civil law in many countries in which Sephardic Jews live.) There is great mutual respect between the Sephardic and Ashkenazic religious authorities (that is, if they qualify as "Orthodox"). Since it is an accepted principle within Judaism that, whenever possible, one should preserve "the customs of our fathers," Sephardic Jews are expected to preserve their own ways of doing things, and Ashkenazic Jews are to do likewise.

One of the largest and most prosperous Jewish communities in the medieval world was that of Spain. Much of Spain was under Muslim hegemony from the seventh century until it was reconquered by Christian forces at the beginning of the thirteenth century. Soon thereafter the Jews of Spain were pushed, in various and sundry ways (including murderous riots), toward the acceptance of Christianity in place of their ancestral faith. Many Jews succumbed to this pressure and became *conversos* or "new Christians." This, however, only made matters worse for many of them. The lower classes of the Spanish population resented the rise to social and economic prominence of the "new Christians," such as marriage of people of Jewish ancestry into noble Spanish families, and bishops of the Church who had originally been Jews. The Holy Inquisition undertook to root out "Judaizing heresy" among the "new Christians," and utilized the cruelest of tortures to force people to confess that they had indeed performed acts that could be construed as Jewish religious rites, such as not eating pork, or lighting a candle on a Friday night. People brought accusations of this kind against neighbors whom they disliked, and the Inquisition took it all very seriously. While there no doubt were some "new Christians" who sought to preserve Jewish rites in their private lives, the majority had sought sincerely to accept their new faith. It was only after they encountered a lack of acceptance on the part of "old Christians" that many reverted to the Jewish beliefs and practices in which they had been raised. The Spanish rulers, in consultation with the Inquisition, resolved that only the expulsion of those Jews who had not accepted baptism could solve the problem of "Judaizing heresy" within the Church. These people were relatives of the "new Christians" and remained in contact with them; their influence was pernicious. The expulsion of the Jewish community in Spain took place in 1492, the same year that the last Spanish city still under Muslim rule fell to the Christians, and the year that Columbus discovered America.

The Sephardic diaspora brought an influx of Jews to North Africa, Italy, Holland, and Turkey (where the Sultan had specifically invited them to settle). The "new Christians," eager to escape the harassment of the Inquisition, also migrated in some number to these communities, where many of them threw off the cover of Christianity and reembraced the Judaism into which they had been born. From Holland, in particular, some of these émigrés, or their children, later journeyed to the Spanish and Portuguese settlements in the New World. The Inquisition, however, was soon established in these places. So it is no surprise that in 1654 twenty-three of these people sought admission to the Dutch colony of New Amsterdam in North America. From that date, the Jewish population of what became the United States of America has come to exceed 8 million.

The Sephardic Jews who came to America were followed in later years by a body of German Jews and, after them, by a massive emigration of Jews from Eastern Europe that was stemmed only by the 1924 legislation specifically designed to limit the number of immigrants from Southern and Eastern Europe. The words of Jacob R. Marcus, the dean and inspiration of all those who research America's Jews, apply with equal force to all three waves of Jewish immigration. "The American Jew has never been obscure. Ever since the days of Peter Stuyvesant his 'high visibility' has been palpable. He has always done business on Main Street. He shares with other groups a wide diversity of roles, as butcher, cattle-dealer, storekeeper, Indian trader, merchant, and shipper, and—in the present—policeman, taxicab driver, garment worker, industrialist, merchant prince, physicist, general, admiral, cabinet officer, Supreme Court justice, and labor leader."

Sources are listed at the back of the book. In addition to Marcus's books, special attention should be paid to the masterly works of Irving Howe (*World of Our Fathers*) and Howard Sachar (*A History of the Jews in America*).

ONE

From the First
Settlement to
the Civil War

*Who were the Jews who came to
New Amsterdam in 1654?*

*What New England city, now a relatively small
town, was a major site of Jewish-American
settlement in the eighteenth century?*

*Why was there no Jewish settlement to speak of in the
oldest and most populous British colony, Virginia?*

*In what Southern city did Jews settle in
significant numbers during the eighteenth and
early nineteenth centuries?*

Why, in 1733, did some fear that
"Georgia [would] soon become a Jewish colony"?

Who was the first Jew to serve in an
American legislative body?

How many synagogue congregations existed
in the British colonies at the beginning of
the American Revolution?

What were some of the occupations in which
Jews engaged during the Colonial period?

Did Jews trade slaves?

Is there any truth to the story that Haym Salomon
advanced $800,000 of his own money to the patriot
cause during the American Revolution, money that
was never repaid, so that, at his death, his young
widow and children were left penniless?

Did the United States Constitution guarantee full
religious equality to Jewish Americans?

Why did Judah Touro, the son of a rabbi, contribute
funds to Christian missionaries for the purpose of
spreading the gospel in Jerusalem?

Where, when, and why was a Jewish state supposed
to be established within the United States?

*What did Uriah Phillips Levy
do for the U.S. Navy?*

*What Jewish-American woman was the
inspiration for the character Rebecca in
Sir Walter Scott's novel Ivanhoe?*

*Why did a significant number of German
Jews immigrate to the United States during the
middle years of the nineteenth century?*

*What Jewish congressman was a spokesman for
the Native American party, advocating an end
to foreign immigration and the restriction of
citizenship to native-born Americans?*

*What American rabbi, while leading the morning
worship service for the Jewish New Year, was
without warning harshly struck by his congregation's
president and, after the ensuing riot, forced to
leave the congregation's employ?*

What was the life of an immigrant peddler like?

*Up to the Civil War, who was the great
organizer and disseminator of Jewish religious
wisdom to America's Jews?*

*What event inspired the founding of the Board of
Delegates of American Israelites in 1859?*

Who was, according to some of his contemporaries, "the greatest native-born American of Jewish origin" in the period prior to the Civil War?

Who were the Jews who came to New Amsterdam in 1654?

When the Portuguese captured the Brazilian city of Recife from the Dutch, most of the Jews who had resided there returned to Holland. Not all of them chose to do so, however. Some went to the islands of the West Indies, but one group of twenty-three showed up, in September 1654, in New Amsterdam on the Hudson. This shipload of refugees had been captured at sea by Spaniards who were in turn driven off by a French privateer. It was this French ship that brought them to New Amsterdam. Though **Peter Stuyvesant**, the governor, wished to send these Jews out of his colony, the directors of the West India Company in Amsterdam instructed him to allow them to remain. They wrote, "These people may travel and trade to and in New Netherland and live and remain there, provided the poor among them shall not become a burden to the company or to the community, but be supported by their own nation." In 1656 the directors reiterated their order to Stuyvesant that the Jews be allowed to trade and, what is more, they were to have the right to buy real estate. They were, however, not yet permitted to open retail stores, practice crafts, or conduct public religious services.

In 1657 **Asser Levy**, a butcher who was one of the 1654 settlers, petitioned the local court to be admitted into the ranks of the burghers of the city. A year and a half earlier Levy and **Jacob Barsimson** had wanted to keep "watch and ward" (periodic military service to protect the city), but they had been told that in lieu of this military service, they would have to pay a special tax. Neither of them could afford to pay the tax, but they were willing to serve. Though at first their request was refused, eventually it was granted. Levy, having served "watch and ward" for some time, thus came to the court to ask to be accepted as a burgher, based as well upon the fact that Jews in Holland were accepted as burghers. After some months of debate, Stuyvesant and the Council of New Netherland authorized the burgomasters of New Amsterdam to grant to the Jews living there the rights of burghership. Stuyvesant was inspired to lament to the directors in Holland that now, "by giving them liberty, we cannot refuse the Lutherans and Papists."

The British took over New Netherland in 1664, and New Amsterdam became New York. The rights granted by the Dutch to the Jews continued under the new regime. Before the end of the seventeenth century Jews were permitted to engage in both wholesale and retail trade and in crafts. By 1695 they openly rented quarters for use as a synagogue, and in 1730 they erected and dedicated a small building for the use of the congregation. The congregation bore the name—and still does to this day—Shearith Israel ("Remnant of Israel"). The first Jewish congregation organized in what was to become the United States of America, it now occupies a large, stately structure in New York City and is known not only as Shearith Israel but as the "Spanish-Portuguese Synagogue." Though today only a minority of its members are of Spanish-Portuguese descent, its services follow the Sephardic rite.

What New England city, now a relatively small town, was a major site of Jewish-American settlement in the eighteenth century?

Nowadays no one would be likely to list Newport, Rhode Island, as one of the great cities of the United States, but in the eighteenth century it was one of the great ports of the British colonies. Between 1739 and 1770 large fortunes were made in the "triangular trade" with Africa and the West Indies, wherein rum from Newport was exchanged for slaves in Africa, who were exchanged for sugar and molasses in the Indies, which were in turn brought back to Newport to be made into rum. By 1770 Newport's foreign trade was greater than that of New York. The city was occupied by British forces from 1776 to 1779, however, and after the success of the Revolution it never regained its previous mercantile prominence.

Newport, having been founded by **Roger Williams**, the apostle of broad religious toleration, attracted Jewish settlers from 1655 on. Its congregation, Yeshuat Israel ("Salvation of Israel"), was organized in 1658. A company of Portuguese Jewish merchants came to the city between 1740 and 1760, the most prominent of whom were **Jacob Rodriguez Rivera** and **Aaron Lopez**. Rodriguez Rivera introduced the manufacture of sperm oil, which soon became one of Newport's leading industries. Newport had seventeen factories producing sperm oil and candles at the outbreak of the Revolution. It dominated the distribution of this essential means of illumination throughout the British colonies. At the beginning of the Revolution, Lopez owned thirty ships engaged in transatlantic and Caribbean trade, and in whaling. At that time the Jewish population of Newport was about 1,175. The synagogue building, erected in 1763, is the oldest in the United States.

Practically all of Newport's Jewish citizens, strong supporters of the Revolution, moved to Massachusetts to escape the British occupation of their city. By the end of the war, New York had become the great commercial center. Newport's important merchants, seeing little continuing opportunity there, thus removed to New York or to Philadelphia, Charleston, and Savannah. Upon its return to Newport in 1780, the General Assembly of the State of Rhode Island held its first session after the war in the synagogue.

In 1790 the congregation sent a formal letter of congratulations to **George Washington** upon his assumption of the presidency of the United States. Washington's reply has been preserved; published many times over the years, it remains one of the salient and significant documents in the history of both the United States and its Jewish citizens. Here is the text of that letter:

While I receive, with much satisfaction, your Address replete with expressions of affection and esteem, I rejoice in the opportunity of assuring you, that I shall always retain a grateful remembrance of the cordial welcome I experienced in my visit to Newport, from all classes of Citizens.

The reflection on the days of difficulty and danger which are past is rendered the more sweet, from a consciousness that they are succeeded by days of uncommon prosperity and security. If we have wisdom to make the best use of the advantages with which we are now favored, we cannot fail, under the just administration of a good government, to become a great and a happy people.

The Citizens of the United States of America have a right to applaud themselves for having given to mankind examples of an enlarged and liberal policy: a policy worthy of imitation. All profess alike liberty of conscience and immunities of citizenship. It is now no more that toleration is spoken of, as if it was by the indulgence of one class of people, that another enjoyed the exercise of their inherent natural rights. For happily the Government of the United States, which gives to bigotry no sanction, to persecution no assistance requires only that they who live under its protection should demean themselves as good citizens, in giving it on all occasions their effectual support.

It would be inconsistent with the frankness of my character not to avow that I am pleased with your favorable opinion of my administration, and fervent wishes for my felicity. May the Children of the Stock of Abraham, who dwell in this land, continue to merit and enjoy the good will of the other Inhabitants; while every one shall sit in safety under his own vine and fig-tree, and there shall be none to make him afraid. May the father of all mercies scatter light and not darkness in our paths, and make us all in our several vocations useful here, and in his own due time and way everlastingly happy.

Why was there no Jewish settlement to speak of in the oldest and most populous British colony, Virginia?

Though there are records of Jews from other colonies who visited or did business in Virginia, no professing Jews seem to have settled there until the second half of the eighteenth century. The most likely reason is the entrenched position that the Church of England held there until after the Revolution and the adoption of Jefferson's Act for Establishing Religious Freedom in 1786. Prior to these events, anyone who refused to profess faith in Jesus as the son of God, or who refused to take the eucharistic sacrament in its Anglican form, was ineligible for citizenship. A law of 1705 excluded all non-Christians, as well as Negroes, Catholics, and convicts, from testifying as witnesses in court. Attendance at Anglican worship services was compulsory. Even Christian Dissenters were frequently persecuted and forbidden to speak or write about religious matters.

In June 1776, however, three weeks before the promulgation of the Declaration of Independence, the Virginia House of Burgesses adopted a Bill of Rights declaring "that all men are by nature equally free and independent, and have certain inherent rights. . . . Religion, or the duty which we owe to our Creator, and the manner of discharging it, can be directed only by reason and conviction, not by force or violence; and therefore all men are equally entitled to the free exercise of religion, according to the dictates of conscience; and that it is the mutual duty of all to practice Christian forbearance, love, and charity towards each other." Despite these noble sentiments, the legislative body passed no laws that would put these ideals into practice until Jefferson's statute was enacted ten years later. This required that "no man shall be compelled to frequent or support any religious worship, place, or ministry whatsoever, nor shall he be enforced, restrained, molested, or burthened in his body or goods, nor shall otherwise suffer on account of his religious opinions or belief; but that all men shall be free to profess and by argument to maintain their opinion in matters of religion, and that the same shall in no wise diminish, enlarge, or affect their civil capacities." In 1789 Richmond's first synagogue, Beth Shalom ("House of Peace") was organized.

In what Southern city did Jews settle in significant numbers during the eighteenth and early nineteenth centuries?

Charleston, South Carolina, was the fourth-largest city in the British colonies, the largest south of Philadelphia. It had a good port, and it was a mercantile and commercial center close to the islands of the West Indies. Many Jews who wished to settle in the colonies came to Charleston for these reasons, particularly since many of them had family or business ties to people in the Indies. In 1816 Charleston had over six hundred Jews in its population, a community larger even than New York's. Commodities bought and sold by the Jewish merchants and shippers based in Charleston included rum, corn, flour, hardtack, butter, beeswax, rice, indigo, deerskins, tanned leather, beer, cider, and slaves.

Moses Lindo came to South Carolina in 1756, convinced that the cultivation and manufacture of indigo, a blue dye derived from plants of the genus *Indigofera*, could become a major source of industry and prosperity in the colony. Within six years he was appointed surveyor and inspector general of indigo, a position that enabled him to enforce high standards of quality for the dye. In 1769 Lindo met an emissary from Rhode Island College, later called Brown University, who had come to Charleston to raise funds for the institution. Other

Charleston Jews contributed, but Lindo was the most generous of all, impressed by the fact that the new college prohibited any type of religious tests. Spurred by Lindo's gift, the trustees of the college in 1771 inserted into its charter the statement that "the children of Jews may be admitted to this institution and entirely enjoy the freedom of their own religion, without any constraint or imposition whatever." They informed Lindo, as well, that Jewish students would be exempt from attendance at Christian religious services; that they would provide a Jewish tutor if a sufficient number of students desired it; and that the Jewish community, if it wished, could establish a chair of Hebrew.

Why, in 1733, did some fear that "Georgia [would] soon become a Jewish colony"?

Col. **James Oglethorpe** was in charge of encouraging English settlers to come to the colony of Georgia in the 1730s, in order to develop its rich potential and protect the Carolinas from the Spanish in Florida and the French to the west. He was particularly interested in bringing over the English poor. In response to Oglethorpe's efforts, some of London's Sephardic elite formed a colonization committee that sent two boatloads of Jews to Georgia in 1733, some ninety men, women, and children. This disturbed some of the colony's trustees, who feared that such a large agglomeration of Jews would keep rich Christians from supporting the colony and poor Christians from settling there. Oglethorpe, however, refused to send the Jews back. He knew that Sephardim from Mediterranean lands were acquainted with the climate and the forms of agriculture appropriate to Georgia, and that they would be an asset to the colony. According to records of land grants allotted in 1733, about 14 percent of the householders in Savannah were Jews. They remained from the beginning, and prospered with the growth of the colony.

Who was the first Jew to serve in an American legislative body?

Francis Salvador, a young Sephardic Jew from England, immigrated to South Carolina in 1773 and soon became a major landowner in the frontier area of that colony. Soon after his arrival he became a fervent patriot. In England, some twenty years before, his father-in-law had been very active in the struggle to secure the passage in Parliament of a naturalization act for the Jews of England. The act was passed, but shortly thereafter was repealed. So it is very understandable that young Salvador embraced the patriot cause; since as a Jew in South Carolina he enjoyed more civic rights than his kinfolk in the mother country, why should he object to a rupture of the tie that bound the colony to its English masters?

Though Salvador had been living in his district for only about twelve months, he was selected to represent the district in the First Provincial Congress in 1775. He continued service in the Second Provincial Congress, which, after the Declaration of Independence, became the first General Assembly of South Carolina in 1776. He was the first identifiable Jew to serve in such a capacity.

How many synagogue congregations existed in the British colonies at the beginning of the American Revolution?

There were five cities within the Colonies with a sufficient number of Jews to support organized synagogue congregations by the beginning of the Revolution. These were **New York**, where the first immigrants in 1654 named their congregation Shearith Israel ("Remnant of Israel"); **Newport**, Rhode Island, whose Jews formed Yeshuat Israel ("Salvation of Israel") in 1658; **Savannah**, Georgia, where the first Jewish immigrants in 1733 called their congregation Mikveh Israel

("Hope of Israel"), honoring the synagogue in Curaçao in the Dutch West Indies that has borne that name since 1656; **Philadelphia**, where the Mikveh Israel synagogue took form about 1745; and **Charleston**, South Carolina, where Beth Elohim ("House of God") was organized in 1749.

Gershom Mendes Seixas, who served as rabbi of Shearith Israel from 1766 to 1816 (except under the British occupation of New York during the Revolution), was one of the fourteen ministers who participated in the inauguration of **George Washington** as President, held in New York on April 30, 1789. Seixas was one of the trustees of Columbia College for twenty-five years during his ministry in New York.

All five "mother congregations" in the Colonies followed the Spanish-Portuguese rite, even though the majority of the Jews affiliated with these bodies were (and still are) of Central or Eastern European ancestry rather than part of the Sephardic dispersion. To this day Shearith Israel in New York, Yeshuat Israel in Newport, and Mikveh Israel in Philadelphia continue as Orthodox synagogues of the Spanish rite. This is no longer true of Mikveh Israel in Savannah and Beth Elohim in Charleston, which, in the nineteenth century, affiliated with Reform Judaism.

What were some of the occupations in which Jews engaged during the Colonial period?

Few Jews were small farmers, since they were by and large accustomed to city life. **Francis Salvador**, though, was a plantation owner in South Carolina, and the Minis and Sheftall families in Georgia combined farming and ranching with commerce. Many Jews were craftsmen—candlemakers, watchmakers, soapmakers, saddlers, bakers, shoemakers, engravers, distillers, and indigo sorters. **Myer Myers** of New York was a master silversmith, as was **Isaiah Isaacs** in Richmond. There were Jewish medical practitioners in the Colonies since 1656, beginning with **Jacob Lumbrozo** in Maryland.

A high percentage of Jews engaged in industry, commerce, and trade. Some large merchants, like **Mordecai Gomez** of New York, also engaged in manufacturing (he was a snuffmaker). **Jacob Rodriguez Rivera** and **Aaron Lopez** in Newport were merchant shippers and whalers who were also major figures in the production of spermaceti candles. More numerous than these wealthy businessmen were the small shopkeepers. Frequently a clerk seeking to open his own shop might get a line of credit from a previous employer, who would also give him his first stock of goods at cost. Women as well as men could be shopkeepers, such as **Hannah Moses** in Philadelphia and **Abigail Minis** in Savannah.

Some Jews participated in what might be considered more exciting ventures, like privateering. Merchant ships would be fitted out with arms to prey on the commerce of England's enemies, usually on a share basis. Several Jewish merchants owned shares in privateers during and after the French and Indian War (1754–63). Some made money; others suffered losses. Purveying goods to the army (first the English, later the American) was a major business. There were sutlers attached to particular military units, as well as important political and financial figures. American Jewish merchants were involved in supplying food to the armed forces at the beginning of the eighteenth century; by the middle of the century they were operating on a large scale, sending supplies to Georgia, the West Indies, and other places. Much of the supplies needed by the English for the conquest of Canada were sold to them by a large consortium in which the Franks family, of New York and London, were major shareholders. **Jacob Franks** of New York and his son **David Franks** of Philadelphia were the American representatives of this company.

During the Revolution David Franks continued to serve as an army purveyor in the American states, representing the English firm in providing supplies for British troops and American Tories held prisoner by American patriot forces.

Suspected of Tory sympathies, he was eventually denied the right to pass through American lines. He suffered severe financial losses because of this, and because the British denied him repayment of much of the funds he had personally spent on their behalf. Other Jewish supplymen worked for the patriot forces. Some were quartermaster and commissary officers, like the Sheftalls of Georgia, who had military status but were expected to operate with their own capital.

Jewish merchants, along with others, participated in the fur trade, one of the oldest forms of business in the Colonies. This involved obtaining furs from Indians in exchange for textiles, kettles, axes, tobacco, guns, ammunition, or liquor. These goods were purchased by men who carried them west to frontier trading posts. It was a hazardous and competitive business.

Did Jews trade slaves?

In 1991 the Nation of Islam, Minister Louis Farrakhan's organization that specializes in "black pride" combined with anti-white and, in particular, anti-Jewish propaganda, published its diatribe, *The Secret Relationship Between Blacks and Jews*. This book, claiming to be documented history, attempts to show that the Atlantic slave system was the creation of Jewish refugees and "secret Jews" (converts to Christianity from Spain and Portugal) who "'procured Black Africans by the tens of thousands and funnelled them to the plantations of South America and throughout the Caribbean."

The truth, according to David Brion Davis, is that the participants in the Atlantic slave system included "Arabs, Berbers, scores of African ethnic groups, Italians, Portuguese, Spaniards, Dutch, Jews, Germans, Swedes, French, English, Danes, white Americans, Native Americans, and even thousands of New World blacks who had been emancipated or were descended from freed slaves but then became slave-holding farmers or planters themselves." While the Atlantic slave trade existed there were a few Jewish slave traders in Amsterdam, Bordeaux, and Newport, Rhode Island (in Newport the names of **Jacob Rodriguez Rivera** and his son-in-law **Aaron Lopez** stand out), but they were far outnumbered by the thousands of Catholics and Protestants who participated and became immensely wealthy from this inhuman system. In the eighteenth century the British slave trade transported the largest share of Africans to the New World; Jews played no role to speak of in this operation.

There was no meaningful protest against the slave system until the late eighteenth century, when the Anglo-American antislavery movement, which embraced both Christians and Jews, began. In the United States relatively few Jews held slaves. In 1830 in the American South, there were only 23 Jews among the 59,000 slaveholders owning twenty or more slaves, and only 4 Jews among the 11,000 slaveholders who owned fifty or more slaves.

Is there any truth to the story that Haym Salomon advanced $800,000 of his own money to the patriot cause during the American Revolution, money that was never repaid, so that, at his death, his young widow and children were left penniless?

Haym Salomon was a Polish Jew, born about 1740, who as a young man traveled across much of Europe and picked up a working knowledge of most of the European languages. Around 1775 he arrived in New York and became solidly attached to the patriot cause. He worked vigorously with Robert Morris, the superintendent of finance in the Revolutionary government, to raise money for the conduct of the war, but did he put out $800,000 of his own money? No, he never had anything approaching funds of this magnitude. Had he possessed anywhere near this amount, he would have been the richest man in the British colonies (soon to be the United States). Salomon was a generous and devoted patriot, but the legend that grew up about him, starting in the 1820s, is, like most legends, a vast exaggeration of the facts.

Some months after his arrival in New York, Salomon was arrested by the British and thrown into a military prison. He was soon released, because his knowledge of languages enabled him to serve as an interpreter with the Hessian mercenary troops who fought alongside the British. He took advantage of his freedom to propagandize for American independence among the Hessians, so it is no surprise that in 1778 he had to flee for his life from New York to Philadelphia. There he settled down to work as a commission merchant and bill broker. He advertised in the local newspapers, emphasizing his financial connections with France and Holland. He worked for the French forces in America allied with the patriot cause, selling their bills of exchange, and recouped the money he had lost when forced to flee New York. In 1781 Robert Morris, newly appointed superintendent of finance for the American government, chose Salomon as his chief agent to help sell the bills that were coming in from France, Holland, Spain, and other countries sympathetic to the Revolutionary cause. Salomon the broker is mentioned more than one hundred times in Morris's diary. After Cornwallis's surrender, Salomon continued to serve Morris in selling bills of exchange, negotiating drafts, and floating securities for the government. By 1782 he was serving as broker not only to the (American) Office of Finance but also to the consul general of France and the treasurer of the French army. From the commissions he earned he lent money, interest-free, to several members of the Continental Congress, including future President **James Madison**.

Salomon became wealthy enough to send money to family members in Europe during the 1780s, but he turned down many requests from other supposed relatives. In 1783 he became a member of the governing board of Congregation Mikveh Israel in Philadelphia. He was a member of this body in 1783 when it addressed a memorial to the Pennsylvania

Council of Censors, requesting that the state's constitution be amended to eliminate the requirement that members of the state House of Representatives take an oath acknowledging "the Scriptures of the Old and New Testament to be given by Divine Inspiration." (This wording disappeared in the new constitution of 1790). In 1784 Salomon returned to New York to rejoin his wife and young children and develop a business. His health was poor, however; after making provision for his aged parents in Poland, he died early in 1785, survived by his wife and four children, all under age seven. Merchants who found it difficult to pay were indebted to him for large amounts. He had made himself personally liable for many of the drafts and bills of exchange that he had handled for the government. He died insolvent.

Jacob R. Marcus, separating fact from legend, sums up the life of Haym Salomon in these words: "At the risk of his own life—in New York, from 1776 to 1778—he helped French and American prisoners to escape; he induced Hessians to desert; he went to prison for his patriotism when he could well have made his peace and fortune with the English in New York; he fled from his home and left behind him wife and infant; he floated securities to the amount of $200,000; he helped keep Madison and others in Congress by lending them money without charge; he fought for political and religious liberty in Pennsylvania; and he gave liberally, munificently, that his fellow Jews might worship the God of their fathers in dignity and devotion in a synagogue of their own. He was Colonial America at its best."

Did the United States Constitution guarantee full religious equality to Jewish Americans?

In a word, the answer to this question is no. Article VI of the Constitution provides that "no religious test shall ever be required as a qualification to any office or public trust under the United States," and the First Amendment to the Constitution, which took effect in 1791, specifies that "Congress shall make no law respecting an establishment of religion, or prohibiting the free exercise thereof." Despite these provisions, however, a strict interpretation understood them to apply only to the federal government, with the various states still being free to enact religious requirements for officeholders within their respective jurisdictions. It took some while before the various state constitutions were rewritten or amended to eliminate religious tests for public office.

Though Maryland, for instance, had been established as the one colony in which Catholics were to be free to practice as they wished, in 1692 the Church of England became its "established" religion. A series of laws passed in the early eighteenth century opened offices of trust only to those able to take the oath "upon the true faith of a Christian." This requirement was retained in the constitution of 1776. Only in 1826 did Maryland enfranchise its Jews. New York was the first state to fully enfranchise its Jewish citizens; its constitution, adopted in 1777, enabled Jews not only to vote but to hold political office. North Carolina was the last state to enfranchise its Jews; only since 1868 have professing Jews had the right to hold political office there.

Why did Judah Touro, the son of a rabbi, contribute funds to Christian missionaries for the purpose of spreading the gospel in Jerusalem?

Judah Touro was born in 1775, the son of the rabbi of the synagogue in Newport, Rhode Island, and died in New Orleans in 1854 as one of that city's most honored and wealthiest citizens. He traveled from New England to New Orleans when he was twenty-seven and, during the entire span of his life from the date of his arrival there, never left that city. He undertook this arduous journey because, after the death of his parents, he lived with his uncle Moses Michael Hays in Boston. He fell in love with Hays's daughter Catherine,

24

and his uncle, disapproving of their marriage, banished Judah from his household. Both Judah and Catherine remained unmarried for the rest of their lives, and, ever faithful to the command of her father, they never saw each other again. This is why Judah sought a new life in New Orleans.

Judah's wealth derived from his career as a merchant shipper and agent for other shippers to and from the port of New Orleans. He was seriously wounded while fighting under the command of Andrew Jackson in the Battle of New Orleans in 1815. During his lifetime he gave munificent gifts to Christian churches, to the fund for the construction of the monument at Bunker Hill, and for the preservation and upkeep of the synagogue in Newport where his father had served as rabbi. This beautiful building, consecrated in 1763, is listed as a national historic site and still functions as a synagogue. Nine years before his death Judah Touro purchased the land and paid for the construction of the synagogue in New Orleans for the followers of the Spanish-Portuguese rite; it is now known as Touro Synagogue, as is the one in Newport. With the publication of his will, Touro achieved posthumous fame throughout the country. In it he dispensed over $500,000 in charitable bequests, the equivalent of many millions of dollars in today's currency. Among them were provisions for founding a hospital and almshouse in New Orleans, gifts to nearly all the Jewish congregations in the country, and benefactions to hospitals and orphanages in Boston and for housing for the poor to be constructed in Jerusalem (with this money Jerusalem began its first expansion outside the old walled city). The provisions of Touro's will were published throughout the United States and in many European periodicals.

It is not surprising that Touro exhibited some eccentric personality traits. He never traveled outside New Orleans (though he was buried in Newport); he never traveled in any vehicle; and though he owned some of the largest ships that came into the port of New Orleans, "he could never be persuaded to go aboard one of them. He would content himself by standing on the levee, and viewing in silent admiration the huge hulks, the tapering masts and snowy sails of his great cotton ships." Touro was quoted as saying that he saved a fortune by strict economy, while others spent theirs on extravagant expenditures. "He had the best wines always by him, without drinking them himself; his table, whatever delicacies it bore, had only plain and simple food for him."

Why, then, did Touro contribute funds for Christian missionaries to use in Jerusalem—ten times more, in fact, than the sum given by any Christian in New Orleans? Perhaps it was one of his eccentricities. Perhaps it was because he was so used to responding to requests for money that he paid little attention to the purposes for which it might be used. More likely, though, he gave because he wished to aid the Christians of Jerusalem in their struggle against persecution by the Turkish rulers of the city. He truly believed that people of all the world's religions could live together as brothers.

Where, when, and why was a Jewish state supposed to be established within the United States?

Mordecai Manuel Noah (1785–1851) was for a time regarded, at least by some, as the most distinguished American Jew of his day. Born in Philadelphia to an old Sephardic-American family, he first worked in a government office but soon entered journalism and achieved some renown as a playwright. Moving to New York, he became active in Democratic party politics and served as sheriff, surveyor of the port, and a judge. During the War of 1812 he was appointed the U.S. consul to Tunis. He was, however, relieved of his post in 1815 on the grounds that his religion was a problem for some of the Muslim potentates with whom he had to deal. Noah denied this by pointing out, correctly, that many of the Muslim rulers had appointed Jews to high government positions. Later on the State Department expressed its regret that it had terminated his consular appointment.

In 1825 Noah staged the proclamation of a "city of refuge" for the persecuted Jews of the world on Grand Island in the Niagara River, between Buffalo and Niagara Falls. He named it "Ararat," after the place where the ark of the biblical Noah had found refuge at the conclusion of the Flood. Noah (the nineteenth-century figure, not the biblical one) thought that the spot he had chosen was "preeminently calculated to become, in time, the greatest trading and commercial depot in the new and better world," this because of its proximity to Niagara Falls, which many assumed could serve as the greatest source of hydroelectric power in the world. Noah, who was himself a journalist, publicized this project widely and chose September 25, 1825, as the date for dedicating the foundation stone of the projected city. This took place amidst the firing of cannon and the participation of federal and state officials, Christian clergy, Masonic officers, and American Indians, whom Noah considered to be "lost tribes" of Israel. Since no structure yet existed at the site, these exercises were held in an Episcopal church in Buffalo.

Noah appointed himself "judge and governor" of Israel and announced this establishment of a Jewish state on Grand Island as the precursor to the eventual restoration of a Jewish state in Palestine. He ordered that a census of Jews be taken throughout the world and levied a tax of three shekels in silver to be paid into the new state's treasury by Jews everywhere each year. He commanded the world's Jews to cooperate with his plans, and named a number of distinguished European Jews as his "commissioners." None of these appointees accepted Noah's proffered honors, and rabbis throughout the world ridiculed and denounced these efforts. Noah himself eventually lost interest, and twenty years later he anticipated the later Zionist movement by appealing to the Christian world to help Jewish resettlement in Palestine. The foundation stone for "Ararat" rests in the collection of the Buffalo Historical Society.

Ridiculous as this scheme appeared to many in Noah's

own time as well as today, it nonetheless reflected a seemingly "practical" approach to solving the problem of the Jews, like the Zionism of the later nineteenth century. Both "Ararat" and Zionism refused to wait for God's supernatural intervention to restore the Jews to their own land. The Ararat scheme also reflects the convictions of perhaps the vast majority of American Jews during the early nineteenth century: the ideals animating and underlying the Declaration of Independence and the Constitution of the United States are intimately related to the anticipated redemption of the Jews, and to the basic principles of Judaism itself.

What did Uriah Phillips Levy do for the U.S. Navy?

Uriah P. Levy (1792–1862), the son of a Philadelphia merchant, was so fascinated by the sea that, at age eleven, he ran away to work as a cabin boy on a sailing vessel. By age twenty he had served on several merchant ships and even become part owner of one. As an American patriot not fully satisfied with his seafaring career thus far, he elected to join the United States Navy and was inducted into the rank of sailing master in 1812. Throughout his naval career Levy faced the animosity of those officers who resented the fact that he had risen through officers' ranks on the basis of his previous experience as a merchant seaman, and thus was not the kind of "gentleman" with whom they felt comfortable in the officers' mess. Some of his opponents also objected to him as a Jew, one who wore his religious identity as a badge of honor. Having risen to the rank of captain, Levy in 1855 received notice that his naval service was terminated. He was not, however, the type to shuffle off quietly. He engaged lawyers and vigorously fought for reinstatement to active duty, and was successful in this effort. He thereafter attained the rank of commodore, at that time the highest grade in the navy.

When not serving in the navy, Levy amassed a small fortune through mercantile activity. He used this money to purchase Monticello, the Virginia home and estate of Thomas Jefferson, and to restore and repair it. He also purchased the statue of Jefferson that stands in the U.S. Capitol. Levy's love for both his country and his religion is demonstrated by these words, which were submitted to the court of inquiry that was considering his appeal for restoration to service in the navy in 1857:

> My case is the case of every Israelite in the Union. I need not speak to you of their number, but I may speak of the fact that they are unsurpassed by any other portion of our people in loyalty to the Constitution and to the Union, by their quiet support of our laws and Constitution, by the cheerfulness with which they contribute their share of the public burthens, and by the liberal donations many of them have made to promote the general interests of education and of charity, in some instances of charities controlled exclusively by Christians and sometimes, exclusively devoted to the benefit of Christians. . . . Are the thousands of Israel and the ten thousands of Judah, in their dispersion throughout the earth, who look to America as a land bright with promise, are they now to learn, to their sorrow and dismay, that we too have sunk into the mire of religious intolerance and bigotry? . . . . What is my case today, if you yield to this injustice, may tomorrow be that of the Roman Catholic or the Unitarian, the Presbyterian or the Methodist, the Episcopalian or the Baptist. There is but one safeguard: that is to be found in an honest, wholehearted, inflexible support of the wise, the just, the impartial guarantee of the Constitution.

Levy took great pride in his work to reduce, and eventually eliminate, the use of the lash as the most common form of punishment within the navy. He wrote, "I admit my aversion to the free and constant use of the cat, much less lacerating the backs of boys of tender age, covering them with stripes and blood, and punishing them as hardened felons, and therefore, governed by the discretion which the law allows the commander of a ship of war, I have studied and practiced all the reforms which mildness could suggest, as substitutes for corporal punishment. . . . What, then, are the results of my system? No ship in the Navy had a better or more orderly set of men, none obeyed orders more cheerfully, in no ship was there less severe punishment, and in none less manifestations of mutiny and disaffection." This was Levy's great gift to the U.S. Navy. At his direction, these are the words carved on his tombstone: "Father of the law for the abolition of the barbarous practice of corporal punishment in the Navy of the United States."

What Jewish-American woman was the inspiration for the character Rebecca in Sir Walter Scott's novel Ivanhoe?

Ivanhoe, a novel by Sir Walter Scott first published in 1819, was included in the curriculum of most American schools until the 1950s (and had a place in schools in England for at least that long). In the story Ivanhoe, a brave Saxon knight in the twelfth century and a favorite of King Richard the Lion-hearted, enters the tournament of Ashby in disguise and defeats five valiant Norman knights. Seriously wounded, he is carried from Ashby by a wealthy Jew, Isaac of York, and is nursed by Isaac's lovely daughter Rebecca. All three, however, are soon captured by the Normans and imprisoned. King Richard and Robin Hood lay siege to the castle where they are being held and rescue all the prisoners except Rebecca. Rebecca is later accused of witchcraft and is sentenced to be burned at the stake unless a champion can successfully defend her. Ivanhoe comes to her aid, and Rebecca is set free. Though she loves Ivanhoe, she knows that she cannot marry him and unselfishly leaves England. Ivanhoe marries his earlier love, the Lady Rowena.

According to a tradition that was preserved within the

wealthy and prominent Gratz family of Philadelphia, Scott's Rebecca was inspired by the example of a flesh-and-blood person, **Rebecca Gratz** (1781–1869). In the period before the Civil War, she was thought of as the outstanding Jewish woman in the United States. Like Scott's Rebecca, she remained unmarried all her life, probably (according to family tradition) because she was in love with a non-Jew but refused to marry out of her faith. She was a beautiful and cultured woman who devoted her considerable energies to philanthropic causes, both Jewish and general. In 1838 she founded the first Jewish Sunday school in the country, modeled after similar Christian Sunday schools. She personally supervised this school until her eighty-third year.

It was related within the Gratz family that Washington Irving, the first American "man of letters," carried the impression of Rebecca Gratz abroad with him. They had been close friends, and Irving had been engaged to a dear associate of Miss Gratz's who had died young and left Irving bereft ever after. When Irving went to England and visited Sir Walter Scott, he told him on one occasion of the Rebecca who was a "Jewess," and who was beautiful and brave in her faith, and who adhered to the one and only God. Scott put her in the story of *Ivanhoe*. He sent a copy of the book to Irving, and asked him how he liked his Rebecca.

Why did a significant number of German Jews immigrate to the United States during the middle years of the nineteenth century?

Civic rights had been granted to the Jews of the various German states only with the conquest of Germany by the forces of Napoleon, inspired by the French Revolution and its ideal of "liberty, equality, fraternity." With Napoleon's defeat at Waterloo in 1815, however, and the restoration to power of the previous ruling families, many civic rights were taken away from Germany's Jews. Having tasted a measure of freedom during the period of French hegemony, many German Jews did not wish to live under the old order, and they set sail for the New World. Even earlier, the first synagogue devoted to the Ashkenazic (North European) rite, rather than the Spanish-Portuguese, had been Rodef Shalom ("Pursuing Peace"), founded in 1802 in Philadelphia. The first congregation in America founded upon the principles and practices of Reform Judaism (which had originated in Germany) was Har Sinai ("Mount Sinai") in Baltimore in 1842; the second was Temple Emanu-El ("God is with Us"), established in New York in 1845. Emanu-El has for some years been the American synagogue with the largest number of enrolled members.

In 1848 and thereafter a large number of German immigrants, Catholics and Protestants as well as Jews, came to the United States in response to the failure of democratic revolutionary efforts in Germany in that year.

What Jewish congressman was a spokesman for the Native American party, advocating an end to foreign immigration and the restriction of citizenship to native-born Americans?

Lewis C. Levin was born in Charleston, South Carolina, in 1808. After becoming a lawyer, he settled in Philadelphia, where, in 1843, he became one of the leading figures in the Native American movement in that city and editor of one of the nativist daily papers. He was elected to Congress as a Native American and served three terms, from 1845 to 1850, "during which time he preached nativism with almost fanatical zeal." He warned, "We stand now on the very verge of overthrow by the impetuous forces of invading foreigners. The day is not distant when the American-born voter will find himself a minority in his own land." In the 1856 presidential campaign he denounced the "Black Republicans" and abolitionists as agents of the Pope. He died in 1860.

The Native Americans insisted that if a foreign immigrant was to be granted naturalization as a citizen, it should take place only after twenty-one years of residence in the country, reasoning that a native-born American attains his right to vote when he reaches the age of twenty-one. The Native Americans were predecessors of the Know-Nothing party, a politically significant group during the 1850s. The example of Congressman Lewis Levin demonstrates that Jews can be found distributed across the complete ideological spectrum.

What American rabbi, while leading the morning worship service for the Jewish New Year, was without warning harshly struck by his congregation's president and, after the ensuing riot, forced to leave the congregation's employ?

Isaac Mayer Wise was born in 1819 in Bohemia, then part of the Austro-Hungarian Empire. Widely read in both Jewish and secular learning, he resolved in 1846 to come to the United States to lead Jewish communities in the way of religious "reform," the philosophy dominant at the time among the Jews of Central Europe. He accepted the call to lead Congregation Beth El ("House of God") in Albany, New York. Wise belonged to the camp of the moderate reformers, rather than that of the radicals. Nonetheless, his open and democratic outlook alienated a segment of the temple's leadership, though the majority of its membership supported and admired his work. The temple's president convened a meeting two days before the Jewish New Year (Rosh Hashana) for the purpose of dismissing Rabbi Wise, whom he charged with "deism," but after eight hours of debate the meeting was adjourned. Following the adjournment, the president and his cohorts remained behind and, illegally, voted to dismiss Wise. Wise and his supporters, of course, did not recognize this action and went to the synagogue on New Year's morning.

In his *Reminiscences* Wise describes what happened next.

Excitement ruled the hour. Everything was quiet as the grave. Finally, the choir sings. At the conclusion of the song, I step before the Ark in order to take out the Scrolls of the Law as usual, and to offer prayer. Spanier [the president] steps in my way, and, without saying a word, smites me with his fist so that my cap falls from my head. This was the terrible signal for an uproar, the like of which I have never experienced. The people acted like furies. It was as though the synagogue had suddenly burst forth into a flaming conflagration. The Poles and Hungarians, who thought only of me, struck out like wild men. The young people jumped down from the choir gallery to protect me and had to fight their way through the surging crowd. Within two minutes the whole assembly was a struggling mass. The sheriff and his posse, who were summoned, were belabored and forced out until finally the whole assembly surged out of the house into Herkimer Street.

Two days later Wise and his supporters organized a new congregation, Anshe Emeth ("People of Truth"). Wise instituted legal action against Beth El's president and was vindicated in his suit. Four years later he went on to lead one of the great temples of Cincinnati, the "Queen City" of the West.

Wise led his Cincinnati congregation until his death in 1900. He also edited a Jewish weekly, the *Israelite*, that was distributed throughout the country. Gifted with almost limitless energy, he was the moving spirit behind the founding of the Union of American Hebrew Congregations in 1873, the first successful effort at establishing a national Jewish religious body in the United States. The union invited all synagogues to affiliate with it, both those embracing reform tendencies and those that rejected them. In a short while, however, it came to represent only Reform Judaism, since the more traditional congregations did not feel comfortable in the company of the reformers. Under the sponsorship of the union, the Hebrew Union College began operation in 1875, under Wise as its president. It is the oldest continuously operating rabbinic seminary in the country. It now has four campuses: one each in Cincinnati, New York, Los Angeles, and Jerusalem. In 1889 the Central Conference of American Rabbis was formed. Isaac Mayer Wise served as its president from its beginning until the day of his death.

What was the life of an immigrant peddler like?

Abraham Kohn came from Bavaria to America at age twenty-three and became a peddler in New England. This was the path followed by many poor newcomers to the United States during the nineteenth century—going on foot from town to town with a pack of merchandise on his back that weighed between thirty and eighty pounds, then, if he earned enough money, graduating to a horse and buggy in which to make his rounds. Kohn left a diary in which he recorded his journeys, thoughts, and impressions during 1842 and 1843. No doubt his words tell us not only about him but about many others who shared a similar life. Here are some excerpts (translated from the German by A. V. Goodman):

> How much more could I write about this queer land! It likes comfort extremely. The German, by comparison, hardly knows the meaning of the word. The wife of an American farmer can consider herself more important than the wife of a Bavarian judge. For hours she can sit in her rocking chair shaking back and forth as she thinks of nothing but beautiful clothes and a fine hairdo. The farmer himself, unlike the German farmer who works every minute, is able to sit down for a few hours every day, reading his paper and smoking his cigar. . . .
>
> Not far from here we were forced to stop on Wednesday because of the heavy snow. We sought to spend the night with a cooper, a Mr. Spaulding, but his wife did not wish to take us in. She was afraid of strangers, she might not sleep well; we should go our way. And outside there raged the worst blizzard I have ever seen. O God, I thought, is this the land of liberty and hos-

pitality and tolerance? Why have I been led here? After we [Kohn and his brother] had talked to this woman for half an hour, after repeatedly pointing out that to turn us forth into the blizzard would be sinful, we were allowed to stay. She became friendlier, indeed, after a few hours, and at night she even joined us in singing. . . .

Business, thanks be to God, is satisfactory, and this week we took in more than $45. We rode horseback for pleasure on Sunday.

> *Things will yet go well,*
> *The world is round and must keep turning.*
> *Things will yet go well.*

So goes an old German song which I once heard an actor sing. . . .

The weather is very bad, and the sleigh sinks two feet into the snow. Money is scarce, but, God be thanked, sleeping quarters have been good. There is much work for little profit, yet God in heaven may send better times that all our drudgery will not have been in vain. . . .

Times are bad; everywhere there is no money. This increases the hardship of life so that I am sometimes tempted to return to New York and start all over again. However, I must have patience. God will help. On Sunday every farmer urges me to attend church, and this week in Williamsburg, at each house where I tried to sell my wares, I was told to go to church. God in heaven, Father of our ancestors, you who have protected the little band of Jews to this day, you know my thoughts. You alone know my grief when, on the Sabbath's eve, I must retire to my lodging and on Saturday morning carry my pack on my back, profaning the holy day, God's gift to his people Israel. . . .

A year ago today I left Fürth in Bavaria. O God, you guide our destinies. I cannot say whether America has misled me or whether I misled myself. How quickly this year has passed! How many sad and bitter hours has it brought me! In Fürth ten years did not bring the worries and troubles that a single year has brought me in this land. Yet you, Father of all, who have brought me across the ocean and directed my steps until today, will grant me your further aid. With confidence in your fatherly goodness, I continue my way of life.

Kohn's patience paid off. Two years later he owned a clothing store in Chicago. He also became active in the Republican party and was visited in his store by Abraham Lincoln in 1860. When Lincoln went to Washington in 1861, Kohn sent him a handmade American flag, on paper, on which he had imprinted words from the biblical book of Joshua: "Be strong and of good courage." Kohn served as the city clerk of Chicago and was active in its Jewish community.

Up to the Civil War, who was the great organizer and disseminator of Jewish religious wisdom to America's Jews?

Very few would dispute the fact that the "spiritual leader" of America's Jews, from 1829 until his death in 1868, was **Isaac Leeser**. Born in 1806 in Germany and educated there, Leeser came to the United States in 1824 and found work with an uncle in Richmond, Virginia, a merchant. While there he wrote a series of articles for a Richmond newspaper defending Jews and Judaism against defamatory attacks. This brought him to the attention of the board of Mikveh Israel in Philadelphia, who were seeking to engage a leader for their congregation. He was offered the position, accepted it, and began his ministry in Philadelphia in 1829, remaining in that city until his death. He was a feverish and innovative worker in all areas of religious leadership, visiting practically every Jewish community in the country and preaching in almost every synagogue. He edited and translated the prayer book of the Spanish-Portuguese rite used in his own congregation, and then proceeded to edit and translate the prayer book of the

Ashkenazic Jews. He wrote textbooks for children, translated the complete Hebrew Scriptures (this was basically a modification of the King James Version for use by Jews), helped organize the Jewish Sunday school in Philadelphia as well as all-day schools for children, and introduced an English sermon as a weekly feature of the Sabbath morning service in his Sephardic synagogue.

He was responsible for the first Jewish publication society in the country and the first Jewish theological seminary (Maimonides College in Philadelphia, which lasted only six years), and served as an officer of the Board of Delegates of American Israelites, which was founded in 1859. In 1843 he founded the first long-lasting Jewish journal in the country, the *Occident and American Jewish Advocate*. He edited this monthly, writing most of its material, until his death in 1868. He advocated Orthodox Judaism and took issue with many of the changes sought by the Reform movement, but his was a religion that sought a synthesis of the ancient teachings with American culture and society.

What event inspired the founding of the Board of Delegates of American Israelites in 1859?

Though the Jews of the United States constituted a very small group far removed from the troubles and persecutions that afflicted, from time to time, their fellow Jews overseas, three events during the middle years of the nineteenth century created a major stir in their midst. The first was the "blood libel" lodged against the Jews of Damascus in 1840. The head of a Franciscan monastery in that city had disappeared, and the tale made its rounds that he had been murdered by Jews for nefarious ritual purposes. Thirteen Jews, including community leaders, were arrested and tortured. Diplomatic protests by European powers and the United States were lodged, and eventually nine of the thirteen were released, the other four Jews having already died while in custody. Unlike the Jews of

Britain and France, the Jews of the United States had no single organized body through which to protest and to express indignation at this hideous event. The Spanish-Portuguese Synagogue turned down a request to hold a community meeting on its premises, its trustees stating that "no benefit can arise from such a course." The meeting was held, instead, at the Bnai Jeshurun Synagogue ("Sons of Jeshurun," a poetic synonym for Israel in the Bible from *yashar*, "upright"), which adhered to the Ashkenazic rite. (It had been formed in 1825 by a group that had withdrawn from the Spanish-Portuguese congregation because they preferred to worship in the Northern European fashion.) Public meetings were also held in Philadelphia and Richmond. Shortly after the Damascus Affair, **Isaac Leeser** sought to create a central American Jewish body, but nothing resulted from it.

American Jews were also alarmed by a proposed treaty with Switzerland in 1855 which provided that the reciprocal admission and treatment of citizens of one country in the other "shall not conflict with the constitutional or legal provisions, Federal as well as State and Cantonal, of the contracting parties." The trouble with this was that, at the time, some of the Swiss cantons did not admit Jews, or placed various restrictions upon them. A year after the treaty's ratification, an American Jew was threatened with expulsion from one of the cantons for this reason. The Swiss changed their policy some years later, but in the meantime, though meetings of protest were held in several American cities, no central Jewish body yet existed to deal with an issue such as this. Isaac Leeser together with **Isaac M. Wise** tried in 1849 to remedy this defect, but again nothing resulted. In 1855 a national rabbinical conference, including both Orthodox and Reform representatives, attempted to set up a central body, but the philosophical differences among them prevented any progress.

At last, in 1858 the indignation unleashed by the Mortara case had an effect. This involved a little boy in Bologna, Italy, who, because a housemaid had secretly baptized him, was torn away from his Jewish parents and placed in a convent so that he might be raised as a Catholic. Church law did not permit the baptism of a child without parental consent, but, nonetheless, once it is done, it is valid and, in the eyes of the Church at that time, such a child had to be raised a Catholic. Not only did Protestants and Jews protest this injustice; even Catholic sovereigns in Europe protested to Pope Pius IX, but he remained adamant. Demonstrations took place in American cities, the one in New York involving two thousand people, Christians as well as Jews. The leading Protestant weekly in the country called on Christians to "make common cause with their Hebrew fellow-citizens in protesting against this Bologna outrage."

Finally, in 1859 a convention met in New York that called into being a body titled the Board of Delegates of American Israelites. The convention was made up of representatives of thirteen congregations, most of them in New York. Several Reform groups stayed away because Isaac M. Wise, a Democrat, did not want groups allied with him to become involved in possible debates over slavery. Shearith Israel of New York and Mikveh Israel of Philadelphia stayed away because they did not wish to be dominated by "newcomers" from Germany and Poland. The Board of Delegates functioned from 1859 to 1878, participating in representations concerning the Swiss treaty and standing up for the Jewish community at various junctures during the Civil War. In 1878 the Board of Delegates gave over its functions to the newly formed Union of American Hebrew Congregations established by Isaac M. Wise.

Who was, according to some of his contemporaries, "the greatest native-born American of Jewish origin" in the period prior to the Civil War?

Presumably there are very few people today who could name the man considered by some during his lifetime to be "the greatest native-born American of Jewish origin." (In later years there were too many contenders for this distinction, so it is unlikely that anyone else was ever proposed for it.) In the years before the Civil War, however, there were not that many native-born American Jews, and **Philip Phillips** stood above the rest. He was born in Charleston, South Carolina, in 1807, and was admitted to the bar of that state at the age of twenty-one. During the same year in which he began his career, he served as the secretary of the Reformed Society of Israelites in Charleston, the first group formed in the United States to emulate the Reform Judaism that had begun to develop a few years earlier in Central Europe. In 1832 Phillips was elected to the South Carolina Nullification Convention on the Unionist ticket, which opposed the secessionist movement that was taking form in the South at that time. He continued to oppose his state's secession from the Union until the outbreak of the Civil War, though his wife, Eugenia Levy Phillips, was a notorious and vocal advocate of secession.

Phillips headed a South Carolina militia regiment (he held the rank of colonel) and served a term in the state legislature. He then sought new opportunities in Alabama, settling in Mobile, where he became one of the outstanding lawyers in the state and edited a volume of digests of Alabama Supreme Court opinions. In 1853 he was elected to Congress and went to Washington. Following his term he chose to remain in Washington to practice law. With the outbreak of the Civil War, the agitations of his wife brought about her arrest and deportation to the South; Phillips, of course, accompanied her there, to New Orleans. After the war he was able to return to Washington, where he became "the most successful Supreme Court lawyer of his generation," appearing before that body in more than four hundred cases. In 1872 he wrote the acclaimed text *The Statutory Jurisdiction and Practice of the Supreme Court of the United States.*

In 1857 Phillips headed the Jewish delegation that went before President **James Buchanan** to protest the anti-Jewish provisions of the American-Swiss Treaty of 1855. Following the Civil War Phillips spoke at the dedication of a new synagogue in New Orleans. He died in Washington in 1884.

TWO

From the Civil War to the Second World War

How did the Civil War affect the Jews of the North?

How did the Civil War affect the Jews of the South?

What was the infamous "General Order No. 11"?

What did Simon Wolf write to William Cullen Bryant, editor of the New York Evening Post, and why did he write it?

What were the achievements of the Seligmans?

How did Henry Hilton, proprietor of the Grand Union Hotel in Saratoga Springs, New York, come to have a major impact upon Jewish-American life, lasting from 1877 until well into the next century?

What did they eat at the "Trefa Banquet" in 1883?

What is the story behind the poem engraved on a tablet affixed to the pedestal upon which the Statue of Liberty stands?

Who was president of the American Federation of Labor from 1886 to 1924?

Who was the first Jew to serve as a cabinet secretary in the United States government?

Who was the greatest banker of them all?

Who was America's outstanding theatrical impresario during the closing years of the nineteenth century and the opening years of the twentieth?

Why did such a dense concentration of Jewish immigrants from Eastern Europe come to settle on New York City's Lower East Side?

What is a landsmanschaft?

When did the Jewish population of New York City reach 1 million?

What were the Yom Kippur balls?

Besides attending Yom Kippur balls,
what else did Emma Goldman do?

When did New York have a "Chief Rabbi"?

Who was "the angel of the East Side"?

What was accomplished by
the Educational Alliance?

Who was the first Socialist to sit
in the U.S. Congress?

When were American Jews important
in the sport of boxing?

Was there more to life on the Lower East Side
than poverty, struggle, and degradation?

Who was looked upon as "probably
the most influential political, cultural,
and literary figure" in the Eastern European
Jewish community in America?

What was the "Bintl Brief"?

What great tragedy befell the people of the
Lower East Side on March 25, 1911?

What is meant by "Jewish labor unions"?

Who was Morris Hillquit?

Who was Meyer London?

*Which clothing manufacturer became
the largest in the world?*

*Who prevented the Rockefellers from controlling
all the copper produced in the United States?*

*How did the daughters of immigrants
advance in the working world?*

Who are the Bnai Brith?

*What inspired the founding of the
American Jewish Committee in 1906?*

*Why did Reform Jews pour money into the
(Conservative) Jewish Theological Seminary?*

What was the "New York Kehilla"?

*What was the unique Jewish
connection to Galveston, Texas?*

*Was there any noticeable Jewish
settlement in the West?*

What was the Sutro Tunnel?

*Who was the first Jewish governor of
an American state?*

*What are, in all likelihood, the two greatest
Jewish-American intellectual achievements of
the early twentieth century?*

What famous Jewish American was "blessed"?

*Who was the first Jewish American
to win a Nobel Prize?*

*Why was an American Jew lynched by
an Atlanta mob in 1915?*

Who is Brandeis University named after?

*Who is considered by many to have been the greatest
Jewish-American woman of the century?*

*When, how, and why were some Jewish
labor unions allied with Communists?*

*How did some unions become involved
with gangsters and racketeers?*

*Who was, even in the judgment of those who
hated him, "the single most influential figure
in twentieth-century urban renewal"?*

Who were the noteworthy Jews from Chicago?

Who was "Greasy Thumb" Guzik?

Who originated "Levi's"?

Are department stores Jewish?

What were Henry Ford's thoughts about Jews?

*Was there ever an instance of the vicious
"blood libel" in the United States?*

*What magician delighted in exposing the fakery and
frauds of other magicians and mind readers?*

*What did the phrase "near churches" mean in real
estate ads during the first half of the twentieth century?*

*What Jewish groups settled in the United States after
immigration restrictions were imposed in 1924?*

*How have Jewish Americans influenced
American music?*

What was so funny about the Marx Brothers?

Who were the first Jewish feminists?

*What dedicated feminist was also active in
the anti-suffrage movement (which opposed
granting women the right to vote)?*

Is The New York Times *a "Jewish" paper?*

Are Hollywood movies a Jewish industry?

*Which studio produced the first feature film
with spoken dialogue?*

Who was the most hated man in the movie industry?

*Was there major Jewish involvement in
the growth of radio and television?*

Who was Stephen Wise?

How did the Civil War affect the Jews of the North?

Before the outbreak of the Civil War in 1861, America's Jews, like the rest of the country's population, were divided over the question of whether the slave system should be permitted to exist anywhere in the United States. With the secession of the Confederate States, however, and the commencement of hostilities between the North and the South, the Jews of the North rallied almost unanimously to support **Abraham Lincoln**'s presidency and the war against the South, while the Jews of the Confederate States enthusiastically supported the government of **Jefferson Davis** and its struggle to preserve the South and its own unique traditions (including slavery). Thousands of Jews served as both officers and fighting men in the armies and navies of both the North and the South. (Since neither side kept records of religious affiliation for its soldiers, exact numbers are impossible to determine.

Researchers can count "Jewish names," but not everyone with a Jewish-type name is Jewish, and not all Jews bear "Jewish names.")

The rabbis in the North, before the outbreak of hostilities, were divided between those who vigorously supported the abolition of slavery and those who chose to keep silent on the issue. There was but one conspicuous exception. **Morris Jacob Raphall** of Bnai Jeshurun in New York early in 1861 preached a sermon in which he maintained that the Hebrew Scriptures approved the institution of slavery. He emphasized that the ancient Hebrews treated the slave "as a person in whom the dignity of human nature was to be respected," in contrast to the frequent practice in the South "which reduces the slave to a thing," but his words were nonetheless widely publicized and praised in the South. In stark contrast to Raphall was the example of **David Einhorn**, rabbi of Baltimore's Har Sinai Congregation (established in 1842 as the first synagogue in the country dedicated to Reform Judaism from its inception). Maryland was a "border state" that did not secede from the Union, but many of its people favored the South and secession. In April 1861 Baltimore withstood days of bloody riots led by secessionists. Einhorn's militant sermons against slavery had made him a marked man among these rioters, and he was forced to flee the city to escape assassination at their hands. He found refuge in Philadelphia and served the Keneseth Israel congregation there, moving on later to a congregation in New York.

After the actual commencement of war between the North and the South, the rabbis of the North were of course unanimous in their support for the Union cause. The considerable number of Jewish soldiers in the Union army brought about a change in the law governing the appointment of military chaplains. This law originally decreed that chaplains be appointed by a vote of field officers and company commanders, and that they be ministers "of some Christian denomination." The unit known as "Cameron's Dragoons" from Pennsylvania, which contained within its ranks a large number of Jews, elected a Jew as its chaplain, and the Secretary of War, following the law, promptly nullified his election. The Board of Delegates of American Israelites thereupon transmitted a Memorial to Congress protesting the regulations governing the appointment of chaplains "inasmuch as they establish a religious test as a qualification for an office under the United States." President Lincoln replied: "I shall try to have a new law broad enough to cover what is desired by you in behalf of the Israelites," and in 1862 the applicable law was amended and the words "some Christian denomination" changed to "some religious denomination."

Despite widespread participation by Jews in the Union military, and general support for the war effort within the community at large, anti-Jewish feeling became very noticeable in the North during the years of the war. This was part of the general resentment of many Americans toward the numerous foreigners who had immigrated to the United States during the 1840s and fifties. Sephardic Jews were by and large accepted as "real Americans," but the German Jews, speaking a heavily accented English along with their native German, were another story. One Northern writer denounced all Jews as "secessionists, copperheads, and rebels." ("Copperheads" were Northerners who sympathized with the South.)

How did the Civil War affect the Jews of the South?

If the strains and privations of the war brought anti-Jewish feelings to the surface in the North, the situation was even more acute in the South. Some Southerners accused the Jews as a group of being "merciless speculators, army slackers, and blockade-runners across the land frontiers to the North." German Jewish peddlers and small merchants were important to the economy of Southern towns and rural areas, particularly as conditions worsened from the destruction wrought by Northern armies and the naval blockade that limited the import of manufactured goods. (The South had little manufacturing of its own.) Thus the Jews, in the minds of some, came to play the role that had been theirs from time immemorial in lands across the sea. When things get rough, blame the Jews.

The frequent and bitter attacks on the Jews were answered in 1863 by **Maximilian J. Michelbacher**, rabbi of Beth Ahabah ("House of Love") in Richmond. In a sermon at a Confederate Fast Day service, he said that he had investigated the conduct of Jewish merchants and was convinced that "the Israelites are not speculators or extortioners." They could not be, he said, because the Jewish merchant specialized in rapid turnover sales, while the speculator made his fortune by hoarding. Besides, Jews for the most part did not deal in the basic commodities in which speculation was most common: "flour, meal, wheat, corn, bacon, beef, coal and wood." If the Jews actually were the extortioners, overcharging without limit, wouldn't the trade go to non-Jewish merchants, who were supposedly free of all taint of profiteering? Michelbacher claimed that the condemnation of the Jews was being deliberately instigated, "cunningly devised after the most approved mode of villainy," to shield the true extortioner and speculator, "who deals in the miseries, life and blood of our fellow citizens." The "monstrous and evil thing that draws its nourishment from the heart's blood of men, women and children" was blamed on the Jews so that those who were actually guilty could escape blame. The rabbi's words were printed in the daily papers of the time.

Individual Jews played prominent roles in the government of the Confederate States, and in several of the member states of the Confederacy. This, too, contributed to the anger and fear directed against the Jews as the South moved closer and closer to defeat at the hands of the North. Before the outbreak of the war Florida had been represented in the United States Senate by **David Levy Yulee**, and Louisiana by **Judah P. Benjamin**. Both resigned their Senate seats upon the secession of their respective states from the Union. Neither one had any religious or community connection to his fellow Jews, but Benjamin in particular was fulsomely denounced as a Jew whenever occasion demanded. While still in the United States Senate he was styled "an Israelite with Egyptian principles," and while an officer of the Confederacy he was routinely referred to as "Judas Iscariot." One Southerner was sure that the "prayers of the Confederacy would have more effect if Benjamin were dismissed." Jefferson Davis, however, would listen to none of this. He retained Benjamin as one of his closest advisers and cabinet officials until the Confederacy came to an end.

In 1861 Salomon de Rothschild visited the Confederate States and wrote to his family, associated with the prominent Rothschild banking house in Paris: "What is astonishing here, or rather, what is not astonishing, is the high position occupied by our coreligionists, or rather by those who were born into the faith and who, having married Christian women, and without converting, have forgotten the practices of their fathers. Judah P. Benjamin, the Attorney General of the Confederate States, is perhaps the greatest mind on this continent. H. M. Hyams, the lieutenant governor of Louisiana, Moyse, the Secretary of the Interior, etc. And, what is odd, all these men have a Jewish heart and take an interest in me, because I represent the greatest Jewish house in the world."

Judah Benjamin had been born in 1811 in St. Thomas, British West Indies. The family settled in Fayetteville, North Carolina, where young Benjamin went to a fine preparatory school; at age fourteen he entered Yale University. Leaving Yale without a degree at age seventeen, he settled in New Orleans and turned to the study of law. At age twenty-one he was admitted to the Louisiana bar. From its very beginning Benjamin's career in the law was an outstanding success. He had great knowledge, eloquence, and force of personality. He became the leading commercial lawyer in New Orleans and developed a national reputation. He entered politics and was elected to the state legislature and the Louisiana constitutional convention. In 1852 he was elected to the United States Senate (in those days senators were elected by the state legislatures rather than by popular vote). Before taking office, President **Franklin Pierce** offered him a seat as a justice of the Supreme Court of the United States, but he accepted his Senate seat instead. Though an apologist for slavery, Benjamin once declaimed these words during a trial relating to slaves: "What is a slave? He is a human being. He has feelings and passions and intellect. His heart, like the white man's, swells with love, burns with jealousy, aches with sorrow, pines under restraint and discomfort, toils with revenge and even cherishes the desire of liberty."

With the establishment of the Confederacy, Benjamin became Attorney General, went on to become Secretary of War (in which position he antagonized many of the generals, who were confident that, through their own strategic brilliance, they could win the war), and was named at last Secretary of State, which post he held from 1862 to 1865. Jefferson Davis wrote of him that he "had a very high reputation as a lawyer, and my acquaintance with him in the Senate impressed me with the lucidity of his intellect, his systematic habits and capacity for labor." Davis also called him "my chief reliance among men." After Gen. **Robert E. Lee**'s surrender at Appomattox, Benjamin acquired a horse and wagon and, disguised as a Frenchman, made his way across Georgia into Florida. There he hired a small fishing boat and reached England. He was called to the English bar in 1866 and in 1872 was named a queen's counsel. To this day the text that he authored, *Benjamin on Sales,* is a principal textbook on its subject. In 1882 he retired to Paris, rejoining his wife, a Catholic of old-French stock from New Orleans, who had been living in Paris since 1843. He died there in 1884.

What was the infamous "*General Order No. 11*"?

The Union army had seen its greatest successes in 1862 under Maj. Gen. **Ulysses S. Grant**. It occupied the western portion of Tennessee, together with southern Kentucky and northern Mississippi, and placed these areas under a military government called the Department of Tennessee. On December 17, 1862, General Order No. 11 was telegraphed from the military headquarters to all post commanders in the department. It read as follows: "The Jews, as a class violating every regulation of trade established by the Treasury Department and also department orders, are hereby expelled from the department within twenty-four hours from the receipt of this order. No passes will be given these people to visit headquarters for the purpose of making personal application for trade permits. By order of Maj. Gen. U. S. Grant."

What gave rise to this order was the fact that the rail and river transportation centers in the department, particularly Memphis, had become sites for illicit trade with the "enemy," namely, Confederate citizens eager to sell cotton to soldiers and others from the North where the mills were idle because they had no cotton. Besides cotton buyers and sellers came smugglers with military and medical goods needed in the South. Of course, there were Jews among both the cotton buyers and the smugglers. But why should Jews have been singled out for penalty under this order? Grant himself had many Jewish friends both prior to this date and in subsequent years. On the date of the general order, however, he wrote a letter to the War Department in Washington, observing that "the Jews seem to be a privileged class that can travel everywhere." This seems to indicate that, in Grant's eyes, the Jews were more successful traders than others, and that the order was due to pressure from other traders, both civilian and military, who wished to be rid of formidable competitors. That this supposition is likely true is borne out by the fact that the day after the order's issuance, the price of cotton fell from forty to twenty-five cents a pound.

In any event, General Order No. 11 constituted the most serious issue ever faced by America's Jewish community in its history. A modest merchant from Paducah, Kentucky, **Cesar Kaskel**, telegraphed Lincoln and then proceeded to Washington with numerous letters and newspaper editorials. The President received him on January 3, 1863, and immediately instructed the general-in-chief of the army to cancel General Order No. 11. The directive issued to Major General Grant was as follows: "A paper purporting to be General Order No. 11, issued by you December 17, has been presented here. By its terms, it expells all Jews from your department. If such an order has been issued, it will be immediately revoked." Thus was the government of the United States spared the shame of summarily expelling a group of people, on the basis of ethnicity alone, from a specific territory in which people of other ethnicities were welcome to remain. The only similar event in the nation's history was the expulsion of Japanese-Americans from the West Coast during the Second World War.

Grant, who subsequently became the commanding general of all Union forces battling the Confederates, and in 1868 was elected President, always regretted the general order that was issued in his name. **Simon Wolf**, who functioned in Washington as a spokesman for major Jewish organizations, wrote the following about Order No. 11: "Having enjoyed the friendship of President Grant and of General Sherman (I was for eight years officially connected with the former, and for a time on intimate social terms with the latter), I can state that I had repeated conversations with them regarding 'Order No. 11,' which was issued over the signature of General Grant, but of which he, at the time, had absolutely no knowledge."

What did Simon Wolf write to William Cullen Bryant, editor of the New York Evening Post, and why did he write it?

Simon Wolf (1836–1923) came to the United States as a young boy and, after working several years for his uncles who were merchants in Ohio, moved on to the study of law. Admitted to the Ohio bar, in 1862 he moved to Washington, D.C., where he spent the rest of his life. He went into politics and held several offices in the District of Columbia government. He was a confidant of presidents, particularly the Republican ones, and soon came to be looked upon as the spokesman for America's Jews in Washington.

In 1864 Wolf wrote to **William Cullen Bryant**, editor of the New York *Evening Post*, in an effort to respond to the constant attacks upon Jews during the course of the Civil War, and to the habit of newspapers generally, including the *Post*, of identifying Jewish malefactors as Jews, without doing the same when the malefactor was Methodist, Presbyterian, etc. Part of his long letter reads as follows: "The war now raging has developed an intensity of malice that borders upon the darkest days of superstition and the Spanish Inquisition. Has the war now raging been inaugurated or fostered by Jews exclusively? Is the late Democratic Party composed entirely of Israelites? Are all the blockade-runners and refugees descendants of Abraham? Are there no native Americans engaged in rebellion? No Christians running the blockade, or meek followers of Christ within the folds of Tammany? We have been branded and outraged for four long years, until discretion has ceased to be a virtue, and it is incumbent upon you, the father of the American press, to give us a hearing through the columns of your valuable journal." Bryant published Wolf's letter in its entirety, and responded that his points were well taken.

When, in 1878, the Union of American Hebrew Congregations organized as a constituent group a Board of Delegates on Civil and Religious Rights (to take up the work of the erstwhile Board of Delegates of American Israelites), Wolf became its spokesman to official Washington. He also represented the Bnai Brith in a similar capacity. Until his death Wolf was involved in almost every action taken to protect the civil rights of Jews both in the United States and in other countries. He worked to secure the intercession of the American government on behalf of persecuted Jews in Russia and Romania. He saved thousands of immigrant Jews in this country from deportation, and strove always to keep the doors of the United States open to the oppressed of Europe. He died before these doors were, to a considerable extent, closed by Congress in 1924.

In 1895 Wolf published his book, *The American Jew as Patriot, Soldier and Citizen,* as a reply to the canard that no Jews had fought in the armed forces during the Civil War. The book lists more than six thousand Jews who fought for the Union and more than one thousand who fought for the Confederacy. His estimate of the Confederate forces is far too low, since their Secretary of War in 1864 had refused to grant Jewish soldiers leave for the High Holy Days—reasoning that there were at least ten thousand of them and too many military units would be disrupted.

What were the achievements of the Seligmans?

David and **Fanny Seligman** were poor Jews living in a small Bavarian town in the 1830s. They are linked to the history of America's Jews because they had eight sons, all of whom either were founders of, or played a role in, J. & W. Seligman and Company, the first great German Jewish banking house to be established in New York. They also had three daughters. **Joseph Seligman**, the oldest son, came to the United States in 1837; by 1841 three other brothers had arrived, and together they decided to seek their fortune as peddlers and, later, as dry-goods merchants in the small towns of Alabama. (**Jesse Seligman**, at age fifteen, owned his own store and had clerks in his employ.) The brothers continued to prosper and in 1848 moved back to New York, where they established an import business. Jesse opened a store in Watertown, in the far north of New York state, and there came to know **Ulysses S. Grant**, then a lieutenant in the army, subsequently the general who headed the Union forces in the Civil War and then served as president of the United States. In 1850 Jesse went with a stock of goods to California, to serve the needs of the hordes flocking there during the Gold Rush. He took possession of the only brick building in San Francisco. When, shortly thereafter, an awesome fire devastated the city, Seligman's stock, in its brick refuge, was all that remained available to the populace of the city. In 1857 Jesse returned to New York, though the San Francisco business continued to operate. By that year the Seligman brothers in New York found that their most profitable import had become gold from California. Without particular effort on their part, they had come to be, as buyers and sellers of bullion, in the banking business.

In 1860 the Seligman firm moved into the manufacture of clothing and, with the outbreak of the Civil War, into supplying uniforms to the Union forces. By 1862 the government owed the company $1 million for uniforms. Joseph Seligman devoted himself to the sale of Union bonds in Europe during the war. According to one calculation, "he placed enormous quantities of bonds in Frankfurt, Munich, Berlin and Amsterdam," amounting to more than $200 million worth between 1862 and 1864. At the conclusion of the war J. & W. Seligman and Company, World Bankers, was officially born. Like the Rothschilds of Europe, the Seligman brothers were to preside in the great financial centers of the world: Joseph, James, and Jesse in New York, and others in London, Paris, and Frankfurt. Houses were later established in Berlin, Amsterdam, New Orleans, and San Francisco. The

Seligman bank in New York was very involved in bond issues for the many railroads that came into being in the years after the Civil War. On some issues it made money; on others, as might be expected, it lost.

In 1891 Jesse Seligman, in summing up his life and work, wrote the following, which applies equally to the entire family:

> My success, whatever it has been, I attribute, first, to the fact that I had the good fortune to become a citizen of this great Republic, under whose beneficent laws the poor and the rich, irrespective of race or creed, have equal opportunities of education and material prosperity; secondly, to the fact that I have always endeavored to extract something good rather than evil from everything that has come before me (which has had the effect of making lighter the cares and tribulations of this life); in the next place, to the great assistance of my good brothers, to the companionship and advice of a loving wife and children, and, above all, to a kind and merciful God.

In 1893 Jesse suffered a blow that, in all likelihood, contributed to his death the following year. After the death of his brother Joseph, he had become the head of the family banking firm, and had also been honored with a vice presidency of the Union League Club in New York. (Both Joseph and Jesse had been members of the club for many years.) While Jesse was serving as vice president, the club's membership committee rejected the application of his son Theodore, a young lawyer, for entry into the club. The committee explained to Jesse that "it was not a personal matter in any way, either as to father or son. The objection is purely racial." Jesse resigned from the club, but its members could not understand what he was so disturbed about; they therefore unanimously rejected his resignation. Jesse's funeral in New York at Temple Emanu-El provided an opportunity for those who lamented what the club had done to him to make amends of a sort. Among the two thousand, including many dignitaries, who attended the funeral, there was a sixty-man delegation from the Union League Club led by its president, which had come on foot from the clubhouse to the temple.

After Jesse's death the firm was headed by another Seligman brother, James. Under his leadership it played a major role in the events leading up to the construction of the Panama Canal, including the formation of an independent state of Panama on territory that had been part of Colombia, the treaty between the United States and Panama agreed to in 1903, and the financing of the Canal's construction.

J. & W. Seligman and Company, no longer an international banking firm with offices around the world, exists today as a small but prestigious investment house in New York.

How did Henry Hilton, proprietor of the Grand Union Hotel in Saratoga Springs, New York, come to have a major impact upon Jewish-American life, lasting from 1877 until well into the next century?

Joseph Seligman was the major German Jewish banking figure in New York City from the early 1860s until his death in 1880. As had been his custom for several years, he, with his family and servants, arrived at the beginning of the summer of 1877 at the Grand Union Hotel in Saratoga Springs, New York, where they had planned to spend the season. This, however, was not to be. The hotel's manager spoke these words to him: "Mr. Seligman, I am required to inform you that Mr. Hilton has given instructions that no Israelites shall be permitted in future to stop at this hotel." Seligman responded, "Are they dirty, do they misbehave themselves, or have they refused to pay their bills?" "Oh, no," came the answer, "there is no fault to be found in that respect. The reason is simply this: Business at the hotel was not good last season, and we had a large number of Jews here. Mr. Hilton came to the conclusion that Christians did not like their company, and for that reason shunned the hotel. He resolved to run the Union on a different principle this season, and gave us instructions to admit no Jew." (This Hilton, it should be noted, had no connection to the family of Conrad Hilton, noted hoteliers of the twentieth century.)

Henry Hilton, in an interview with a *New York Times* reporter, indicated that he did not consider Joseph Seligman a "Hebrew." Years ago, he said, he absolutely threw overboard the Hebrew Bible and Moses, and now "he belongs to the Adler sect of Liberals, and this being the case, he but plays the mountebank if he attempts to arouse the prejudices of the Orthodox Hebrew Church by circulating any stories or insinuations to the effect that he was turned out of the Grand Union Hotel simply because he belonged to that ancient faith. Mr. Seligman is a Jew in the trade sense of the word, and the class of Jews he represents, while they are not forbidden to come to the Grand Union, are not encouraged to come."

Hilton continued:

The wishes and prejudices of the only class of people who can or will support a hotel like this must be consulted and followed. The hotel is run for them, and not for those they dislike. Mr. Seligman belongs to a class of not Hebrews, but Jews, with whom this class of guests, particularly the female portion of them, will not associate and whom they do not wish to be forced to meet. Families like the Hendricks and Nathans are welcome everywhere, while these Jews, not Hebrews, of whom Joseph Seligman is a representative, are not wanted any more at any of the first-class Summer hotels. They have brought the public opinion down on themselves by a vulgar ostentation, a puffed-up vanity, an overwhelming display of condition, a lack of those considerate civilities so much appreciated by good American society.

Hilton's remarks attempt to differentiate between "Hebrews," that is to say, truly religious Jews of Spanish-Portuguese stock who had resided in America for several generations, and "Jews," those of German derivation who had come to the United States much later and prospered fairly quickly in banking and mercantile activities. Some of the latter, like Seligman, supported the "Adler sect of Liberals," Hilton's term for the Ethical Culture Society founded by **Felix Adler** in the 1870s. This group, which still exists, emphasizes a devotion to ethical ideals rather than worship of a personalized deity. It sought to attract both Jews and Christians who questioned the efficacy of the ancient religions. Hilton's antipathy to such "liberals" should be considered in conjunction with his remark that it was the female portion of his favored guests who did not wish to associate with "Jews" like the Seligmans. "Liberals," it was implied, might have little compunction about seeking to take advantage of such female guests or, even worse, proposing marriage to them. Truly religious "Hebrews," on the other hand, members of the Spanish-Portuguese Synagogue, would not be suspected of having such proclivities since marriage to a non-Jewish woman could be cause for their expulsion from the synagogue. Hilton, however, was not telling the truth when he said that Sephardic families like the Hendricks and the Nathans would still be welcome at his hotel. Members of the Hendricks family were also turned away.

Subsequent journalistic inquiry discovered that Hilton's antagonism to Joseph Seligman was traceable to a disagreement between the management of the A. T. Stewart and Company dry-goods emporium, over which Hilton presided as trustee, and the Seligman bank. Without doubt another factor was Seligman's membership on the "Committee of Seventy"—a group of prominent New Yorkers devoted to "clean government" and the eradication of the Tweed Ring, with which Hilton was associated. Seligman's treatment at the hotel was written up and discussed as a cause célèbre in newspapers throughout the country; it was the subject of sermons at both synagogues and churches; meetings passed resolutions denouncing what had occurred. Except for isolated incidents in out-of-the-way inns, nothing like this had happened in the United States before. People removed their accounts from A. T. Stewart, and not long thereafter the store went out of business.

Though elements of polite society decried what had happened, as did many clergy and intellectuals, there were also people in all parts of the country who approved of Hilton's behavior. Since what New York society did was often copied elsewhere in the country, it now became acceptable for Jews to be turned away from hotels and resort accommodations, if such places wished to demonstrate that they catered to an "exclusive" clientele. Various city and country clubs also adopted such policies, even if Jews had been among the founding members of such groups in the past. A case in point is that of the Union League Club in New York, which rejected the membership application of Jesse Seligman's son while Jesse himself was serving as a vice president of the club. A change of policy had been quietly introduced, preventing the introduction of any new Jewish members into the club.

In 1872 **Louis J. Salomon**, a Jew who was the great-grandson of **Haym Salomon** of Revolutionary War fame, had been chosen as the first Rex of Mardi Gras in New Orleans. After Hilton's exclusion of Joseph Seligman from the Grand Union Hotel, however, no Jew could any longer be considered for that honor, nor were they eligible for membership in that city's exclusive clubs. New Orleans, after all, could not allow itself to be less discriminating than New York.

Exclusionary policies based on race and religion were quite common in much of America until after the Second World War. In subsequent years they were set aside at clubs and resort hotels, though not everywhere. Now, of course, there is federal and state legislation that prevents the implementation of such policies at places of public accommodation.

What did they eat at the "Trefa Banquet" *in 1883?*

Rabbi **Isaac Mayer Wise** was the organizing genius behind the founding of the central religious institutions of American Judaism during the last quarter of the nineteenth century: the Union of American Hebrew Congregations in 1873 and the Hebrew Union College, a rabbinic seminary, in 1875. Both of these institutions were based in Cincinnati (the union's headquarters is now in New York and the college now has four campuses, in Cincinnati, New York, Los Angeles, and Jerusalem).

As might be expected, the Jewish elite of Cincinnati arranged a celebration to fete the members of the first graduating class of the college (four students who were ordained rabbis), together with the delegates of the union, under whose auspices the college had been established. This took the form of a dinner for two hundred people at a hilltop restaurant overlooking the Ohio River. The banquet consisted of nine courses, interspersed with seven wines and liqueurs. This should have been an elegant, convivial evening for all in attendance, but with the appearance of the first course several visiting rabbis from the East Coast fled the room in horror. What had been placed before them were littleneck clams on the half shell, a food definitely not acceptable within kosher cuisine. Had these rabbis remained for later courses, they would have had the opportunity of selecting, among other things, soft-shell crabs, shrimp salad, or frog's legs—items equally at odds with Jewish dietary custom. This occasion came to be known as the "*trefa* banquet," from the Hebrew and Yiddish *taref,* "unkosher." (In biblical Hebrew the word refers to an animal "torn" to death by wild beasts, and hence unfit for Jewish consumption.)

Wise had conceived of the union and the college as institutions that could encompass all types of synagogues and Jews in the country, from the most liberal to the most traditional.

To serve nonkosher foods at a banquet of this type was a calculated insult to the traditionalists. Wise and others close to him always maintained that the Jewish caterer supervising the meal, though he had been instructed to provide only kosher foods, failed to do so and was solely responsible for what had happened. Others claim, however, that the menu that was served had been dictated by some of the Cincinnati laymen who were hosting the occasion, and that they wished, through this action, to drive away the traditionalists and preserve both the union and the college as instruments of the Reform tendency within Judaism. Whether the suspect foods appeared at the banquet through error or by design, the traditionalists did cease to cooperate with Wise, and the union and the college have, since 1883, been identified solely with Reform Judaism.

When Wise's critics demanded an apology for the *trefa* banquet, he wrote in his newsletter that the Jew's religion "centers not in kitchen and stomach," and that "the fact is that the chief cook, himself a Jew, was placed there to bring before the guests a kosher meal. So it was understood in Cincinnati all along, and we do not know why he diversified his menu with multipeds and bivalves. If any of the committee gave him such orders, they are responsible to those who appointed them, not to us, not to any newspaper, not to the Union of American Hebrew Congregations, none of whom had anything to do with the entertainment given to the guests." One of Wise's defenders went so far as to describe his critics as "ignorant fanatics," and then proceeded to inquire, "Why should a dozen men whose religion depended upon abstention from oysters and lobsters decide what others, who like these dishes, should eat? Who forced them to eat *trefa* dishes when so many fine kosher foods had also been available? The humbug of the dietary laws must go, for they promote clannishness, Jewish exclusiveness, even fanaticism, and they make Judaism ridiculous, Lilliputian, demeaning."

While the majority of today's Reform Jews probably do

not observe the Jewish dietary restrictions, what happened at the *trefa* banquet would not recur today. In practically all communities it is understood that at meals sponsored by official Jewish groups, the basic restrictions encoded within the biblical dietary laws will be observed.

What is the story behind the poem engraved on a tablet affixed to the pedestal upon which the Statue of Liberty stands?

The Statue of Liberty was meant to be the gift of the people of France to the people of the United States to commemorate the centennial of American independence in 1876. It was an additional ten years, however, before this great sculpture, fashioned in France, was transported, erected, and dedicated upon the island in New York Harbor, where it now stands. Since the 1930s a sonnet inspired by this statue has been taught to schoolchildren in many parts of the country. It captures, in the judgment of many, what the statue, and maybe even the American nation itself, is supposed to represent.

The author of this poem was **Emma Lazarus**, born in New York in 1849 to a well-to-do family. Her father was Sephardic, her mother from a German Jewish family affiliated with the city's Spanish-Portuguese Synagogue. Emma was one of seven children—one boy, the rest girls. (Her first cousin, **Benjamin Cardozo**, served on the U.S. Supreme Court from 1932 to his death in 1938.) The Lazarus family was an extremely close-knit one. She never married and remained devoted to her father until his death in 1885. She herself died two years later at the age of thirty-eight.

Lazarus was educated through home tutoring, a common practice among upper-class families. She and her siblings studied literature, arithmetic, history, geography, and music, and she became quite proficient in French, German, and Italian. At age fourteen she began to write poetry, much of it rooted in Greek and Roman mythology. Her father had some of her early work printed for circulation among family and friends. In 1868 at a social gathering she met Ralph Waldo Emerson, whom she had long admired. He asked for her volume of poems and, of course, she sent one to him. He advised her on her writing, and they corresponded for years afterward. He recommended that she use Shakespeare as a model of language economy, since she often used more words than necessary to convey her thought. He also advised that life experience was as important for a poet as reading. Lazarus continued to write, and her work was published in various magazines and journals. Her first poem on a Jewish theme was inspired by a family visit to the Touro Synagogue in Newport; it was published in a Jewish journal. When asked by the rabbi of Temple Emanu-El in New York to translate and author some pieces for a new hymnal he wished to publish, she agreed to do the translations but declined to write the original poems that he wanted, writing, "I should be most happy to serve you in your difficult and patriotic undertaking, but the more I see of these religious poems, the more I feel that the fervor and enthusiasm are lacking in me."

Not long afterward, however, Lazarus read about the bubonic plague that had ravaged Europe in the fourteenth century. Known as "the Black Death," in many communities it had been blamed on Jews who were thought to have poisoned the wells, and Jews in consequence had been given over to slaughter. Lazarus was inspired by her research to write a verse drama in five acts, *The Dance to Death*, based on the condemnation and death of the Jews in one German town. Not long after completing this work, Lazarus came to learn about the terrible pogroms against the Jews that broke out in Russia in 1881 and the consequent mass migration of Russian Jews to New York. **Gustav Gottheil**, the rabbi of Temple Emanu-El, was active within the Hebrew Emigrant Aid Society, and one day he brought Lazarus and some others to Ward's Island, where the immigrants were temporarily housed, to view firsthand "the wretched fugitives, the victims of Russian barbarity." From that day on, Lazarus not only worked with the refugees by tending to their needs and giving monetary support, but found in them a new sense of purpose that fueled her poetry. "I am all Israel's now," she said. "Till that cloud pass, I have no thought, no passion, no desire save for my own people." Lazarus, together with the publisher of one of the city's Jewish journals, brought out an inexpensive pamphlet available to the general populace, containing *The Dance to Death* and some of her Jewish poems, under the title *Songs of a Semite.*

By 1883 the sculptor Frédéric Auguste Bartholdi had completed his statue in Paris, but the pedestal upon which it was to stand, for which Americans were supposed to raise the funds, could not even be begun because of lack of funds. **Joseph Pulitzer** (Hungarian-born, of part-Jewish ancestry), who had come to the United States to join the Union army during the Civil War, was the publisher of the *New York World.* He wrote, "New York ought to blush at this humiliating spectacle. The statue, the noble gift of our sister republic, is ready for us, and we stand haggling and begging and scheming in order to raise enough money." His efforts day after day in his paper brought thousands of gifts, but still it was not enough. The pedestal committee decided, among other things, to ask writers to submit pieces that would be published in a portfolio and auctioned off for the pedestal fund. Mark Twain and Walt Whitman were to be included. Emma Lazarus was also asked. At first she refused, saying, "I cannot write to order." But one of the women on the committee suggested that Lazarus think of the statue as holding out her torch to the Russian refugees. This struck home, and she began to work. She wrote two poems, but neither satisfied her. Then she drew upon the store of classical imagery that she had used in so much of her earliest work, and she remembered the Colossus, the huge bronze statue of the sun god that had stood in the harbor of Rhodes in ancient times. And she wrote her greatest, most memorable work, titling it "The New Colossus."

Not like the brazen giant of Greek fame,
With conquering limbs astride from land to land;
Here at our sea-washed, sunset gates shall stand
A mighty woman with a torch, whose flame
Is the imprisoned lightning, and her name
Mother of Exiles. From her beacon-hand
Glows world-wide welcome; her mild eyes command
The air-bridged harbor that twin cities frame.
"Keep, ancient lands, your storied pomp! cries she
With silent lips. "Give me your tired, your poor,
Your huddled masses yearning to breathe free,
The wretched refuse of your teeming shore.
Send these, the homeless, tempest-tost to me,
I lift my lamp beside the golden door!"

The portfolio in which Lazarus's sonnet was included was on exhibit with other works of art to be auctioned off by the pedestal committee. It was purchased by the highest bidder for fifteen hundred dollars, and he took it home.

James Russell Lowell had seen the portfolio before its sale, and he wrote to Lazarus as follows: "I like your sonnet about the Statue much better than I like the Statue itself. But your sonnet gives its subject a *raison d'être* which it wanted before quite as much as it wants a pedestal. You have set it on a noble one, saying admirably just the right word to be said, an achievement more arduous than that of the sculptor."

The poem was not read at the statue's dedication in 1886, nor was it placed on or inside the pedestal at that time. In 1903 Georgina Schuyler, a patron of the arts, came across the portfolio in a used-book shop in New York. She was struck by "The New Colossus." She purchased the portfolio and arranged for the last five lines of the poem to be engraved on a plaque, which was placed inside the second story of the pedestal. In 1945 this plaque was removed and the entire sonnet was engraved upon a new tablet and placed over the pedestal's main entrance, where it remains today.

Who was president of the American Federation of Labor from 1886 to 1924?

Samuel Gompers was born in London in 1850, to Jewish parents who had come from Holland. His father was a cigar maker who earned a meager living. Gompers remembered hearing voices from his childhood, the voices of men as they tramped in groups through the streets of his London neighborhood: " 'God, I've no work to do. Lord, strike me dead— my wife, my kids want bread, and I've no work to do.' Child that I was, that cry taught me the world-wide feeling that has ever bound the oppressed together in a struggle against those who hold control over the lives and opportunities of those who work for wages. That feeling became a subconscious guiding impulse that in later years developed into the dominating influence in shaping my life." Young Gompers was indentured to a cigar maker and learned his father's trade in London. He continued in the trade after his family came to New York in 1863; he was thirteen years old.

Early in his adult life Gompers became a union organizer, eschewing Marxism and any attempt to form a political movement. He and his associates were conservative and cautious, and formed the American Federation of Labor in 1886. He became its president and, except for one term, served in that office until his death in 1924. Gompers believed in a large measure of autonomy for local unions, in organizing by crafts rather than by industries, and in effective collective bargaining. His efforts were concentrated on working for better wages and shorter hours. He advocated workmen's compensation laws, free state education, and the prohibition of child labor. It took the Depression of the 1930s to bring all the elements that Gompers had fought for to fruition, but now, of course, Americans take them for granted.

Gompers as an adult did not pay very much attention to his Jewish heritage. In his autobiography, however, he recalled his beginnings: "When six years of age, I was sent to the Jewish Free School and learned rapidly all that was taught there: reading, writing, arithmetic, geography, and history. The school was an old institution when I attended it. It provided instruction for both boys and girls, as well as for select students known as the Talmud boys, twenty-one in number. When I was ten years and three months I had to go to work. When I left school I stood third to the highest in my classes. As I made rapid progress in my studies, the teacher told father that it was wrong to rob me of an education, particularly as I showed ability. But father could not do otherwise."

Who was the first Jew to serve as a cabinet secretary in the United States government?

Oscar S. Straus, a lawyer educated at Columbia College, was appointed in 1887 by President Grover Cleveland to be United States minister to Turkey. He functioned so well in that very demanding position that three succeeding presidents appointed him to the same post. In 1902 President **Theodore Roosevelt** appointed Straus the American member of the Permanent Court of Arbitration at The Hague. Four years later Roosevelt appointed him his Secretary of Commerce and Labor, the first choice of a Jew to head a cabinet department. When he asked him to take this position, the President told Straus, "I want to show Russia and some other countries what we think of the Jews in this country." (Now, at the end of the twentieth century, no one pays attention to the appointment of Jews to significant government positions, nor do we normally calculate the numbers drawn from other religious groups. At the beginning of the century, though, these were considered interesting and significant matters.)

In 1887 Oscar's brothers, **Nathan** and **Isidor Straus**, had become owners of the R. H. Macy department store in New York. Isidor held several political posts in the city and state, served a term in Congress, and was president of the Educational Alliance, the organization that worked toward the integration of immigrants into American life. In 1912 Isidor and his wife, Ida, were on the liner the *Titanic* when it struck an iceberg and sank. Women and children had been offered space on the lifeboats that were available, but Ida insisted on remaining with her husband and they died together.

By 1900 Nathan Straus was recognized as a major philanthropist, particularly in the field of public health. He campaigned tirelessly for the pasteurization of milk to remove the disease germs that would otherwise be present. In 1914 New York City made the pasteurization of milk compulsory, and the death rate among infants and small children plummeted. All three of the Straus brothers were interested in Jewish affairs and philanthropies as well.

Who was the greatest banker of them all?

Of the German Jewish families who settled in the United States from the 1830s to the 1870s there were a number who became prominent in investment banking. The Seligmans, of course, were the best known of this group in the earlier years. But there were others whose names live on in the various Wall Street investment and brokerage firms that they founded. Among the names are Bache; Carl M. Loeb of Loeb, Rhodes and Company; Goldman, Sachs; Lehman Brothers; and Abraham Kuhn and Solomon Loeb of Kuhn, Loeb and Company. The single most outstanding banker who flourished during the days of these great firms, however, was not one whose name is perpetuated in a company title. By common consensus this was **Jacob Schiff**, who came to New York from Frankfurt in 1873 at the age of twenty-six. Abraham Kuhn of Kuhn, Loeb had met him in Germany and suggested that he write to his partner, Solomon Loeb, about a position with the firm. Schiff came on board, married Therese Loeb, the daughter of Solomon Loeb by his first wife, Fanny Kuhn Loeb (who had died), and became a partner in Kuhn, Loeb and

Company. Schiff was active in financing many of the railroads that were expanding their reach throughout the country during his time. He personally investigated every aspect of operation, and every mile of track, of every railroad within his purview. He was the only German Jewish banker whom J. P. Morgan the elder treated and respected as his own peer.

Schiff was much more serious about his religious observances than most of the Jewish banking crowd. Friday night, the Sabbath eve, was strictly reserved for the family. His wife and children would gather in a circle about him, and he would bless each individually. Then he read a short service in German, after which the group would move from the drawing room to the dining room. At the table Schiff each week recited a grace he himself had put together from traditional Jewish materials: "Our God and Father, thou givest food to every living being. Thou hast not only given us life, thou also givest our daily bread to sustain it. Continue to bless us with thy mercy so that we may be able to share our own plenty with those less fortunate than ourselves. Blessed be thy name forevermore. Amen."

Through his contacts with the Warburg family and bank in Hamburg, Schiff brought Felix Warburg, who became the husband of his daughter Frieda, into Kuhn, Loeb. His brother Paul Warburg was for some years associated with both Kuhn, Loeb and the Warburg bank in Germany, to the mutual benefit of both. He later became the intellectual force behind the establishment of the Federal Reserve System. Schiff also brought in Otto Kahn as a partner, and he became a noted patron of the Metropolitan Opera.

In 1905 Schiff was instrumental in arranging massive loans to Japan to support its war against czarist Russia. (After Japan's victory, President Theodore Roosevelt mediated the peace between the two empires.) Schiff, of course, despised the Russian government because of its unrelenting persecution of the Jews within its domain.

In 1906 Schiff sponsored the meeting that called into

being the American Jewish Committee, an organization still in existence dedicated to protecting the rights and bettering the condition of Jews throughout the world. (The committee now sponsors projects for all sorts of intergroup understanding.) In 1914, as the First World War began, over a million Jews fled the countries of Eastern Europe to escape the warring armies. Schiff brought together the leadership of the American Jewish Committee with other people of wealth to organize the Joint Distribution Committee of American Funds for the Relief of Jewish War Sufferers. By the end of the war "the Joint" was distributing over $16 million a year.

Schiff fervently believed in the Jewish principle that charitable giving was an obligation (*sedaka*, meaning "justice"). He voluntarily tithed 10 percent of his income as a minimum for charitable causes; until he exceeded this 10 percent obligation, he did not consider that he had yet disbursed any of "his money." Whenever possible he kept the amount of his benefactions a secret. He supported the Jewish Theological Seminary so that East European Jews streaming into New York could be "Americanized" through exposure to the seminary's Conservative Judaism. These newcomers would not have been comfortable in the Germanic Reform temples of the time. He gave to colleges in this country, Germany, and Palestine. He gave to hospitals and was a founder of the Provident Loan Society. He originated the "matching gift," a concept prevalent in charitable fund-raising to this day. He gave to individuals to get them started in enterprises of their own. For one man who wanted to be a merchant he bought a candy store; for a man who had cut hair in Europe he bought a barbershop. Except during the last seven years of his life, there was no federal income tax. Schiff took no "deductions" for his benefactions; he gave because he wished to follow the commandment of his God. There is no way to calculate how much his gifts amounted to. It has been estimated at $50 million to $100 million, at a time when this was still "real money."

Jacob Schiff died in 1920. Inside the temple the dignitaries and his German Jewish colleagues came to bid him farewell. Outside the temple, on both sides of Fifth Avenue, hundreds of Eastern European Jews had come from the Lower East Side to do him honor, for in his good works he had given them life and sustenance.

Who was America's outstanding theatrical impresario during the closing years of the nineteenth century and the opening years of the twentieth?

David Belasco (1854–1931) was characterized by his biographer as "the most conspicuous figure in the contemporary theater: his career has been long, picturesque, adventurous, and brilliant." Belasco was born to Sephardic Jewish parents whose ancestors had settled in London early in the sixteenth century. In the 1850s, drawn by the Gold Rush, they journeyed to San Francisco, where David was born. The family then moved to Victoria, British Columbia. When David was seven a Catholic priest friendly with the family, noticing that the young boy was uncommonly intelligent and precocious, proposed that he be placed under his care and receive his education in a monastery in Victoria. His father, a religious Jew, objected vigorously, but David and his mother gave their consent. Soon thereafter, however, David fled the monastery and joined a traveling circus. He rejoined his family in 1862, and they moved back to San Francisco.

Early on Belasco was attracted to the stage, as a child playing juvenile roles and doing some dramatic writing. He became a "theatrical vagabond," serving as callboy, actor, stage manager, and adapter and writer of plays. When he left San Francisco at age twenty-nine, he had played more than 170 parts, written or adapted more than one hundred plays, and directed more than three hundred of them. Settling in New York, he became a producer and director of productions noted for their lavish scenery, costumes, and lighting effects. Among his greatest successes were *Madame Butterfly* and *The*

Girl of the Golden West, both of which were made into operas by Puccini.

Throughout his career Belasco fought the Theatrical Trust, a combination of theater owners that attempted to control theatrical bookings throughout the country and took for itself an exorbitant percentage of the profits of all productions presented in its theaters. In 1904 the trust dictated that none of the theaters it controlled in Washington was permitted to book any Belasco production. Rather than give in to the demands of the trust, Belasco rented Convention Hall in Washington and rebuilt its interior "in strict observance of the legal requirements of the District of Columbia departments, and with every regard for the comfort and safety of his patrons." There he presented his work to large and appreciative audiences. Even though he lost twenty-five thousand dollars as a result of these arrangements, Belasco nonetheless rejoiced that his production was a success.

The stranglehold of the Theatrical Trust on American theater production was not broken until the ascendancy of the Shubert brothers as major theater owners and producers in 1916.

How did such a dense concentration of Jewish immigrants from Eastern Europe come to settle on New York City's Lower East Side?

New York was the primary port of entry for Europeans coming to settle in the United States. Eastern European Jews began to come in noticeable numbers beginning in the 1870s. A major influx of Jews from Russia came in response to the pogroms there in 1881, the subsequent laws forbidding Jewish residence in many areas, and the disturbances of 1905. Thousands upon thousands continued to pour in each year (except during the First World War, 1914–18) until immigration was restricted by an act of Congress in 1924. The vast majority of these "greenhorns" (as newcomers unfamiliar with the language and ways of America were called) settled on New York City's Lower East Side.

German Jews had been part of New York's population for at least two generations before the masses of Eastern Europeans began to arrive; many of them had become active in the garment trades, both wholesale and retail. Mass-production techniques were already widely used in men's clothing; it took somewhat longer for them to come into play in the manufacture of women's garments. The shops of many German Jewish garment entrepreneurs were concentrated on streets on the Lower East Side, and it was here that the first Eastern Europeans arriving in the 1870s settled. Many of them were tailors who brought work home from the shops of the German Jewish merchants who farmed it out to them, and it was convenient to live close to these shops. The Jews who poured into New York in the 1880s and thereafter followed in the footsteps of their predecessors. Thus the Lower East Side, until perhaps the 1950s, was looked upon by many as the major Jewish center in the United States and as the source of Jewish creativity, both material and spiritual, that spread to the rest of the Jews of the country.

Some of the "greenhorns" would start out with a pushcart, attempting to sell articles of clothing, or even scraps of ribbon and cloth gleaned from the wholesale shops, to people on the street. A step up was "customer peddling," going door to door taking orders for secondhand clothing and buying such clothing for resale. The successful peddler might save enough money to eventually open a store of his own.

Most clothing manufacturers, who in the early days were still the German Jews, would farm out part of the manufacturing process. Merchant-manufacturers bought the raw textiles and cut them in their shops. They would give the cut material to contractors, who took it to their own shops (in most cases, these were the tenement rooms in which they themselves lived with their families) and oversaw the sewing and other procedures that produced finished goods. The contractor resold the garments to the manufacturer, who would sell them to buyers, wholesale or retail. The largest segment of Jews in the garment industry were those who worked for the contractors. In most cases, the people—men or women and sometimes children—who labored for the contractors had to buy their own sewing machines. The center for the daily hiring of laborers by contractors was the intersection of Hester and Ludlow streets at eight o'clock each morning—the "Pig Market," called in its day "the noisiest and most densely crowded spot in New York."

Here is how Jacob Riis described the living conditions of many on the Lower East Side in the 1880s: "The homes of the Hebrew quarter are its workshops also. You are made fully aware of it before you have travelled the length of a single block in any of these East Side streets, by the whir of a thousand sewing machines, worked at high pressure from earliest dawn until mind and muscle give out together. Every member of the family, from the youngest to the oldest, bears a hand, shut in the qualmy rooms, where meals are cooked and clothing washed and dried besides, the live-long day. It is not unusual to find a dozen persons—men, women, and children—at work in a single small room." This was a typical "sweatshop."

What is a landsmanschaft?

A *landsmanschaft* (Yiddish; plural *landsmanschaften*) is an association of Jewish immigrants to the United States, and their descendants, who stem from a particular town or village in Eastern Europe. Hundreds of such fellowships were formed in New York and other cities in which Eastern European Jews settled during the 1880s, when massive immigration began, and thereafter. Members of such associations often receive health and death benefits, loans of money, and aid in finding employment or housing. Some *landsmanschaften* also function as synagogues. In 1938 there were about three thousand *landsmanschaften,* with a combined membership of half a million people. These groups were important in aiding new immigrants during the early twentieth century; in the years following the Second World War they took in survivors of the Holocaust and in many instances published books of remembrance about European communities that had been destroyed. In later years many *landsmanschaften* went out of existence, as the services they rendered were taken over by various governmental and private social agencies.

When did the Jewish population of New York City reach 1 million?

In 1870 there were roughly 80,000 Jews in New York City. With the major movement of Jews out of the Russian Empire, however, by 1907 there were some 90,000 Jews arriving every year. The result was that by that year the Jews numbered almost 1 million, composing a quarter of the city's population. By 1915 there would be nearly 1.5 million Jews in New York.

In 1904 there were 306 synagogues on the Lower East Side, as compared to but 22 churches. There were 48 public schools, and 307 Jewish schools that met in the afternoons after public school hours, to give instruction in Hebrew reading and Jewish religion to 8,616 boys and 361 girls. (The obligation to teach Hebrew to girls was less compelling for religious Jews in those days.)

The huge immigration brought not only simple working people but also businessmen, doctors, lawyers, and other professionals. Even gangsters, pimps, and prostitutes sought refuge in the "golden land." As Ronald Sanders noted, "Increasing social mobility had brought with it new opportunities for public vice as well as for public virtue."

What were the Yom Kippur balls?

In her autobiography the famous anarchist **Emma Goldman** wrote, "When I first came to New York, I used to attend the joint gatherings of anarchists and socialists. One occasion of these days had been particularly memorable. It was a Yom Kippur celebration, held as a protest against Jewish orthodoxy. Speeches on free thought, dances, and plenty of eats took the place of the traditional fast and prayers. Religious Jews resented our desecration of their holiest Day of Atonement, and their sons came down in strong force to meet our boys in pitched battle. While the affray was going on in the street, anarchist and socialist orators were holding forth inside the hall."

These "Yom Kippur balls" had their beginning around 1890 and continued for a number of years. As the Lower East Side community matured, however, there was less and less interest in them. Abraham Cahan of the *Jewish Daily Forward* newspaper was an opponent of these affairs and advocated a more tolerant attitude toward the feelings of religious Jews than some socialists wished. In one column of his he described the "three stages in the life of a freethinker: (1) when he passes a synagogue and gnashes his teeth; (2) when he passes a synagogue and smiles; (3) when he passes a synagogue and, though inclined to sigh because the world is still in such a state of ignorance, nevertheless finds himself taking an interest in such moments as these, when men stand together immersed in a feeling that has nothing to do with the egoistic life."

Besides attending Yom Kippur balls, what else did Emma Goldman do?

Emma Goldman (1869–1940) was, in the estimation of some during the late nineteenth and early twentieth centuries, the most dangerous woman in the United States. Born in Lithuania, she came to the United States in 1886 and worked in factories in Rochester (New York) and New Haven before settling in New York City. She became an enthusiastic follower of the anarchist Johann Most, who advocated violence and the overthrow of all government. She became the lover of Alexander Berkman and aided him in testing explosives before his attempt on the life of steel magnate Henry Clay Frick in Pittsburgh in 1892 (this in revenge for the killing of nine striking workers at the Homestead steel plant). Berkman went to prison for fourteen years. "Red Emma," as she was known, traveled the country lecturing about the virtues and benefits of anarchism. She was sent to prison for ten months in 1893 for telling people that if they had no bread, they should take it. She opposed military service and censorship, and was convinced that the voting process was a sham that helped preserve control by the wealthy. She opposed marriage, saying, "If two people care for each other, they have a right to live together as long as that love exists. When it is dead, what base immorality for them still to keep together."

It was one of Goldman's more deluded followers who assassinated President **William McKinley** in 1901. In 1915 Goldman added birth control to the list of causes that she favored. She spoke on the subject and distributed pamphlets about it. During the First World War she turned her energies to opposing the military draft. She and Berkman were arrested and convicted of trying to prevent draft registration and advocating violence. They served two years in prison. In 1919 they and other "dangerous" radicals were deported from the United States. She and Berkman went to Soviet Russia, hoping that it might prove to be the workers' paradise that it claimed to be. After two years they discovered that Russian Communism was every bit as repressive as the regimes in the Western world. Disillusioned, they went first to England and then to Canada, where Goldman died in 1940.

When did New York have a "Chief Rabbi"?

In 1888 several Orthodox congregations brought **Rabbi Jacob Joseph**, a respected talmudic scholar and pietist, from Vilna in Lithuania to New York, to serve as "Chief Rabbi" and bring some order out of the chaos that characterized Jewish religious life on the Lower East Side. A primary task was to impose some level of supervision over the slaughter, preparation, and sale of kosher meat. He imposed and sought to collect a penny tax on poultry killed by *shohetim* (ritual slaughterers) under his supervision, but few were willing to pay this tax and there was no enforcement authority to collect it. Disputes between butchers and slaughterers and some rabbis were frequent: "Fist fights were not uncommon and disregard for both Jewish law and Board of Health ordinances was rampant." Some congregations appointed a rival "Chief Rabbi" of their own. A third came from Moscow and hung out a sign, "Chief Rabbi of America." When asked who had given him this title, he replied, "The sign painter."

Rabbi Joseph's reign as Chief Rabbi was an unhappy one, and he died in 1892. There was no attempt to appoint a successor, but in 1896 elements in the Orthodox community opened a seminary for the training of rabbis, the Isaac Elchanan Yeshiva. This institution is now part of Yeshiva University.

Who was "the angel of the East Side"?

Lillian Wald (1867–1940) grew up in a comfortable German Jewish family in Cincinnati and Rochester, New York. She could have married well and, it may be presumed, lived a life of ease and wealth. For some reason, however, she felt the need for "serious, definite work," specifically work as a "professional nurse." She entered the nursing program at New York Hospital in New York City and, in 1893, began teaching

EXEMPLARY RABBIS

Moshe Feinstein	An Orthodox rabbi known as the great "decisor of the generation." Rabbis throughout the country and the world sent him complex questions of Jewish law for his analysis and decision.
Abraham Joshua Heschel	Professor at the Jewish Theological Seminary of the Conservative movement; he authored several bestselling books that disseminated Jewish spiritual teachings to a wide readership.
Joshua Loth Liebman	A Reform rabbi in Boston; his book *Peace of Mind* swept the country during the 1940s; he offered effective "pastoral counseling" on a nationwide, nonsectarian scale.

a class in home nursing to Lower East Side women. One day a little girl burst into the room, begging Wald to come with her. In Albert Vorspan's words, she led her "into an unheated, dark hovel of a flat, where rough boards lining the walls served as 'beds' for boarders. [Many tenement dwellers took in boarders, who ate with the host family and slept in whatever small space might be available to them.] Lying in the shadows on a blood-stained rag was the mother, virtually at death's door. For a moment the young nurse was transfixed by the stark poverty and grinding misery which lay revealed before her. Then she went to work, ministering to the hemorrhaging woman, scrubbing the floors, cleaning the children, preparing the meal, and making the sick woman and her children more comfortable. She stayed through the day and into the evening."

Wald, in fact, did not stay merely through the day and into the evening. She spent the rest of her life in residence on the Lower East Side. She recognized that what the immigrants needed was not so much a parade of social workers and "do-gooders" who would come into their neighborhood to perform occasional good works and then leave, but rather people who would live in their midst and share the actual conditions of their lives. Wald and a nursing companion, **Mary Brewster**, took a fifth-floor apartment out of which they worked, seeking above all "to make their own impression as friendly souls before whom all the confidence and problems of living might be safely opened." **Jacob Schiff**, the investment banker and philanthropist, sent the nurses a monthly stipend for living expenses, and they could request additional emergency funds if needed. Their apartment became known far and wide throughout the East Side as a combination employment agency, nursing home, and food distribution center.

Wald learned that many children were refused admission to public school because their parents could not read the instructions for administering various medications needed by the children; she made it her business to show them how to do so, and then oversaw the registration of these children in school. She also found that children with contagious diseases often remained in school; Joey, for instance, in the last stages of scarlet fever would entertain his classmates by peeling off his skin in class. In an effort to deal with both these contingencies, Wald was instrumental in bringing about the appointment of school nurses, and physicians who visited the schools regularly.

Within two years Lillian Wald and Mary Brewster could no longer accommodate the throngs who came to their apartment. They moved to a three-story house on Henry Street. Eventually more than fifteen nurses staffed this house, which came to be known as the Henry Street Settlement. In these expanded quarters there came to be playgrounds for children and adult clubs for art, theater, housekeeping, cooking, political discussion, dancing, sewing, mechanics, and English. Children were taken on trips to the zoo, the parks, and to the country. Wald's work led her to campaign for the placement of "public health nurses" in communities throughout the country; she served as the first president of the National Association for Public Health Nursing. Jacob Riis wrote, "The poor trust her absolutely, trust her head, her judgment, and her friendship. She arbitrates in a strike, and the men listen. When pushcart peddlers are blackmailed by the police, she will tell the mayor the truth, for she knows."

She herself wrote:

The visitor who sees our neighborhood for the first time at the hour when school is dismissed, reacts with joy or dismay to the sight, not paralleled in any part of the world, of thousands of little ones on a single city block. Out they pour, the little hyphenated Americans, more conscious of their patriotism than perhaps any other large group of children that could be found in our land; unaware that to some of us they carry on their shoulders our hopes of a finer, more democratic America, when the worthy things they bring to us shall be recognized, and the good in their old-world traditions and culture shall be mingled with the best that lies within our new-world ideals. They open up wide vistas of the many lands from which they come. The multitude passes; swinging walk, lagging step; smiling, serious—just little children, forever appealing, and these, perhaps, more than others, stir the emotions. As a nation we must rise or fall as we serve or fail these future citizens.

What was accomplished by the Educational Alliance?

While the Henry Street Settlement was, in origin, largely the embodiment of the dream of one great soul, **Lillian Wald**, the

Educational Alliance was a project initiated by the uptown German Jewish community for their Eastern European "coreligionists" on the Lower East Side. It was the result of the merger in 1889 of three agencies—the Hebrew Free School Association, the Young Men's Hebrew Association, and the Aguilar Free Library Society—in one large five-story building. Many uptown Jews felt that their downtown brethren had to be "Americanized in spite of themselves." In the words of one uptown publication, they were "slovenly in dress, loud in manners, and vulgar in discourse." According to a report of the Educational Alliance's Committee on Moral Culture, "Within the contracted limits of the New York ghetto medieval Orthodoxy and anarchistic license are struggling for mastery. A people whose political surroundings have entirely changed, who are apt to become intoxicated with liberty of action which has suddenly been vouchsafed to them, is apt to depart from its mooring and to become a moral menace."

Between the turn of the century and the First World War, the alliance sponsored morning classes for children who needed tutoring before entering public school; night classes for adults in English; daytime classes for waiters, watchmen, and bakers who worked at night; classes in Yiddish and Hebrew, cooking and sewing, and Greek and Roman history; classes in music and art (attended by Jacob Epstein, Ben Shahn, Chaim Gross, Moses and Isaac Soyer, and William Zorach, who developed into world-renowned artists); classes taught by Morris Raphael Cohen, who was to become the great professor of philosophy at the City College of New York, in such subjects as the Book of Job and social evolution. Cohen later wrote, "A window of my life opening on the soul-strengthening vista of humanity will always be dedicated to the Educational Alliance."

The alliance sponsored orchestras and singing societies, low-cost lessons in violin and piano, art exhibitions, literary clubs, a summer boys' camp and a girls' camp, a legal aid bureau to serve deserted wives, and theatrical performances. It was, in the words of one of its annual reports, the "immigrant's university and club." Though today relatively few Jews remain on the Lower East Side, the alliance continues its work among all the ethnic communities that make their home in the area.

Who was the first Socialist to sit in the U.S. Congress?

In 1910 **Victor Berger**, of Milwaukee, Wisconsin, was elected as the first member of the Socialist party in the U.S. House of Representatives. Berger had been born in Austria in 1860, and immigrated to Milwaukee in 1878. In 1900 he edited a socialist newspaper and became active in the faction of the socialist movement led by **Eugene Debs**. He lost bids for reelection in 1912 and 1914, and in 1918 was indicted for sedition because of his opposition to American entry into the First World War. In that same year he was once again elected to Congress, but because of the indictment the House refused to seat him. Berger was found guilty and sentenced to twenty years in prison, but the U.S. Supreme Court reversed this decision in 1921. In 1922 he was reelected to Congress. He served there, and as a member of the national executive committee of the Socialist party, until his death in 1929.

During his years in Congress, Berger was a vigorous advocate of child labor laws, the eight-hour workday, and old-age pensions—reforms that finally became law during the New Deal administration of Franklin Roosevelt which took office in 1933.

When were American Jews important in the sport of boxing?

During the 1920s and 1930s Jews made up the largest single ethnic group of contenders in all weight divisions. **Al McCoy (Harry Rudolph)**, son of a kosher butcher in Brooklyn, was middleweight champion from 1914 to 1921. **Abe ("Battling") Levinsky** was light-heavyweight champion from 1916 to 1920. **Benny Leonard**, perhaps for a time the most famous Jew in the country, was lightweight champion of the world from 1917 until his retirement in 1925. **Barney Ross** was the great Jewish boxer of the 1930s. Reared in Chicago's Maxwell Street, he won both the lightweight and junior welterweight championships in 1932. In 1934 he won the welterweight title. Ross, like **Max Baer**, the heavyweight champion in 1933–35, insisted on wearing a Star of David on his boxing trunks.

SPORTS

During the early years of the twentieth century, Jews were usually not noted for their prowess in any sport except boxing and basketball. The immigrants, and many of their children, were apt to be short, and systematic exercise was rarely emphasized. A joke from those years: A man goes into a bookstore and asks for a very short book. The salesman responds: "I have just what you're looking for, a book one page long—*Jewish Sports Figures.*"

Over the years, however, Jews, like people in other immigrant groups, improved their nutritional habits and developed a love for physical exercise. Jews today are found in all areas of sport—college and professional, women as well as men—and many have achieved national or regional prominence in football, baseball, tennis, golf, and other sports. Nowadays people, Jews or others, for the most part do not seek to specify who is Jewish on the playing fields, or distinguish among athletes by religion or ethnic background.

Here are some of the better-known Jewish-American sports figures of the twentieth century:

Nat Holman	One of the most celebrated basketball players of all time. During the 1920s he played for the Celtics (then a New York team) and simultaneously coached at the City College of New York. He was

	head coach at CCNY for thirty-six years, into the 1950s.
Dolph Schayes	Played basketball for New York University in the late 1940s, then went pro with the Syracuse Nationals in the 1950s. His son Danny continued the tradition, playing for Syracuse University, and pro teams during the 1970s, 1980s, and 1990s (Utah Jazz, Denver Nuggets, Milwaukee Bucks, Orlando Magic).
Red Auerbach	Coach who led the Boston Celtics to nine National Basketball Association championships between 1956 and 1966, making him the most successful pro basketball coach in history
Nancy Lieberman	Acclaimed female basketball player from the 1960s into the 1980s
Red Holzman	Basketball coach who led the New York Knicks to a record of 696 wins from 1968 to his retirement in 1982
Hank Greenberg	Praised by the *Detroit News* as the "greatest player the Jews have contributed to baseball and an illustrious torch bearer of his people," the acclaimed Detroit Tigers first baseman led the American League four times in home runs and runs batted in. Jews everywhere rejoiced in his feats on the field, and in his refusal to play ball on Yom Kippur. Greenberg was with the Tigers from 1930 to 1947, except for four years of military service during World War II.

Sandy Koufax	One of the greatest pitchers in major league baseball, Koufax signed with the Brooklyn Dodgers in 1954. Hitting his stride after the team's move to Los Angeles, he led the Dodgers to three National League pennants and two World Series victories between 1961 and 1966. His best single season was 1963, when he won 25 games and lost 5, struck out 306 batters, and pitched 11 shutouts. A sore arm forced him to retire in 1966.
Benny Friedman	Sportswriter Grantland Rice called him "a great quarterback, a marvelous passer and a brilliant field director who deserves equal rank with Red Grange." Friedman served as quarterback, safety, and placekicker while leading the University of Michigan to Big Ten football championships in 1925 and 1926. He played professional football for the old New York Giants and Brooklyn Dodgers in the 1930s and coached at Yale, City College of New York, and Brandeis.
Marv Levy	Pro football coach; with the Kansas City Chiefs from 1978 to 1982, and with the Buffalo Bills from 1986 to the present, leading them to four Super Bowls
Marshall Goldberg	An all-around athlete who was captain of his high school football, basketball, and track teams in a small West Virginia mountain community, Goldberg

went on to play football at the University of Pittsburgh. He led the team to three victorious seasons in 1936–38, including a national championship in 1937. One football magazine in 1938 called him "college football's No. 1 Star." He played a ten-year pro stint with the Chicago Cardinals.

Sid Luckman

Quarterback for Columbia University who went on to lead the Chicago Bears to four National Football League championships between 1940 and 1946.

Marty Glickman

A star in both football and track at high school, Glickman went to Syracuse University on an athletic scholarship. Selected as a member of the United States track and field team at the 1936 Berlin Olympics, he had been promised a slot in the 400-meter relay. In Berlin, the day before the event, he and the other Jewish member of the relay team were removed by Olympic officials. Glickman, as well as many others, are convinced that this was the work of Americans, themselves anti-Semites, who wished to spare the Nazis the embarrassment of having to honor Jewish runners on the winning American team. Back in Syracuse, Glickman resumed football and track, but took advantage of an opportunity to begin a career in sports broadcasting. He graduated in 1939, and except for the length of his military service during World War II, this has been his career ever since. In 1945 he became "the voice of the New York Knicks" basketball team, an association that lasted twenty years. He has also done extensive coverage of pro football and horse racing. He was the first sports director for the HBO cable TV network, and continues to give supervision and instruction to fledgling sportscasters.

Mark Spitz

Winner in 1971 of an award as the outstanding amateur athlete in the United States, Spitz won eight gold medals in swimming at the 1972 Munich Olympics. In every event he set a new world record.

Dick Savitt

A tennis champion, Savitt won the Australian Open in 1951, and then the men's singles title at Wimbledon.

Aaron Krickstein

A professional tennis player in the 1980s and 1990s, he, like others on the circuit, has earned millions.

Amy Alcott

A professional golfer, she was a consistent winner during the 1980s on the Ladies' Professional Golf Association's Tour and at other events.

Rod Carew

A convert to Judaism, Carew is one of the all-time great hitters in baseball. During the 1970s and 1980s he played first or second base for the Minnesota Twins and the California Angels.

Was there more to life on the Lower East Side than poverty, struggle, and degradation?

In spite of overcrowding and the hard labor required to eke out a living, the immigrants on the Lower East Side, if they were so minded, could participate in a vigorous social and cultural life. **Hutchins Hapgood**, a journalist, wrote *The Spirit of the Ghetto* just as the twentieth century was beginning. He described the situation this way:

> The Jewish quarter of New York is generally supposed to be a place of poverty, dirt, ignorance and immorality—the seat of the sweatshop, the tenement house, where 'red-lights' sparkle at night, where the people are queer and repulsive. Well-to-do persons visit the 'Ghetto' merely from motives of curiosity or philanthropy; writers treat of it 'sociologically,' as of a place in crying need of improvement. That the Ghetto has an unpleasant aspect is as true as it is trite. But I was led to spend much time in certain poor resorts of Yiddish New York not through motives either philanthropic or sociological, but simply by virtue of the charm I felt in men and things there.

He gave this example:

> Four men sat excitedly talking in the little cafe on Grand Street where the Socialists and Anarchists of the Russian quarter were wont to meet late at night and stay until the small hours. An American, who might by chance have happened there, would have wondered what important event had occurred to rasp these men's voices, to cause them to gesticulate so wildly, to give their dark, intelligent faces so fateful, so ominous an expression. In reality, however, nothing out of the ordinary had happened. It was the usual course of human affairs which kept these men in a constant glow of unhappy emotion; an emotion which they deeply preferred to trivial optimism and the content

founded on Philistine well-being. They were always excited about life, for life as it is constituted seemed to them very unjust.

It was nearly midnight, and the men in the cafe, although they had drunk nothing stronger than Russian tea, talked on, seemingly intoxicated with ideas.

Hapgood was describing a vigorous intellectual life centered on political ideas. Other Jews could apply the same intensity and emotion in discussing religious texts.

Those who were not intellectuals or philosophers could find recreation and even inspiration in the many offerings that were available in Yiddish theater. Hapgood writes, "Poor workingmen and women with their babies of all ages fill the theater. Great enthusiasm is manifested, sincere laughter and tears accompany the sincere acting on the stage. Peddlers of soda water, candy, of fantastic gewgaws of many kinds, mix freely with the audience between the acts. Conversation during the play is received with strenuous hisses, but the falling of the curtain is the signal for groups of friends to get together and gossip about the play or the affairs of the week. Introductions are not necessary, and the Yiddish community can then be seen and approached with great freedom."

Who was looked upon as "probably the most influential political, cultural, and literary figure" in the Eastern European Jewish community in America?

This distinction, according to many of his contemporaries as well as later researchers, belongs to **Abraham Cahan** (1860–1951). Cahan was born in Russia to a religious family, but in his teens he began to question Jewish Orthodoxy and pursue secular learning. At age twenty he became part of a revolutionary circle. Learning that the Russian police were investigating his group, Cahan procured a forged passport and made his way to the United States. On board ship he taught himself English, using an old grammar book. In New York he took work in a cigar factory.

One evening in 1882 Cahan attended a socialist meeting on the Lower East Side and was chagrined to find that all the lecturers made their presentations in either Russian or German. Why did no one speak to the group in Yiddish, the language of the listeners? He expressed his dissatisfaction, and was invited to give the featured presentation at the next meeting. He spoke in Yiddish for two hours, holding his audience of four hundred in rapt attention. Thereafter he was in great demand as a speaker. He also honed his English style, writing stories and articles that were published in New York papers. William Dean Howells admired his writing and championed its publication. (In 1917 Cahan published a highly acclaimed novel, *The Rise of David Levinsky*.) For a time he worked as a reporter for the New York *Commercial Advertiser*, with Lincoln Steffens as his editor. At that paper he became friendly with **Hutchins Hapgood**, who toured the Lower East Side with Cahan as his guide. Hapgood later wrote *The Spirit of the Ghetto*, an admiring look at the life and culture of the immigrant Jews to which he had been introduced by Cahan.

Cahan wrote for Yiddish papers and campaigned for Henry George in the New York mayoral election of 1886. George, who advocated a single tax on ownership of land as a cure for all social ills, would have won if Tammany had not rigged the vote in favor of the Democratic candidate. Cahan's political affiliation had been anarchist, but he moved over to the Socialist Labor Party headed by **Daniel DeLeon**, of Sephardic ancestry, and edited a Yiddish paper affiliated with the party. DeLeon was an autocrat, however, and Cahan resigned his position, proceeding instead to found a new paper in 1897, the *Jewish Daily Forward*, which became the major literary and cultural institution of Yiddish-speaking Jews in America. Cahan switched his political affiliation to the Socialist party headed by Eugene Debs, a group deeply rooted in the democratic tradition and opposed to the so-called "dictatorship of the proletariat" that developed in the Soviet Union.

Cahan remained the editor of the *Forward*, a daily Yiddish newspaper, except for short periods, until his death. Under his leadership the paper's circulation grew as long as there remained a sufficient number of Yiddish-language readers to appreciate it. It covered political topics from a democratic socialist perspective and vigorously supported the work of labor unions. It also presented wide coverage of cultural news, including plays and books. In its early years it was widely known for columns and editorials giving advice to new Americans about American ways, thus helping them adjust and acculturate to their new society. The paper serialized works of great writers like **Sholem Asch** and **Isaac Bashevis Singer**. Cahan's wide personal interests and his understanding of what his paper's readers needed enabled them to develop as educated Jewish Americans.

Cahan's feud with the famous Yiddish playwright **Jacob Gordin** was well known on the Lower East Side. After a derogatory review of one of Gordin's plays by Cahan, Gordin wrote the following: "It is clear that we are working for the sake of the selfsame people. But I want to lead them forward, and he drags them backward through the *Forward.* I say to them, a man must be upright and defend his principles unequivocally. He teaches them to be politicians. I say, a revolutionary should not be two-faced. He says, you have to keep the circulation in mind. I say, an honest man should never kowtow to anybody. He says, you've got to make friends. I say, you have to lift the masses up to your level. He says, you have to stoop down to the level of the masses, cater to them and accommodate yourself to their basest instincts." Gordin speaks here as the uncompromising idealist. Cahan is the practical man, in search of results that will bear fruit.

Cahan always remained committed to the democratic socialism exemplified by Eugene Debs, but in 1936 he joined with **Sidney Hillman** and **David Dubinsky** and other labor figures in organizing the American Labor party, a New York organization that would make it possible for democratic socialists to vote for Franklin Roosevelt's second term without having to pull the lever for the Democratic party, which in New York's local politics was associated with the corruption of Tammany Hall. During the 1940s the American Labor party was largely taken over by Communists. In response, many of its original founders established the Liberal party, which still plays a marginal role in local New York City elections.

The *Forward* continues today as a weekly paper published in Yiddish. It now produces in addition a weekly paper in English.

What was the "Bintl Brief"?

In 1906 the *Jewish Daily Forward,* the leading Yiddish-language newspaper in New York, edited by Abraham Cahan, initiated the "Bintl Brief" ("Bundle of Letters"), a regular column featuring letters that, for the most part, requested advice from the editor about common, or sometimes not-so-common, situations in which the writers, recent immigrants to this country, found themselves. It soon became the most popular feature in the paper. One correspondent reported that "neighbors began to whisper that my wife was having an affair with our boarder, but I had no suspicion of her, whom I love as life itself." A Jewish detective could not find it in his heart to arrest a poor restaurateur who was selling liquor without a license; was he violating his duty? An abandoned wife declared, "I will sell my children to people who will give them a home. I will sell them for bread, not money."

A writer who signed himself "The Unhappy Fool" revealed that he loves "a fine girl who has a flaw that keeps me from marrying her. She has a dimple in her chin, and it is said that people who have this lose their first husband or wife." The editor answered, "The trouble is not that the girl has a dimple in her chin but that some people have a screw loose in their heads."

Hayim Zhitlovsky, a vigorous critic of both the socialist *Forward* and the vulgarity of mass culture, nonetheless admitted that the "Bintl Brief" satisfied "the need of the Jewish radical immigrants to extract some ethical lessons from their muddled experiences. Sex and family problems had not yet been dealt with in Yiddish literature. In a moral crisis the ordinary man was bewildered and anguished. He had lost the old compass of traditional religion, and now had to look to the foggy generalizations of Jewish radicalism and his new synagogue, the *Forward*. Of course, it would have been better if the advice given in the 'Bintl Brief' were more serious and on a higher intellectual level."

What great tragedy befell the people of the Lower East Side on March 25, 1911?

On March 25, 1911, a fire broke out at the Triangle Shirtwaist Company, located in the vicinity of Washington Square in New York City. (A "shirtwaist" is a woman's blouse.) The company occupied the top three floors of a ten-story building. On these three floors there were about 850 workers, most of them Jewish women between the ages of thirteen and twenty-five, together with a smaller number of Italians. Some escaped the flames, but 146 died, some at their sewing machines, some at the doors to the exit stairways which had been locked to prevent workers from leaving their jobs early.

The Yiddish-language poet **Morris Rosenfeld** was commissioned by the *Jewish Daily Forward* to describe the scene, as pieced together from eyewitness reports. He wrote:

> One girl after another fell, like shot birds, from above, from the burning floors. The men held out a longer time, enveloped in flames. And when they could hold out no longer, they jumped too. Below, horrified and weeping, stood thousands of workers from the surrounding factories. They watched moving, terrible, unforgettable scenes. At one window on the eighth

floor appeared a young man with a girl. He was holding her tightly by the hand. Behind them the red flames could be seen. The young man lovingly wrapped his arms around the girl and held her to him a moment, kissed her, and then let her go. She leaped, and fell to the sidewalk with great impact. A moment later he leaped after her, and his body landed next to hers. Both were dead. It took a whole hour before the firemen could enter the burning building, and by then it was all over. The sidewalks were full of dead and wounded, and no one could be seen at the windows any longer. The poor girls who had remained inside the building lay all about burnt or smothered to death by fire and smoke. The ambulances and patrol wagons that arrived were not sufficient for the job. Grocers, butchers and peddlers contributed their wagons and pushcarts.

The labor unions utilized this terrible tragedy to strengthen their ties to the working people of the Lower East Side, where the great majority of the victims had lived. A *Forward* headline proclaimed, THE MORGUE IS FULL OF OUR DEAD, and the paper urged all its readers to attend the memorial for them ten days later, to march "every union man with his trade, with his union." One hundred thousand people marched through the streets of the Lower East Side. Rosenfeld's poem in memory of the dead reads in part:

> *Over whom shall we weep first?*
> *Over the burned ones?*
> *Over those beyond recognition?*
> *Over those who have been crippled?*
> *Or driven senseless?*
> *Or smashed?*
> *I weep for them all.*
>
> *Now let us light the holy candles*
> *And mark the sorrow*
> *Of Jewish masses in darkness and poverty.*

> *This is our funeral,*
> *These our graves,*
> *Our children.*

Rose Schneiderman, a small but stormy union activist, said this at a meeting:

> The old Inquisition had its rack and thumbscrews and its instruments of torture with iron teeth. We know what these things are today: the iron teeth are our necessities, the thumbscrews are the high-powered and swift machinery close to which we must work, and the rack is here in the firetrap structures that will destroy us the minute they catch fire. This is not the first time girls have been burned alive in this city. Every week I must learn of the untimely death of one of my sister workers. Every year thousands of us are maimed. The life of men and women is so cheap and property is so sacred. I can't talk fellowship to you who are gathered here. Too much blood has been spilled. It is up to the working people to save themselves.

What is meant by "Jewish labor unions"?

In 1885 Russian and Hungarian Jewish socialists formed the Jewish Workers Association for the purpose of organizing labor unions. Two years later the group affiliated with the Socialist Labor party. The following year Jewish elements within the Socialist Labor party decided to create a union federation, even though there were no unions seeking to federate; they called it the United Hebrew Trades. Within a year, however, it contained ten participating unions with twelve hundred members, and within two years there were twenty-two unions with six thousand members. In 1890 a spontaneous strike by sewers of knickers (then called kneepants) broke out. The United Hebrew Trades assumed control of the strike, which lasted a week; the clothing contractors settled on the workers' terms. In like manner, the UHT took over a strike against shops that made women's cloaks. This strike lasted eight weeks, but in the end the manufacturer, a German Jew, gave in to the workers' demands. The UHT became weak and ineffective, however, because of the rivalry that broke out in the various unions between "DeLeonists" (followers of **Daniel DeLeon**'s militant political approach) and "Gompersists" (followers of **Samuel Gompers** and the American Federation of Labor, who emphasized negotiation for improved working conditions over efforts at political activity). In an attempt to start anew, the United Brotherhood of Cloak Makers was formed in 1896. Four years later its leadership called a conference of labor representatives from around the country to found a national group, the International Ladies Garment Workers Union. Upon its formation this union affiliated with the American Federation of Labor, though because of the strong socialist influence in the New York group, it was one of the more "radical" AFL unions. The ILGWU successfully organized the women's clothing industry and became one of the largest unions in the country.

In 1909 strikes had been called at several individual shirtwaist (blouse) companies, but within ILGWU ranks there was uncertainty about the wisdom of a general strike. At a mass meeting of thousands of workers and labor leaders, a teenage girl, **Clara Lemlich**, suddenly raced to the platform and, in eloquent Yiddish, proclaimed, "I am a working girl, one of those striking against intolerable conditions. I am tired of listening to speakers who talk in generalities. What we are here for is to decide whether or not to strike. I offer a resolution that a general strike be declared—*now*." Thousands of people chanted their approval. The chairman of the meeting, taken aback, cried out, "Do you mean it in good faith? Will you take the old Jewish oath?" The oath to which they subscribed was, "If I turn traitor to the cause I now pledge, may this hand wither from the arm I raise," a variation upon the verse in Psalm 137, "If I forget you, Jerusalem, may my right hand forget." The strike lasted three months. A reporter described watching "a picket line form in front of a struck shirtwaist-factory. The girls, headed by teen-age Clara Lemlich, described by union organizers as a pint of trouble for the bosses, began singing Italian and Russian working-class songs as they paced in twos before the factory door. Of a sudden, around the corner came a dozen tough-looking customers, for whom the union label 'gorillas' seemed well-chosen. 'Stand fast, girls,' called Clara, and then the thugs rushed the line, knocking Clara to her knees, striking at the pickets, opening the way for a group of frightened scabs to slip through the broken line." In the end the ILGWU settled for improved conditions, but without the formal union recognition it had wanted. In Lower East Side lore, this strike is known as "the uprising of the twenty thousand."

Five months after the shirtwaist strike, the cloak makers declared a general strike. The union asked for a forty-nine-hour week; the employers countered with fifty-three hours. The union was also asking for a "union shop," forbidding the employers to hire anyone who was not a member of the union. This strike lasted nearly two months; it was settled through the intervention of public figures from the Jewish community, who recommended that **Louis Brandeis**, then an attorney in Boston noted for his work on labor issues, be appointed to negotiate between the two sides. He had the assistance of **Louis Marshall**, also an attorney, and **Jacob Schiff**, the investment banker, who were associated with the American Jewish Committee. Brandeis proposed that, in place of a union shop, there be a "preferential union shop," which is to say, a shop in which "union standards prevail and the union is entitled to preference." The *Jewish Daily Forward* at first called this "a scab shop with honey," but both sides were eager to settle. A "Protocol of Peace" was signed, providing for a fifty-hour week, wage increases, the abolition of inside subcontracting, and the "preferential union shop."

The organization of a powerful union for workers in the men's clothing industry took longer to take shape than the process of doing so in women's wear. In 1910 a general strike was called in Chicago against the men's clothing manufacturers, the largest of which was Hart, Schaffner and Marx. Its leader was young **Sidney Hillman**, an immigrant from Russia who had settled in Chicago. The grandson of a rabbi, he had received a traditional Jewish education in Russia but, like young Abraham Cahan, had joined a revolutionary movement. Working as a cutter at Hart, Schaffner and Marx, he became a member of the United Garment Workers, an AFL affiliate. The UGW as a whole, however, was distrustful of "radical Jewish tailors," and did little to support the cause of the strikers. Hillman himself negotiated an agreement with Joseph Schaffner, who took to heart the unrelenting criticism of rabbis, ministers, and social workers as the strike went on, and wondered whether he was a "moral failure." In 1914 Hillman moved to New York to pursue full-time union organizing, and when members of the United Garment Workers left that union to found the Amalgamated Clothing Workers of America, he became its president. This union left the AFL, affiliating in 1938 with the Congress of Industrial Organizations (CIO), which, years later, merged with the older AFL to form today's AFL-CIO.

The Amalgamated in its early days was, like the ILGWU, a "Jewish union." It pioneered in introducing a multitude of auxiliary services for its members: educational programs, unemployment insurance, health centers. It built cooperative apartment houses and low rental housing, and established banks in New York and Chicago to promote its projects and serve the union's members. During the administration of Franklin Roosevelt, Hillman became a major figure in American political life. He was an active adviser to the President both in the days of the National Recovery Administration and during World War II, when he served as director of the labor section of the War Production Board. He, together with **David Dubinsky**, president of the ILGWU from 1932, were the two most distinguished leaders of Jewish labor. Hillman's importance in American politics is illustrated by what occurred at the Democratic National Convention in 1944, when Roosevelt was nominated for a fourth term. Left-leaning Democrats sought the renomination of Henry Wallace as Vice President, while conservatives were pushing the candidacy of James F. Byrnes. The name of **Harry Truman** was suggested as a moderate alternative palatable to both wings of the party. When the party's national chairman approached Roosevelt to ascertain his preference, the President's response was, "Clear it with Sidney." Hillman and the CIO had been strongly for Wallace but, realizing that the majority of convention delegates would accept Wallace only if extreme pressure were applied, Hillman shifted his support to Truman. Hillman is thus responsible for Truman's becoming President of the United States upon Roosevelt's death in 1945, rather than Henry Wallace.

The memberships of both the ILGWU and the Amalgamated Clothing Workers remained over 50 percent Jewish until the First World War. By 1923 the Jewish percentage had dropped to 40 percent. During subsequent years the Jewish membership of these unions has been overwhelmed by Italians, blacks, Puerto Ricans, and other groups. For many years, though, the leadership of both unions remained predominantly Jewish, but official union business was no longer conducted in Yiddish.

In 1995 the ILGWU and the Amalgamated joined to form a single union bearing the name UNITE (Union of Needletrades, Industrial & Textile Employees).

Who was Morris Hillquit?

Morris Hillquit (1869–1933) served for a time during the 1920s as national chairman of the Socialist Party of America. He was born in Riga, Latvia, a city founded by Germans. German was his native tongue, but he received his later education in Russian, thus becoming fluent in both languages.

His family came in 1886 to the United States, to New York's Lower East Side. Though intellectually gifted, he did not want his education to be a drain upon them. He took work as a shirtmaker, became a member of the Socialist Labor party and was on the committee that founded the United Hebrew Trades. In a short time his abilities as both a writer and a speaker came to be recognized, and he was a featured speaker not only at socialist gatherings but also, after leaving the Socialist Labor party for the more moderate Debs group, at "establishment" spots like the Republican Club, the Colony Club, and the Chamber of Commerce. He was instrumental in winning a number of well-known liberals and social workers over to the socialist cause, Christians as well as Jews. He taught English to foreigners and, in his free time, studied law. He was admitted to the bar in 1903 and became a very successful attorney.

Hillquit ran as the Socialist candidate for Congress from the Lower East Side in 1906. He described his district this way: "It is the home of the tenements, pushcarts, paupers and tuberculosis. It is the experimental laboratory of the sentimental moralist, and the chosen prey of the smug philanthropist. Geographically, it is located in the slums; industrially it belongs to the sweatshop; politically it is a dependency of Tammany Hall." Tammany's candidate, **Henry Goldfogle**, won by a small margin (Tammany was always able to rig the vote in its favor in close elections). In 1908 Hillquit ran again, losing this time because he had joined some other labor leaders in advocating restrictions on immigration, a position opposed by the vast majority of Lower East Side voters. In 1916 Hillquit was the Socialist nominee for Congress from Harlem, then an area in which Jews and others were moving to escape the poverty and crowded conditions of the Lower East Side. As the results came in, Hillquit was ahead of his rivals, but then the returns from two precincts favoring him were held up. The Republican and Democratic bosses were negotiating a "deal." The deal involved falsifying Hillquit's plurality of 500 votes into a loss of 350 votes. The bosses again had won.

In the mayoral campaign of 1917 Hillquit was the Socialist candidate. His supporters thought he had a good chance of winning, reasoning that the incumbent mayor, John Mitchel, a Fusion "good government" candidate, would draw Democratic votes away from the Tammany candidate, "Silent" John Hylan, while the Republican candidate would deprive Mitchel of Republican votes. They also anticipated that the sentiment of many Jewish, Irish, and German voters against American entry into the First World War would draw them to vote for Hillquit, the antiwar candidate. Tammany sent speakers into Jewish neighborhoods, warning that a Hillquit victory would inflame anti-Semitism; he was also pilloried as a socialist who lived well, earning high legal fees. Hylan won the election, though Hillquit's vote was five times that of the Socialist mayoral candidate in the previous election. The Socialists, however, elected five state assemblymen, seven city aldermen, and a municipal judge. In 1918 he ran again for Congress from his Harlem district and lost, as he did in 1920. This time he was opposed by a single Republican-Democratic candidate, and got 40 percent of the vote. During the 1920s Hillquit devoted much of his energy to the internal problems besetting the Socialist party. In 1928 he stated, "There is no difference between the Soviet government and the Communist party here. We must dissociate ourselves from the Soviet government and thereby make clear that Social Democracy has no connection with it."

After the war Hillquit was active in the effort to bring about the release of American political prisoners. (In 1918 Congress had passed amendments to the Espionage Act which made writing or speaking against the conduct of the war criminal offenses. Dozens of well-known socialists were indicted, convicted, and imprisoned under this law. Others were imprisoned under similar state laws.) President **Woodrow Wilson** refused to release anyone sentenced under the

Espionage Act. **Warren Harding**, however, did receive a committee appealing for an amnesty; Hillquit was its spokesman. He said, "The men and women whose cause we are pleading have been tried and convicted solely on the basis of speeches or writing in support of their political convictions or for participating in the struggle of organized labor. They spoke and acted in their courageous performance of what they deeply and sincerely felt to be their civic duty." Though he came to the trade union movement in his capacity as an attorney quite late in his legal career, from 1915 until shortly before his death he was the chief legal adviser to the International Ladies Garment Workers Union.

Who was Meyer London?

While Morris Hillquit never made it to Congress, **Meyer London** (1871–1927) was a Socialist candidate who did. (He was not the first. That distinction belongs to **Victor Berger**, a Jewish immigrant from Austria who was elected from Wisconsin in 1910.) London was born in Russian Poland. His father had trained to be a rabbi, but embraced radical ideas instead. In 1888 his father and younger brother immigrated to America; Meyer stayed behind to finish his studies, both Jewish and Russian. In 1891 he and the rest of the family joined those already in New York, where his father, who was running a small printing shop, had become associated with an anarchist group. Meyer tutored pupils in various subjects and then got a job in a circulating library. In the evenings he studied law. As soon as he learned English, he read everything he could put his hands on about English and American history and politics. He became a fluent debater, went to law school at New York University, and in 1898 was admitted to the bar. Beginning around the turn of the century, London became a perennial candidate for state assemblyman on the Socialist ticket. According to Melech Epstein,

A Socialist nominee at that time had no illusions of winning. Tammany Hall ruled the East Side from the saloons, gambling houses, pool parlors, and red-light district. The only thing permitted the Socialist candidate was to address crowds on street corners, thundering against injustices and advocating socialism. London did not play up to immigrants by referring to events in the old country. He spoke as an American to Americans, basing his arguments on day-to-day happenings in the political and industrial life of the country. He spoke in English, and avoided the histrionics indulged in by other speakers. He attracted chiefly the younger, more Americanized, elements. He was the only Jewish Socialist to venture into the outlying districts of the East Side, inhabited by Germans and Irish often unfriendly to Jews. His courage, sincerity, and eloquence overcame their prejudice, and they stopped to listen.

London's law practice was very much involved with the struggling trade unions. He also took on the cause of tenants fighting landlords, and other poor people's cases. He got very little remuneration. His family, for the most part, lived off his wife's earnings as a dentist (she had been trained in Russia). London often gave away the little money he had to those he thought needed it more than he. During a long strike of the fur workers in 1912, the union's funds were exhausted and a group came to London lamenting their plight. London looked at his bankbook, remarked that his bank balance was thirty-four dollars, and wrote out a check to the union for that amount. In addition, "during the agonizing weeks of the strike London forsook his law office, his home, his friends and his personal affairs and gave himself to us wholly and utterly. He was there to inspire the men with his oratory; he was there to comfort and guide the strike leaders; he was there to plead with the bankers for loans and with fellow labor organizations for help. He was there at the end to negotiate the peace terms with the employers." The union subsequently sent him a check for two thousand dollars and a gold watch. London became angry at these gifts which he had not requested. The money he gave to the socialist movement and the watch he gave away to help a needy worker.

London ran for Congress in 1910 and 1912, losing both times. In 1914, however, things were looking good for the Socialists and their charismatic candidate. Tammany worked hard to produce a victory for their man Goldfogle. A Socialist poll watcher said that on election night, he had objected to the way the votes were being counted. A Tammany politician told him, "You look like a nice fellow, so I will be frank with you. Your candidate will get a fair vote, but not an honest one." When the watcher persisted in his objection, he was bodily ejected as a policeman looked on. Tammany was not able to deliver this time, though. London won because the Socialists learned from their experience in previous races to wage a vigorous and methodical campaign. Union membership had grown strongly, and union people were for London. Unions mobilized hundreds who had received their training on picket lines to serve as watchers at the polls, and some of them were large, strong types.

As crowds waited for the election results to be flashed on the screen in front of the *Jewish Daily Forward* building, Tammany was trying to delay the final count. At about eleven o'clock the Orthodox Yiddish paper put out an extra announcing Goldfogle's victory. (The Orthodox hated the Socialists.) But the crowds refused to accept this as the final word, and kept their vigil. At about two o'clock Tammany conceded London's election. Thousands sang and danced in the streets; many more rose up from their beds and came to join them. London was brought to the square at 4:00 A.M. for an impromptu demonstration. Melech Epstein, who was there in person, remembers the triumphant march through the streets in the early dawn, when one of the *Forward*'s editors, standing on the balcony of the paper's building, lifted his arms to the rising sun and exclaimed, "Perhaps the sun will shine on the East Side from now on."

In Congress London sought justice for Puerto Rico, introduced bills against child labor, for a national unemployment insurance system, and a minimum wage law (all goals that were finally achieved as part of **Franklin Roosevelt**'s New Deal). He opposed **Woodrow Wilson**'s "punitive expedition" against Mexico in 1916, and wished to keep the United States out of World War I. He was reelected to a second term in 1916 in spite of a united opposition and a hostile press. He voted against the declaration of war in 1917, but once it was passed, he could not in good conscience oppose any measure that would strengthen the country's position in the war. The Socialist party, however, maintained its totally pacifist stance with regard to the war, and London was regarded by many as a traitor to his party because of his support of the war effort. During Hillquit's campaign for the mayoralty in 1917, with its rigid antiwar platform, London was the "odd man out." At a party meeting he said, "We Socialists must not be demagogues. We must not appeal to ignorance. It is absurd to say that if a large Socialist vote is polled the war would stop. This war will not be over until there is a firm foundation for world peace. It is nonsense to say that we are neutral to the outcome of the war once we are in it. Socialists cannot afford to hope for the war to end until Belgium is restored and every German soldier has been removed from the soil of revolutionary Russia. I don't want the Kaiser to misinterpret the Socialist vote."

In the 1918 campaign for a third term in Congress, London was opposed by the left wing of his own party because of his stand on the war, by conservatives of all stripes, and by many Zionists who objected to his lack of enthusiasm for Britain's Balfour Declaration, supporting a Jewish homeland in Palestine. The Orthodox complained that he had attended a session of Congress on Yom Kippur. Prominent Jewish leaders from uptown urged his defeat. Democrats and Republicans agreed on a single candidate to oppose him—**Henry Goldfogle**, the old Tammany reliable. London was attacked both for "compromising his socialist principles and for stead-fastly adhering to them; for being too much of a patriot and for not being patriotic enough." At the opening of his cam-paign he said, "I wonder whether I am to be punished for having had the courage to vote against war or for standing by my country's decision when it chose war." London was defeated by seven hundred votes. In 1920 London was once again sent to Congress with a larger majority than ever. He remained true to his principles, but there was little sympathy for them among his colleagues. As he said, "This is a busi-nessman's Congress, and it is ultraconservative." For the elec-tion of 1922, redistricting drew the lines on the Lower East Side in such a way that there would be little chance of voters ever selecting a Socialist representative again.

Crossing a street on June 6, 1927, Meyer London was caught in heavy automobile traffic. He became confused and was struck by a taxi. The driver recognized London and rushed him to Bellevue Hospital, where London's daughter, an intern, was on duty in the emergency room. She recog-nized her father as he was brought in. London had only one thought—that the driver of the taxi not be prosecuted. "It is not his fault," he said, "and he is a poor man." London died that night.

The people of the entire Lower East Side lined the streets when London's funeral procession passed, estimated by the police at half a million. In Epstein's judgment, "A child of the radical enlightenment that was sweeping Russia in the second half of the nineteenth century, London never wavered from his youthful concept of social morality and ethical standards. No one of London's moral stature has appeared either in the Jewish community or in the labor movement since his passing."

Which clothing manufacturer became the largest in the world?

During the 1870s the Hart family of Chicago, German Jews, enlisted a cousin, Marcus Marx, and another one, Joseph Schaffner, to join them in the manufacture and distribution of men's clothing. Their company was the first to adopt an all-wool policy and to guarantee colorfastness. It also developed tactics of advertising, marketing, and distribution that were adopted, eventually, by the entire industry. By the end of the nineteenth century **Hart, Schaffner & Marx** was the largest manufacturer of men's clothing in the world.

Who prevented the Rockefellers from controlling all the copper produced in the United States?

Meyer Guggenheim came with his family from Switzerland to the United States in 1856. While peddling in the Pennsylvania coal country, he noticed that housewives were frequently burned by the caustic stove polish they had to use. With the help of a chemist, Guggenheim was able to remove the sting from the polish and became wealthy from his sales of the reconstituted product. He and his family invested in lead and silver mines in Colorado. Earning millions, he and his seven sons formed the Colorado Smelting and Refining Company, which by 1898 was producing (with other Guggenheim enterprises) almost half of the world's copper supply. This is the company that the Rockefeller interests wished to absorb into their American Smelting and Refining Company, with the aim of controlling nearly all of the world's copper supply. The Rockefellers and their allies offered to buy Colorado Smelting and Refining, but the Guggenheims outsmarted them. After some complicated stock transactions, the Guggenheims consented to the purchase of their interests by American Smelting and Refining, with the proviso that **Daniel Guggenheim** become president of the enlarged company, and four other Guggenheims occupy seats on its board. The Rockefellers were in no position to contest this, so, in effect, their copper interests ended up being taken over by the Guggenheims.

During the twentieth century the Guggenheims acquired other mining properties in the Yukon, Mexico, South America, and Africa, producing silver, gold, copper, zinc, lead, and nitrates. For a time they were among the five wealthiest families in the United States. The Guggenheim Fund for the Promotion of Aeronautics offered the prize that inspired Charles Lindbergh to fly across the Atlantic in 1927. The John Simon Guggenheim Memorial Foundation has supported the work of thousands of scholars, writers, and artists. The Solomon R. Guggenheim Museum in New York is known throughout the world for its collection of modern art.

How did the daughters of immigrants advance in the working world?

The *Jewish Daily Forward* in 1905 wrote the following:

> When a grown girl emigrates to America, she becomes either a finisher or an operator (in the garment industry). Girls who have grown up here do not work at these "greenhorn" trades. They become salesladies or typists. A typist represents a compromise between a teacher and a finisher. Salaries for typists are very low—some work for as little as three dollars a week. But typists have more status than shopgirls; it helps them get a husband; they come in contact with a more refined class of people. Typists, therefore, live in two different worlds: they work in a sunny, spacious office, they speak and hear only English, their superiors call them "Miss." And then they come home to dirty rooms and to parents who aren't always so courteous.

Beginning about 1915 many girls from the Lower East Side were graduating high school; ten years later a noticeable number were going to college. Many of those with higher education entered the teaching profession, initiating a major influx of Jewish women (and men, too, particularly in the high schools) as teachers in the public schools of New York City. During the previous forty years many of the Irish and Anglo-Saxon teachers in the public schools had shown great kindness toward and interest in the Jewish immigrant children coming by the thousands into the neighborhood schools. Now the offspring of these immigrants were following in the footsteps of their parents' teachers, entering their profession to guide the growth and development of future generations of children. A number of them subsequently rose to positions of eminence in the city's school system.

Who are the Bnai Brith?

Bnai Brith means "Sons of the Covenant." It is a nationwide Jewish fraternal order, founded in 1843 in New York by twelve young Jewish men who used to meet one another regularly at Sinsheimer's saloon. From the Masons and Odd Fellows, to which some of the original Bnai Brith belonged, they adopted such devices as secret handshakes and passwords, and exalted Hebraic titles for the lodge officers. By 1861 Bnai Brith lodges existed in almost every Jewish community in the country. Bnai Brith Women began operating in 1895.

In 1870 a Jewish lawyer from San Francisco, **Benjamin Franklin Peixotto**, was serving as the national president of Bnai Brith. He used this post as leverage to campaign for appointment as U.S. consul to Bucharest, where the Romanian government had introduced harsh restrictions against Jews and encouraged mob actions against them. Peixotto got the position and carried with him a letter from President **Ulysses S. Grant** stating that the United States, "knowing no distinction of her citizens on account of religion or nativity, naturally believes in a civilization the world over which will secure the same universal views." During Peixotto's five-year term in Bucharest, anti-Jewish acts were sharply curtailed.

Though many members of Bnai Brith joined for the fellowship that lodge activities provided, others were more interested in the civic and educational work that the group encouraged. In 1913, after the **Leo Frank** trial in Atlanta, Bnai Brith sponsored the formation of its Anti-Defamation League, whose duty it was to expose and counteract the effects of anti-Semitic bigotry. The ADL from the beginning interpreted its mandate as encompassing the defense of other racial and religious groups besides Jews; to this day it remains one of the most effective organizations on the American scene in the fight against hate. Over the years Bnai Brith, particularly in the South and Midwest, served as a venue in which German and Eastern European Jews could mingle. It sponsored several youth programs, and in 1925 assumed responsibility for the work of the Hillel Foundations with Jews on college campuses.

What inspired the founding of the American Jewish Committee in 1906?

Anti-Jewish legislation and murderous anti-Semitic riots in the Russian Empire during the early 1900s prompted American Jewish leaders to urge the White House to lodge representations with the Russian government. This was done, but the czarist regime remained unmoved. In 1905 a group of New York Jewish leaders decided that a permanent "Jewish committee" was needed to deal with such matters; they sent invitations to fifty-nine prominent Jews, including men from Milwaukee, New Orleans, Chicago, and San Francisco, as well as a contingent from the East Coast. Thirty-nine attended a meeting in February 1906; three were of Eastern European stock. After some additional meetings, the group decided to establish an "American Jewish Committee," with an executive board of fifteen that could, if it chose to do so, increase its membership to fifty. The purpose of the committee was "to prevent infringement of the civil and religious rights of Jews, and to alleviate the consequences of persecution."

The first major project undertaken by the committee concerned the Russian-American Treaty of Commerce and Navigation that dated from 1832. The treaty guaranteed citizens of either country freedom of movement and residence within the territory of the other, subject to "the laws and ordinances there prevailing." Since Jews were prohibited by Russian law from residing in many localities, American Jews visiting Russia were thus excluded from these localities as well. Congress passed resolutions demanding that this provision of the treaty be renegotiated; Democratic and Republican party platforms demanded that this be done. The Russians, however, were unmoved. In 1912 the Congress voted to abrogate the treaty, and the Secretary of State thereupon notified the Russian government that, in accordance with the provisions of the treaty itself, it would expire. Though the committee's effort did not bring about a change in Russian policy, it demonstrated both an attachment to principle and the ability of the committee to flex its muscle in Washington.

From 1912 until his death in 1929, the president of the American Jewish Committee was **Louis Marshall**. The son of German immigrants, he had grown up in Syracuse and graduated from Columbia Law School (he completed its two-year program in one year). He achieved prominence in the legal community of Syracuse and New York State, and was then invited to join a New York City firm. He fit easily into the German-Jewish aristocracy and served for years as the president of Temple Emanu-El. He was a conservative Republican, but at the same time was devoted to the civil rights of all individuals and groups in the nation, no matter how fervently he might disagree with their views. He worked tirelessly to keep the doors of the United States open to immigrants.

Though a Reform Jew, Marshall was instrumental in funding the Jewish Theological Seminary of Conservative Judaism, enabling it to become a major center of scholarship. He took up the case of **Leo Frank**, convicted of murder in Atlanta through perjured testimony, before the U.S. Supreme Court. He served as a member of the delegation that went to the Versailles Peace Conference to speak for American Jewry. He arranged the retraction by Henry Ford of the anti-Semitic "conspiracy theories" that had been published in his Michigan newspaper. He became a director of the National Association for the Advancement of Colored People and, in court, argued the cases of Japanese-Americans who were prohibited from buying land in California, and of Catholic nuns who had been prohibited from operating a parochial school in Oregon. Though not a Zionist, just before his death he was elected chairman of the Jewish Agency for Palestine, the international body of Zionists and non-Zionists that had been set up to facilitate Jewish settlement in Palestine.

Why did Reform Jews pour money into the (Conservative) Jewish Theological Seminary?

The Jewish Theological Seminary in New York began in 1886, meeting in a room made available at the Spanish-Portuguese Synagogue, under the auspices of the Sephardic scholar **Sabato Morais** and some colleagues who objected to the radical reforming tendencies that seemed to hold sway at the Hebrew Union College. Morais died suddenly in 1897, however, and it seemed that the school would not continue. Men from the German Jewish establishment, most of them affiliated with the stately Reform congregation Temple Emanu-El, came to the seminary's rescue. They realized that neither the type of Orthodoxy that many remembered from Eastern Europe nor the kind of Reform Judaism with which the Germans were comfortable could serve the great mass of Eastern European immigrants in their new American environment. The newcomers needed spiritual roots in a traditional Judaism at home in America; this was the kind of Judaism that the

Jewish Theological Seminary represented. Therefore, Cyrus Adler in 1901 was able to persuade **Jacob Schiff**, **Louis Marshall**, the Warburgs, the Guggenheims, and other people from the German Jewish establishment to contribute half a million dollars for a seminary endowment fund. Representatives of this group took seats on the seminary's board, and they set about engaging **Solomon Schechter** to come to New York and head the revitalized institution.

Schechter was one of the great Jewish academics in the world. From a Romanian Hasidic family, he studied at the seminary in Vienna and then went to Berlin to study at both an advanced Jewish institution and the University of Berlin. He then went to England, studied at Oxford, and accepted an appointment as lecturer in Talmud at Cambridge. He published widely in academic journals, and was famous for his discovery, in the attic of an old Cairo synagogue, of the original Hebrew text of Ecclesiasticus (Sirach), previously known only from the Greek version that is part of the Old Testament Apocrypha. In the same attic he also discovered the Zadokite Document (known also as the Damascus Covenant), copies of which were found fifty years later among the Dead Sea Scrolls.

Schechter died in 1915, leaving behind an institution with a respected and distinguished faculty, and a vibrant Conservative Judaism.

What was the "New York Kehilla"?

The Hebrew word *kehilla* means an organized Jewish community (it is sometimes used to mean a synagogue congregation). In 1908 the Jewish community of New York City, encompassing both the Americanized "uptown" German Jews and the "downtown" Eastern European immigrants, formed a new body that sought, in a democratic way, to exert control over, and coordinate the activities of, the multifarious Jewish organizations working among, and on behalf of, the city's

Jews. This body was called the "New York Kehilla." Its creation was inspired by the publication, in that year, of remarks by New York's police commissioner asserting that perhaps half the criminals in the city were Russian Jews. "They are burglars, firebugs, pickpockets and highway robbers—when they have the courage; but though all crime is their province, pocket-picking is the one to which they take most naturally." While among the city's million Jews there were of course a number of delinquents and criminals, the commissioner's statistics were highly exaggerated. Russian Jews were indignant that their group had been slandered in such a way, and German Jews feared being associated in public opinion with "coreligionists" alleged to have spawned such a large criminal element. Jewish leaders from both uptown and downtown spoke out over a two-week period, and Police Commissioner Theodore Bingham acknowledged that his remark had not been completely accurate. In the meantime, however, the community leaders set about organizing a permanent organization that would be qualified to respond on behalf of its constituent members. Thus the Kehilla was born.

The hundreds of Jewish groups within the community were entitled to send delegates to meetings of the Kehilla; these delegates chose twenty-five persons to serve as an executive board. (All types of organizations within Jewish New York were welcome to be part of the Kehilla; the only groups that decided not to participate as a matter of principle were the labor unions and socialist bodies.) In 1906 the American Jewish Committee had been organized by some of the leading "uptown" German Jews, including **Jacob Schiff** and **Louis Marshall**; the executive board of the Kehilla was accepted by the committee as its New York district, and was to "defer to the Committee [which was a national organization] in all national and international affairs while retaining autonomy in local matters." This organic connection between the Kehilla and the AJC brought the German and Eastern European communities together. It was advantageous to both groups because, while the Kehilla would be "self-governing in all local matters, it would exercise a potent influence upon all matters of general interest coming within the jurisdiction of the American Jewish Committee." In fact, many delegates from Eastern European groups voted for AJC people to serve on the executive board, admiring them for their philanthropic work and unselfish interest in meeting Jewish needs.

Chosen to serve as president of the Kehilla was a very unusual man—**Judah Magnes**, one of the rabbis on the staff of Temple Emanu-El. Magnes had been born in California to German Jewish parents and received his early education there. He was ordained at Reform Judaism's Hebrew Union College in Cincinnati, where, as a student, he had been one of the few advocates of Zionism on that campus during the 1890s. He studied in Germany for his doctorate and then returned to teach at the college before deciding to enter the pulpit rabbinate. After serving at a temple in Brooklyn, he accepted the call of New York's Emanu-El, though he realized that most of its members were decidedly unenthusiastic about Zionism and the type of culturally rich Judaism that he himself believed in. Magnes always remained true to his convictions, preaching what he believed whether those who listened to him approved of it or not. He formed a close personal bond with many in the Russian Jewish community and valued the store of Jewish tradition that they retained. Among his close friends and associates in New York were **Solomon Schechter**, **Henrietta Szold**, and **Mordecai Kaplan** of the Jewish Theological Seminary, leaders of a "modern Orthodoxy" that was in process of becoming the Conservative movement. He was the perfect choice to head the New York Kehilla, bridging as he did the differences between German Reform Judaism and Eastern European traditional Judaism.

Magnes was involved in all aspects of the Kehilla's activity from its origin in 1908 until his resignation in 1922. (The Kehilla's demise followed in 1925.) Its greatest success was probably in the field of Jewish education. Under the leadership of educator **Samson Benderly**, it brought modern educational techniques to the teaching of Hebrew and Jewish religion and history. Young men and women were trained as teachers in these fields, and books published for use in Sunday and afternoon schools. The Kehilla also made progress in supervising the provision of kosher meat, and worked with the city's police and district attorneys to combat crime on the Lower East Side. And though the Jewish labor unions were not part of the Kehilla, they and employers turned to arbitrators and other experts supplied by the Kehilla to settle a number of labor-management disputes. For several years it looked as if the Kehilla concept would prove to be a great success. With the outbreak of World War I, however, New York's Jews turned their energies away from local problems toward satisfying the needs of the war-torn Jewish communities of Europe, from which most of the immigrants had come. In 1914 the American Jewish Committee took the lead in forming the American Jewish Relief Committee. This soon federated with the Central Relief Committee, set up by Orthodox Jews, to form the Joint Distribution Committee. In 1915 Jewish socialists and trade unions established the People's Relief Committee, which also joined the Joint Distribution Committee. ("The Joint" exists to this day as a major focus of Jewish giving for the needy throughout the world. In what is likely its greatest accomplishment, the Joint in the aftermath of the Second World War provided relief and rehabilitation to some 750,000 impoverished Jews in Hungary, Poland, Romania, Bulgaria, Czechoslovakia, Yugoslavia, Germany, Austria, and Italy. Two thousand Joint personnel provided meals and operated schools, kindergartens, hospitals, orphanages, sanatoria, and clothing warehouses.) During the World War I years the Joint's relief efforts took away both people and funds from the various projects of the Kehilla. In 1917 the Federation of Jewish Philanthropies was formed, further weakening the Kehilla. After America's entry into the First World War, the Jewish Welfare Board, serving Jews in the

U.S. military forces, was organized. Following the war the JWB expanded its role to serve as an auxiliary and coordinating agency for the numerous Young Men's (and Young Women's) Hebrew Associations that had arisen in various cities, and the Jewish Community Centers that were organized in later years. (The first YMHA, modeled on the Young Men's Christian Association, had been organized in Baltimore in 1854.)

Magnes, as a dedicated pacifist, opposed U.S. entry into the war. Not the kind of person to relinquish deeply held principles, he continued to oppose the war even after America's entry in 1917. Many Jews objected to his antiwar stance, and his influence declined. With both the Kehilla as an organization and Magnes's stature as an American Jewish leader at a low ebb, he submitted his resignation as the group's president in 1920. It was not accepted until 1922. Many of the activities sponsored by the Kehilla, such as its work in Jewish education, were taken over by other Jewish organizations. The philosophy and outlook of both Magnes and the Kehilla found a home in the Jewish Reconstructionist movement founded by **Mordecai Kaplan**. The attempt to centralize organized Jewish life was, however, not repeated. Magnes and his family immigrated to Palestine in 1922.

The Hebrew University opened its doors in Jerusalem in 1925. Judah Magnes was its chancellor from its inception to his death in 1949. He was also active in Brit Shalom ("Covenant of Peace") and a founder of Ihud ("Unity"), groups seeking peace and reconciliation between Arabs and Jews in Palestine and the formation of a binational state. Magnes remains a testimony and example to all who seek to live an uncorrupted life.

What was the unique Jewish connection to Galveston, Texas?

During the early twentieth century there was widespread opposition to unrestricted immigration into the United States. In some circles, including political officeholders and some upper-class German Jews, the feeling developed that perhaps such opposition to immigration could be dissipated by the dispersal of immigrants to different parts of the country. If Russian Jews, for instance, were not so tightly packed into the Lower East Side of New York and similar neighborhoods in other large cities, maybe the "nativist" movement might lose some of its support. **Jacob Schiff**, the banker and philanthropist, was one of those who thought that dispersion of Jewish immigrants should be attempted. He contacted **Israel Zangwill**, an English Jewish writer who had founded the Jewish Territorial Organization, a non-Zionist group dedicated to the mass resettlement of Russian Jews in areas willing to accept them (other than Palestine). If Zangwill's group, he said, could arrange passage for groups of Russian Jews aboard ships from Europe directly to Galveston, a Gulf Coast port within easy reach of cities in the American Southwest, fewer immigrants would end up in New York and other East Coast cities. They would, rather, find accommodation and work in a much less crowded area of the country. Schiff himself would take care of expenses for the immigrants once they reached Galveston. Jobs would be found for them through the network of Bnai Brith lodges in the Southwest, working with the Industrial Removal Office supported by Bnai Brith. On paper all of this looked like a very effective plan.

Henry Cohen had been the rabbi of Galveston's Reform temple since 1888, as well as a circuit-riding rabbi for other Texas towns. He was beloved by Christians as well as Jews, by blacks as well as whites. He provided a "decent Christian burial" for a prostitute whom other clergy refused to bury; he interceded with President William McKinley to save a Russian Christian immigrant from deportation. In 1907 he was ready to receive the first shipload of Russian Jewish immigrants to come to Galveston. He arranged for a brass band to welcome the ship when it docked, and for the mayor to give a speech of welcome. Cohen saw to it that the immigrants got hot meals and baths at a local hotel. The next day they went by train, with escorts, to the West or the South, where housing and jobs awaited them. Other immigrants in subsequent months were processed in the same way. The program should have been a great success.

During the seven years of its existence, however, relatively few immigrants came through Galveston. The financial panic of 1907 eliminated many jobs. The Jewish Territorial Organization did not function too well in Europe, unable as it was to cope with large numbers of people. Immigration officials stationed in Galveston did not cooperate as they had been expected to. Most significantly, however, many immigrants did not want to come to Galveston. They had relatives in New York who sent them money for passage to New York. New York was where they wanted to be. And in 1914 World War I curtailed most immigration.

The Galveston experiment is still fondly remembered in that city, as is Rabbi Cohen. For Jews and Christians alike, according to Albert Vorspan, Henry Cohen "served at once as employment agency, marriage counselor, parole board, nurse, immigration service, and social reformer. In effect, Cohen was the spiritual leader of his city. In 1938, the fiftieth anniversary of his service in Texas was observed in a public celebration that lasted all day and half the night, and five thousand citizens of all religions packed the city auditorium to honor him."

Was there any noticeable Jewish settlement in the West?

Jewish settlers moved west across the United States as the frontier itself moved west. They were to be found in practically every city and town in the Midwest, the Southwest, California, and the Northwest. Some were merchants; others were prospectors, fur trappers, miners, hotelkeepers. **Henryk Sienkiewicz**, a noted Polish writer, traveled across the country and in 1877 wrote this description of California: "At the recently discovered gold mines where adventurers quickly congregate, where the knife, the revolver, and the terrifying lynch law still prevail, where an American merchant hesitates to open shop out of fear both for his merchandise and his life, the first stores are generally established by Jews. By their courtesy, kind words, and, above all, extension of credit, they win the favor of the most dangerous adventurers. And once having the revolvers of the desperadoes on their side, the storekeepers conduct their affairs with complete safety." These settlers, and their descendants, came to play a prominent role in the communities in which they lived. Many of them served as mayors, or as other political officeholders, in cities and towns large and small. **Michael Goldwater** came to California from Europe in 1853. Settling finally in Arizona, he and his family opened a general store in Phoenix that developed, later on, into a chain of department stores covering the entire state. His grandson, **Barry Goldwater**, served as Arizona's senator and ran as the Republican nominee for the presidency in 1964. He was an Episcopalian, having been raised in his mother's faith.

What was the Sutro Tunnel?

Adolph Sutro (1830–1898) came to the United States from Germany and in 1850 responded to the lure of California gold by taking a steamer to Nicaragua, crossing fever-infested Panama, and journeying north to San Francisco. By the time he arrived there, the gold boom was over, but he stayed and opened a tobacco shop. In Germany he had been an engineer at his father's textile factory, so when, in 1859, he learned of a silver strike at the Comstock Lode in Virginia City, Nevada, he sold his business and went there. He opened a small mill to extract secondary minerals from discarded ore.

Sutro soon learned of the poor ventilation and underground floods that endangered the miners working the Lode. He developed plans to bore a five-mile tunnel parallel to the mines, at a depth of sixteen hundred feet, which would provide ventilation. He sought financing for this vast project for nine years, investment coming at last from the miners' union, a British bank, and the U.S. Congress. The project was not completed until 1879, but it did not take long for the Sutro Tunnel to be recognized as a work of engineering genius.

After some years Sutro sold his share in the tunnel company for $5 million and returned to San Francisco. There he became a real estate developer and, like many others in that city's German Jewish community, become prominent in civic affairs and philanthropic work. He served as mayor from 1895 to 1897. At one time he owned one tenth of San Francisco's real estate. He deeded the area known as Sutro Heights to the city as a park, and also gave the land for the University of California Hospital.

Who was the first Jewish governor of an American state?

The earliest Jewish governors were to be found in the West, where several politically active Jews served in the gubernatorial office of their home states during the early years of the twentieth century. The first was **Moses Alexander** in Idaho (1915–19). After him came **Simon Bamberger** in Utah (1917–21). Nowadays Jewish governors, mayors, and senators are no longer novelties, and few people bother to keep track of their number.

What are, in all likelihood, the two greatest Jewish-American intellectual achievements of the early twentieth century?

Between 1901 and 1905 the twelve massive volumes of *The Jewish Encyclopedia* appeared, published by the Funk & Wagnalls Company of New York. It includes contributions by over six hundred scholars from all over the world. The first project of its kind to appear in any language, its chief editor was **Isidore Singer**; its board included Jewish scholars associated with the Jewish Theological Seminary, the Hebrew Union College, Columbia University, the University of Pennsylvania, and a Christian professor of Hebrew and Hellenistic literature from Harvard. Nothing to equal it has yet appeared in any language. During the later years of the century other encyclopedias devoted to Judaism and Jewish life have been published in the United States and other countries, but *The Jewish Encyclopedia* still dwarfs them all.

In 1888 the Jewish Publication Society of America began operation in Philadelphia. This was a nonprofit society, inspired by several rabbis and community leaders, whose purpose was the publication of a wide range of English-language texts (as well as a few in Hebrew) that would promote an understanding of all aspects of Jewish culture, history, and religion among a wide readership. The JPS is still going strong. It continues to turn out translations of classical Jewish works from the rabbinic and medieval periods, original scholarship, fiction, and an array of children's books.

In 1892 a group of scholars, most of them associated with the Jewish Theological Seminary or the Hebrew Union College, in consultation with the Jewish Publication Society initiated work on a new translation of the Hebrew Scriptures. It was published by the JPS in 1917, and quickly became the most widely used version of the Bible among English-speaking Jews, in the United States and elsewhere. Isaac Leeser's translation had been in use before, but it had been deemed too dependent upon the King James Bible. In actuality, the 1917 JPS translation also has much in common with the King James Version. It was not until 1962, when the JPS issued the first volume (*The Torah*) of a brand-new Bible translation, that the King James influence was at last left far behind. This version uses contemporary American English and incorporates some interpretations of medieval rabbinic commentators. For instance, instead of "In the beginning God created the heaven and the earth," the 1962 version opens Genesis this way: "When God began to create the heaven and the earth—the earth being unformed and void, with darkness over the surface of the deep and a wind from God sweeping over the water—God said, 'Let there be light'; and there was light."

What famous Jewish American was "blessed"?

Actually, it was a famous father-and-son team that was "blessed," since the family name Baruch means "blessed" in Hebrew. The father was **Simon Baruch** (1840–1921), born in Germany and an immigrant to the United States at age fifteen. He studied medicine in South Carolina and Virginia, and during the Civil War became a surgeon to South Carolina troops. After the war he once again settled in Camden, South Carolina, and by 1880 was one of the outstanding physicians in the South: he served as president of the state medical association and chairman of the State Board of Health. Baruch was closely associated with the passage of legislation requiring vaccination as a means of controlling smallpox in his state. In 1881 Baruch moved to New York and there became known for his work and his medical treatises on appendectomy, and on the uses of water in the treatment of disease. He was largely responsible for the construction of free public baths in New York City.

One of Simon Baruch's sons was **Bernard Baruch** (1870–1965). Bernard's mother was of mixed German Jewish and Sephardic parentage. (Her Sephardic ancestors had arrived in this country in the 1690s and settled in South Carolina about 1800.) After the family's move to New York, Bernard attended the City College of New York, where he did well academically and served as senior class president. He did not enter one of the learned professions, however. Bernard Baruch's destiny was, first, to make an enormous amount of money as a stock trader on Wall Street and, subsequently, to serve either as an officeholder or unofficial adviser to every President of the United States from Woodrow Wilson to Harry Truman. For over thirty years he was one of the most admired, and in some circles, one of the most resented, public figures in the country.

Baruch's profits as a trader on the floor of the New York Stock Exchange were legendary. Though not a religiously observant Jew, his mother in 1901 reminded him that the Day of Atonement was to fall on September 23. Baruch had been, in the week leading up to that date, "selling short" the stock of the Amalgamated Copper Company, which is to say, contracting to deliver stock in the company that he did not yet own, in anticipation that its price would drop and he would be able to buy it at a lower price prior to delivery. On the Day of Atonement, however, his mother expected him to absent himself from the Exchange and take no part in business activities like buying or selling. In accordance with her wishes, he spent the day at a seaside resort in New Jersey with his family. His absence from the Exchange enabled him to make a profit of $700,000 on Amalgamated Copper stock. Had he been there observing the stock's decline, he would have purchased it at the price it reached at 11:00 A.M. that morning. The stock continued its decline into the afternoon, however, and fell even further during the next days, and he was able to buy at a much more advantageous price than he had anticipated. This was one time when observing a religious obligation brought not only spiritual comfort but great material benefit as well.

Baruch, continuing the tradition of his South Carolina family, was a Democrat. He was introduced to **Woodrow Wilson**, Democratic candidate for President, during his campaign in 1912, and the two came to respect and admire each other immediately. Baruch was also generous in his financial support of the campaign. After Wilson's election and inauguration as President, Baruch was a frequent visitor to the White House. Following American entry into the First World War, he sold his seat on the New York Stock Exchange and was asked to serve as chairman of the raw materials and minerals committee of the Advisory Commission of the Council of National Defense. During the last eight months of the war Baruch served in a very high-visibility position: chairman of the War Industries Board. During the peace negotiations at Versailles he was a member of the reparations committee.

As might be expected, Baruch was often the target of wild accusations and invective. A Republican congressman accused him of stealing $50 million worth of copper from the government during the war, and it was rumored that he was "secretly running the White House" after Wilson suffered a stroke. Henry Ford's paper, the *Dearborn Independent*, called him the "pro-consul of Judah in America" and a "Jew of Super-Power." When reporters asked him to comment, he said, "Boys, you wouldn't expect me to deny that, would you?" The good feeling that many had for him is shown by the request he received in 1920 from the Kansas State Board of Agriculture asking him to investigate the marketing problems of the state's wheat farmers. This led him to publish a pamphlet, *Putting Farming on a Modern Business Basis*, encouraging the move toward cooperative farming.

Baruch's relationship with President **Franklin Roosevelt** was complex; they often disagreed about policies the President wished to implement. Baruch often relaxed on a park bench opposite the White House and from time to time conferred with officials or reporters there. When the country entered the Second World War, however, Baruch was ready to offer his services. In 1943 he was named a special adviser to James F. Byrnes, the Director of War Mobilization. The following year he drafted plans for American reconversion to a peace-time economy. In 1946, as the United States representative to the United Nations Atomic Energy Commission, he presented the country's proposals for international control of atomic energy, based on worldwide inspection procedures. This was called the Baruch Plan.

The reputation that Baruch had during his years in Washington is dramatized by the skit presented in 1941 at the press corps' Gridiron Dinner. It parodied the Office of Production Management and its joint directors, William Knudsen and Sidney Hillman, who sang these lyrics to the tune of "O, Susanna":

> *When any problem gets so large*
> *It might end in a fluke,*
> *We take it straight to FDR—*
> *Who takes it to Baruch.*

> *OPM, that is the place for me,*
> *We'll take our troubles to Baruch*
> *AND SAVE DEMOCRACY!*

Baruch College of the City University of New York was named in his honor.

Who was the first Jewish American to win a Nobel Prize?

The first Jewish American to win a Nobel Prize was also the first American to win a Nobel Prize—**Albert Abraham Michelson** (1852–1931). Michelson was born in Germany but received his early education in San Francisco, where his parents had settled.

A SAMPLING OF JEWISH-AMERICAN NOBEL PRIZE WINNERS

Physics
1979   Sheldon Glashow and Steven Weinberg (with Abdus Salam of Pakistan), "for their contributions to the theory of the unified weak and electromagnetic interaction between elementary particles, including *inter alia* the prediction of the weak neutral current"

Chemistry
1989   Sidney Altman (with Thomas Cech), "for their discovery of catalytic properties of RNA"

Physiology or Medicine
1977   Rosalyn Yalow, "for the development of radioimmunoassays of peptide hormones"

Literature
1976   Saul Bellow, "for the human understanding and subtle analysis of contemporary culture that are combined in his work"

Peace
1986   Elie Wiesel, chairman of the President's Commission on the Holocaust

Economic Sciences
1970   Paul Samuelson, "for the scientific work through which he has developed static and dynamic economic theory and actively contributed to raising the level of analysis in economic science"

He graduated from the U.S. Naval Academy in Annapolis and then pursued postgraduate studies in physics in Germany and France. He held chairs in physics at several American universities and in 1907 was awarded the Nobel Prize in physics. The achievement for which he is best known throughout the world is his determination of the velocity of light.

Nobel awards are made annually in six categories: Physics, Chemistry, Physiology or Medicine, Literature, Peace, and the Nobel Memorial Prize in Economic Sciences. From 1907 to 1995 over sixty American Jews have won Nobel Prizes, constituting more than one quarter of the awards that have gone to Americans. (Jews are estimated to constitute no more than 3 percent of the population of the United States.)

Why was a Jewish American lynched by an Atlanta mob in 1915?

Leo Frank was, in 1913, the superintendent and part owner of his uncle's pencil factory in Atlanta. Though born in Texas, Frank had grown up in Boston and been educated at Cornell University. He was married to the daughter of a prominent Atlanta Jewish family, and had served as president of the local Bnai Brith lodge (a Jewish fraternal order).

Mary Phagan was a "little factory girl" who worked part-time at Frank's factory. On the night of April 27, 1913, her mutilated body was found in the factory basement. Suspicion centered chiefly on the black nightwatchman, who had found the body, and on Leo Frank, who had been alone with the girl earlier in the day when she had come to his office to pick up $1.20 in earnings for the ten hours she had worked that week. Frank was charged with the murder and convicted in 1913. At the trial Jim Conley, a black sweeper who had been employed at the National Pencil Factory, alleged that Frank had murdered the girl and that he had helped him move her body to the factory basement. Frank was sentenced to hang. The verdict and sentence were greeted with joy by many of Atlanta's citizens, relieved that at last "the Jew" would get what he deserved. Frank's lawyers appealed the case to the higher Georgia courts and to the U.S. Supreme Court, but the verdict and sentence were not overturned. Georgia's governor, however, had his doubts about the case, and in 1915 he commuted the sentence to life imprisonment. Two months after his decision a band of men stormed the prison in which Frank was held, kidnapped him, and hanged him. It was in response to the Frank case that, in 1913, Bnai Brith organized its Anti-Defamation League, to combat and expose unjust and malicious acts rooted in racial or religious hatred.

In 1982 Alonzo Mann, who was a fourteen-year-old office boy in Frank's factory in 1913, came forward to reveal that he had seen Jim Conley carrying Mary Phagan's body, and that Conley had threatened to kill him if he talked. In 1986 the Georgia Board of Pardons and Paroles awarded a posthumous pardon to Leo Frank.

Who is Brandeis University named after?

Rabbi Stephen S. Wise, one of his contemporaries, characterized **Louis Brandeis** (1856–1941) as "indisputably and incomparably our greatest Jew." Brandeis was born in Louisville, Kentucky, to parents who had come to America from Bohemia. In a book of "Reminiscences" his mother wrote, "I do not believe that sins can be expiated by going to divine service and observing this or that formula; I believe that only goodness and truth and conduct that is humane and self-sacrificing towards those who need us can bring God nearer to us, and that our errors can only be atoned for by acting in a more kindly spirit. Love, virtue, and truth are the foundation upon which the education of the child must be based. God has blessed my endeavors." At age sixteen Louis began three years of study in Germany, after which he entered Harvard Law School. He began his legal career in St. Louis, but when invited to join a partnership in Boston, he eagerly availed himself of the opportunity. By 1890 he was one of the most eminent corporate lawyers in the country, and he mingled easily at the highest levels of society. In that year, however, he was deeply troubled by the violence that broke out between strikers and armed strikebreakers at the Carnegie steel plant in Homestead, Pennsylvania. He wrote that it was this affair "which first set me to thinking seriously about the labor problem. It took the shock of that battle, where organized capital hired a private army to shoot at organized labor for resisting an arbitrary cut in wages, to turn my mind definitely toward a searching study of the relations of labor to industry."

Brandeis now began to channel his career toward protecting the public interest, securing the rights of working people, and encouraging good government both in his state and on the federal level. He took on many controversial cases. In 1910 he was the chief arbitrator in the garment workers' general strike in New York, crafting the "Protocol of Peace" to which both employers and unions subscribed. Through his involvement in this task he for the first time met Jews who retained an intense attachment to Jewish traditions and culture, including a passion for social justice which stemmed from the biblical prophets. He came to the conclusion that American Jews could play their full role as Americans only when they expressed themselves as Jews. "The twentieth century ideals of America have been the ideals of the Jew for more than twenty centuries," he said. These feelings led him in 1912 to embrace Zionism. He did not envision the return of all Jews to the ancient homeland in Palestine. For him Zionism sought to affect Jews and Jewish life throughout the world—to enhance Jewish dignity and pride in a glorious heritage. Brandeis was in great demand as a speaker in behalf of his newfound cause. At the beginning of World War I he was elected chairman of the Provisional Executive Committee for General Zionist Affairs, the leading position in the Zionist movement in the United States. He gave up the official position in 1921 but remained devoted to the Zionist cause for his entire life. According to biographer A. T. Mason, Zionism "fired Brandeis's imagination and captured his heart. It was for him no dream, but a beautiful reality." Under Brandeis's leadership the Zionist Organization of America grew from 12,000 members to 186,000 between 1912 and 1917.

In 1916 President **Woodrow Wilson** nominated Brandeis to a seat on the Supreme Court. It took five months before the Senate Judiciary Committee would recommend approval of this nomination. Opposition to Brandeis was rooted in two considerations: first, he was a liberal whose activities as a lawyer and an advocate of social reform had garnered him many enemies among the wealthy and powerful; second, he was a Jew. Wilson fought hard for his confirmation, rejecting out of hand a petition sent to him by some "leading" American Jews requesting that he withdraw the nomination because the continuing agitation over it would "hurt" the Jewish community.

Brandeis retired from the Court in 1939. His time on the bench gave him the opportunity to struggle for a better America, where, according to Albert Vorspan, "monopoly would be checked and small business prosper; where trade unions would be protected so that they could spell decent living standards for workers; where human values would never be subordinated to property values; where the government would not be a neutral observer but an eager buttress of social welfare; where a man's right to think, to write, to exercise religious freedom, and to associate with like-minded persons, would be secured and reverenced; where the law would be a handmaiden of social progress; where the dreams which reflect the spirit of America would find the richness of fulfillment."

Brandeis University, a nonsectarian institution under Jewish auspices, opened in 1948 in Waltham, Massachusetts, a suburb of Boston. Its name honors the justice.

Who is considered by many to have been the greatest Jewish-American woman of the century?

Henrietta Szold (1860–1945) was born in Baltimore, the first of eight daughters of Rabbi and Mrs. Benjamin Szold. The elder Szolds had immigrated to America after the failure of the revolutionary movement in Germany in 1848, and had come to Baltimore in 1859 to assume the pulpit of one of its temples, a Conservative-Reform congregation. He was a fervent abolitionist and supporter of the Union. Henrietta was raised with a reverence for learning, a faithfulness to the highest standards of conduct, and a commitment to Jewish religious tradition. The household was one filled with love, culture, and an appreciation of all things good, true, and beautiful. Henrietta was valedictorian of her high school class, but since the idea of sending a girl to college was much too revolutionary for all but a courageous few, she took up a career as a teacher—German, algebra, French, Hebrew—when she was but seventeen years old. She was also a columnist for several English-language Jewish journals. During the 1880s Jewish refugees from Russia began to come to Baltimore. Szold had the idea of establishing a night school for them. Classes were held in a loft; she was the principal. About 650 men and women enrolled in the first semester, learning English and other practical subjects. Szold took a liking to the spirit of these Eastern European Jews; her contact with them was one of the factors that made her a Zionist.

In 1893 Szold was hired as a full-time editor by the Jewish Publication Society, and as secretary of its publication committee. She held this position for twenty-three years, during which time she did translations and annotations for almost one hundred volumes published under the society's auspices, in addition to proofreading, indexing, and publicizing these works. In her spare time she was a member of the Executive Committee of the Federation of American Zionists and served as its honorary secretary and honorary vice president. Noticing her many abilities and capacity for hard work, several generous benefactors undertook to grant her a stipend so that she would no longer have to depend on employment for a livelihood. She was thus able, from 1915 on, to devote herself fully to Zionist and Jewish activity of her own choosing. At age fifty-five she was about to enter the most significant period of her life.

For a few years Szold had been associated with a group of women in New York (where she had gone to live in 1903) called the Hadassah Study Circle. Their avocation was to hear and discuss papers on academic Zionist and Jewish topics. In 1909 she and her mother visited Europe and Palestine and were saddened to encounter the widespread poverty and disease among both Jews and Arabs in the ancient homeland. Her mother commented that the ladies of the Hadassah Study Circle could be doing better things with their time than reading papers and drinking tea; they could instead do something practical to improve the living conditions of real people. Szold thereupon set out to convert the Hadassah Study Circle into a national organization of Jewish women to undertake practical work in Palestine. The new organization held its first meeting in 1912; Szold was elected president. The group would later be known as Hadassah—the Women's Zionist Organization of America. It became the largest and most active Zionist group in the country, pioneering in providing and subventioning nursing and medical care in Palestine for both Jews and Arabs. The Hadassah Hospital in Jerusalem is to this day one of the premier medical institutions in the world. For the remainder of her life Henrietta Szold was the driving force behind Hadassah and all of its accomplishments.

Szold went in 1919 to Palestine, assuming that she would in a short while return to her own country, the United States. As matters turned out, however, her services and leadership were needed on site by those who looked to her for leadership and guidance. Instead of returning to the United States and making occasional visits to Palestine, it was to the United States that she would make the occasional visits. This was especially true after the rise of Nazism and the Second World War. She organized Youth Aliyah, a project that by the end of the war had saved the lives of eight thousand European Jewish children, rescuing them for a new life in the Jewish settlements in Palestine. She never stopped considering herself an American, though, even as she dedicated her life to her responsibilities of saving and healing the Jewish people.

Henrietta Szold died before the founding of the state of Israel, but her work helped prepare the way for that event. She wrote, in discussing Arab-Jewish conflict in Palestine, "If our cause is wholly just and righteous, we are bound to find just and righteous and peaceful means of conciliation." And, in regard to the work to which she devoted her life (she never married or had children), she said, "We are promised a place in the sun—not to ravage and dominate, but to serve, our people, ourselves, our world. Standing in the sun we shall be seen clearly as never before. Our abilities will be on trial before a world full of nations, who will judge us in the light of a glorious past of ideal service to mankind. For Israel, election has never meant anything but obligation. Clearly, rehabilitating a nation is not a pastime. It is a task, a heavy task, a holy task."

When, how, and why were some Jewish labor unions allied with Communists?

The victory of Lenin and his hard-line Communist followers in Russia in 1917 brought about a split among socialists in the United States, many of whom were active in the trade union movement. The majority remained committed to the ideals of democratic socialism, but a militant segment looked to the Soviet Union for leadership and inspiration. Among the Jewish unions in the garment industry, the Amalgamated

Clothing Workers under **Sidney Hillman**'s leadership was able to keep the Communists under control. The International Ladies Garment Workers, however, was a more diffuse organization, and several locals were taken over by Communists. Violent words and acts marred union meetings, with the Communist elements looking upon union members who were less radical with even greater antipathy than they did the employers. Sometimes the violence was merely symbolic: leftist women, forming "fainting brigades," would pretend to faint when a right-wing speaker had the platform at a meeting and create so much commotion that he was unable to continue. Then there were the "spitting brigades"—groups of women who would ostentatiously spit into the gutter when a right-wing unionist passed by. During the 1920s and early 1930s these relatively harmless amusements were replaced by physical attacks with fists and weapons. Communist leadership in the ILGWU locals forced a general strike in the cloak trade in 1926. During the six months that the workers remained out, the local Communist leadership refused to approve a settlement. Only when the International leadership suspended the local leaders was a settlement finally arrived at. This bitter experience turned the ILGWU rank and file against the Communists, and **David Dubinsky**, who assumed the International presidency a few years later, was able to keep their influence to a minimum.

One union in which the Communists for a time achieved dominance was that of the fur workers. Militant Jewish workers, joined by some Greeks in the industry, battled in the streets and in the shops against non-Communist workers. They had no qualms about resorting to knives, belts, and pipes. The Communist leader of the fur workers was Ben Gold. In 1926 he was able to win a forty-hour week for the furriers, the first in the garment industry. According to Irving Howe, he was a "virtuoso of invective, pouring endless scorn on the heads of 'Socialist fakers' and 'AFL misleaders.' When Gold would reach the tenth floor of the *Forward* building, where Abraham Cahan had his office, there tumbled out of him arias of abuse as his voice rose to a piercing shriek. His hysteria ate into his audiences, and they reveled in it." After the Second World War and the rise of widespread anti-Communist feeling in the country, the Fur Workers Union realized it could no longer operate as it had. Over Gold's vigorous opposition, it gave up its independence and became the fur and leather division of the Amalgamated Meat Cutters.

How did some unions become involved with gangsters and racketeers?

In the mid-1920s racketeers began infiltrating the garment industry and other industries dependent upon trucking. During the 1926 general strike by the cloak makers, the employers hired the Legs Diamond mob to terrorize union pickets. In response, some union locals hired a mob led by Jacob ("Little Augie") Orgen. The violence and bloodshed between these rival gangs was put to rest through the intervention of **Arnold Rothstein**, the overall boss of the New York rackets. He had achieved this position because, in Irving Howe's words, "The political bosses (of Tammany Hall) and outlaw elements concluded that the financial arrangements between their two groups would have to be put on a more businesslike basis, a resolution that caused them to install Arnold Rothstein as the czar of the New York underworld."

Rothstein began his career as a protégé of the Tammany leader "Big Tim" Sullivan. He used his connections to move into gambling, bootlegging, drug dealing, and labor racketeering. He financed some of the Communist locals in the garment industry and mediated labor disputes in which they were involved. He was shot to death in 1928 at the age of forty-six.

By 1930–32, during the Great Depression, the underworld's hold on some key union positions had become a factor to be reckoned with. The gunmen and racketeers worked with corrupt union officials and were protected by corrupt police officers and judges. After Rothstein's death the most notorious mobster in New York was **Louis ("Lepke") Buchalter** who, with **Jacob ("Gurrah") Shapiro**, headed what some law enforcement people called "Murder Incorporated." Lepke's base in the men's garment industry was Cutters Local 4. Lepke's mob collected union dues and kept a percentage for themselves. He persuaded management to be "reasonable" by threatening to call strikes, destroy merchandise, and injure or kill those who would not cooperate with him. He exacted a small fee on each garment or construction contract, and by the mid-1930s was collecting $40 million a year. He was reputed to have 250 "enforcers" working for him.

Lepke had grown up on the Lower East Side and had been active in extortion, industrial sabotage, the protection racket, and loan-sharking all of his professional life. When at last the time was right, **Sidney Hillman**, president of the Amalgamated Clothing Workers, arranged, with the aid of New York's police commissioner, a raid on Local 4's offices. The corrupt officials were removed bodily from the premises, and the gangsters driven out of the union. Lepke surrendered to the FBI through the mediation of columnist Walter Winchell. He was turned over to state authorities in 1939, convicted of murder, and executed in 1944 at the age of forty-seven.

Who was, even in the judgment of those who hated him, "the single most influential figure in twentieth-century urban renewal"?

Robert Moses (1888–1981) was not an architect, planner, or lawyer. He never held elective office. Yet he was the great master builder of much of New York City and New York State. He was proud of his ability "to get things done." Appointed to almost countless offices in city and state government over a span of time exceeding fifty years, beginning in 1914, he once held twelve city and state positions simultaneously.

What did Moses do? He revised and revamped much of the infrastructure of the city and state for the age of the automobile. He was responsible for the building of parks, highways, bridges, housing, tunnels, beaches, playgrounds, zoos, exhibition halls, sports stadiums, electric power projects, and the 1964–65 New York World's Fair. Without Robert Moses, much of New York City and neighboring areas would not look at all like they do today.

Who were the noteworthy Jews from Chicago?

Chicago's Maxwell Street neighborhood was that city's equivalent of New York's Lower East Side. Journalist Ira Berkow's book *Maxwell Street; Survival in a Bazaar,* celebrates the life and legacy of the immigrants who settled there, and their offspring, most of them Jews. He writes that to the immigrants, "Maxwell Street appeared a welcome step, a chance to climb up in the New World, or 'Columbus's land,' as they called it. And if they themselves couldn't make it, they dreamed that opportunities would be created for their children."

Joseph Goldberg came to Maxwell Street from Russia. Buying a blind horse, he peddled vegetables and fruit in the streets. His son, **Arthur Goldberg**, however, would serve in Washington as a cabinet secretary and a Supreme Court justice. Another denizen of Maxwell Street was **Samuel Paley**. His son, **William Paley**, was born in the back room of the family cigar store, and became founder, president, and chairman of the board of the Columbia Broadcasting System. Another cigar maker in the street's environs was **Max Guzik**. His son **Jake Guzik**, called "Greasy Thumb," rose to be the brains behind the Capone gang and one of the top three on the FBI's list of public enemies.

Two of the immigrant tailors who took jobs in Chicago were **David Goodman** and **Abraham Rickover**. The former became the father of musician and composer **Benny Good-man**. The latter fathered Admiral **Hyman G. Rickover**, who headed the U.S. Navy's nuclear submarine program. His submarines could cruise around the world without surfacing. **Barney Ross**'s father operated a small grocery store near Maxwell Street, as did **Barney Balaban**'s father. Barney Ross became lightweight boxing champion of the world, while Barney Balaban became president of Paramount Pictures.

Also on Maxwell Street was the father of actor **Paul Muni**; he owned a Yiddish theater there. Working as a carpenter in the neighborhood was the father of **Jack Ruby**, who in 1963 killed **Lee Harvey Oswald**, the assassin of President John F. Kennedy.

And, in Berkow's words, "it was around Maxwell Street at the turn of the century that the phenomenal con man Joseph 'Yellow Kid' Weil, son of immigrant parents, learned to inveigle people to gladly hand him their money for nothing but a sweet song."

Who was "Greasy Thumb" Guzik?

Jake ("Greasy Thumb") Guzik was the business manger for Al Capone's criminal organization operating out of Chicago from the 1920s into the 1940s. He was short and fat, measuring about sixty inches high and almost sixty inches around. In Berkow's words, he was a "short, penguin-shaped man, wattled, dew-lipped and pouchy-eyed, who wore a perpetually plaintive air." His criminal dossier lists his occupation as gambler, and the charges against him included tax evasion, bootlegging, and pandering. Guzik said, "I don't know why they call me a hoodlum. I never carried a gun in my life." During Prohibition in the United States, the organization's main source of income was the illegal importation and distribution of liquor. When Prohibition ended in 1933, the organization turned to operating a nationwide racing wire, transmitting descriptions of horse races from all tracks to illegal book-making establishments throughout the country. This was largely the brainchild of "Greasy Thumb," and it resulted in the creation of a nationwide crime syndicate.

Guzik died at the age of seventy in 1956. At his funeral the rabbi who officiated said, "Jacob Guzik never lost faith in God. Hundreds benefited from his kindness and generosity. His charities were performed quietly. And he made frequent and vast contributions to my congregation."

Who originated "Levi's"?

Levi Strauss (1829–1902) came to San Francisco in 1853 with a limited supply of heavy cloth which he thought would be useful to miners needing tents during the pandemonium of the Gold Rush. He easily sold what he had, but he noticed that the miners' pants wore out very rapidly. He took his remaining bolt of tenting canvas to a tailor and had it made into a dozen pair of pants. These he sold immediately, and then sent instructions to his brothers in the East to buy up all the tenting canvas they could find and ship it posthaste to him. Thus was Levi Strauss and Company born. His brothers and brothers-in-law joined him in San Francisco, and the company became the world's greatest producer of heavy workclothes. The work-pants were of course the characteristic "dungarees" or "jeans" (short for "Genoa Fustian," a cotton fabric) that are known throughout the world as "Levi's." In 1873 the company patented the copper riveting it had added to the pockets of its Levi's, and advertised that these pants were "so tough even a team of plough horses could not tear them apart."

Are department stores Jewish?

According to Howard Sachar, "It was the omnibus, one-stop department store, virtually synonymous with German Jewish merchandising in the late nineteenth century, that emerged as a central feature of the American urban landscape in both the North and the South. **Jacob Kaufmann**, son of a Rhenish cattle dealer, pack-peddled in western Pennsylvania before setting up a little general store in Pittsburgh in 1868. Twenty years later, with his two brothers, Kaufmann proudly opened the city's first 'emporium.' " Other department stores opened by successful Jewish merchants during this period were Filene's in Boston; Gimbel's in Milwaukee, later in Philadelphia, and in 1909 in New York; Altman's, Abraham and Straus, and Bloomingdale's in New York; and, with the move of **Lazarus Straus** and his family from Georgia to New York, came the development of Macy's in the early twentieth century as the largest department store in the world.

In 1895 **Julius Rosenwald**, who grew up in Springfield, Illinois, and had become a successful clothing manufacturer in Chicago, purchased a part interest in the Sears, Roebuck mail-order operation. He became the company's marketing director and established high standards of quality control. In 1907 Sears floated a stock issue that transformed it into a major public corporation. Rosenwald, as chairman, opened a large number of retail outlets throughout the country. By the 1930s Sears was the largest mass-merchandising business in the nation. During the depression of 1921–22 Rosenwald eliminated his own salary and, from his private funds, paid cash dividends to small stockholders of Sears until the economy recovered. Throughout his career he was a munificent donor to educational institutions, hospitals, and medical research. Rosenwald developed a unique program to expand educational opportunities for Southern blacks during a time when black education was still strictly segregated. He offered half the cost of a new school for blacks to any Southern community whose members would contribute the other half. Individual citizens and county governments in fifteen Southern states together with Rosenwald built over five thousand schools, libraries, health clinics, and YMCAs.

What were Henry Ford's thoughts about Jews?

Henry Ford (1863–1947) discovered how to make the automobile one of the indispensable possessions of the average American. Ford's method of industrial organization enabled him to reduce the cost of manufacturing automobiles; he passed on these savings to the purchasing public and sold the cars he produced at an affordable price. It is not surprising, therefore, that he was, during the later years of the nineteenth century and the early years of the twentieth, one of the most admired and beloved of America's citizens.

From 1920 to 1922 Ford sponsored the publication of a series of articles in a weekly paper that he owned in the Detroit suburb where he had been born, the *Dearborn Independent;* these pieces were later published in book form under the title *The International Jew.* This collection attempts to blame Jews for all the ills that afflict the modern world. It accepts as factually accurate the notorious forgery titled *The Protocols of the Elders of Zion*, which purports to expose a Jewish plot to take over the world, a work widely circulated in czarist Russia at the end of the nineteenth century.

In Ford's articles the Jews, or at least the wealthy element within the community, seek not to "make" money but to "get" money; that is to say, they have no interest in producing high-quality products but rather are intent on manipulating industries and the financial and banking systems so that they control them and enrich themselves. Jews are responsible for the debasement of the American theater and the movie industry. Jewish composers introduced jazz and sexually suggestive lyrics into American music. Jewish control of the liquor industry caused the displacement of good American wines and liquors by brands of such inferior quality that violent crime, sickness, and death became the lot of those who consumed them. For this reason, according to the *Dearborn Independent* and *The International Jew*, the Eighteenth Amendment prohibiting the manufacture and distribution of alcoholic beverages was added to the Constitution (it was repealed with the advent of the Roosevelt administration in 1933). The Jews, however, were ready for Prohibition; they became the leaders and organizers of bootleg liquor distribution in the United States. All of this, according to Ford's articles, was part of the age-old Jewish conspiracy to weaken and debase the cultures of all countries so that Jews could step into leadership everywhere, as they were already doing in Russia through its Bolshevik regime. The Jesuits and the Masons had in earlier centuries been accused of seeking to take over the world. In the opinion of Ford's paper, it had been Jews who had infiltrated the ranks of both the Jesuits and the Masons for their own nefarious purposes. Now they were taking over Christian churches and seminaries through modern scientific study of the Bible. Ford, or the authors who wrote these materials for him, were quite naive about many aspects of culture outside the United States. They thought that German-type names were most likely Jewish, and insisted that the great German Protestant scholars who pioneered scientific biblical research in the nineteenth century were Jews. This would have been surprising news to these scholars, their families, and their contemporaries.

As might be expected, the publication of drivel of this type in association with the name of Henry Ford was the cause of great consternation not only to Jews but to many other Americans as well. By 1927 their protests bore fruit and Ford issued the following statement:

> To my great regret I have learned that Jews generally, and particularly those of this country, not only resent these publications as promoting anti-Semitism, but regard me as their enemy. Trusted friends with whom I have conferred recently have assured me in all sincerity that in their opinion the character of the charges and insinuations made against the Jews, both individually and collectively, contained in many of the

articles which have been circulated periodically in the *Dearborn Independent* and have been reprinted in the pamphlets mentioned, justifies the righteous indignation entertained by Jews everywhere toward me because of the mental anguish occasioned by the unprovoked reflections made upon them. . . . Had I appreciated even the general nature, to say nothing of the details, of these utterances, I would have forbidden their circulation without a moment's hesitation, because I am fully aware of the virtues of the Jewish people as a whole, of what they and their ancestors have done for civilization and for mankind and toward the development of commerce and industry, of their sobriety and diligence, their benevolence and their unselfish interest in the public welfare. Of course there are black sheep in every flock, as there are among men of all races, creeds and nationalities who are at times evildoers. It is wrong, however, to judge a people by a few individuals, and I therefore join in condemning unreservedly all wholesale denunciations and attacks.

Ford was a great industrialist, but it took him six years to realize that these attacks upon the Jews reflected adversely upon his character and intelligence (and that, in addition, they did nothing for the continuing profitability of his automobile business). As the twentieth century comes to its end, however, there are still people who promulgate conspiracy theories of human history. Instead of speaking of "international Jews," as Ford's articles did, in an attempt to escape the charge of blatant anti-Semitism, they speak of "international bankers," some of whom happen to be Jews.

Was there ever an instance of the vicious "blood libel" in the United States?

In various European countries the "blood libel," alleging that Jews use the blood of Christians in religious rituals, has from time to time arisen to spread terror and consternation in

Jewish communities. The Damascus Affair (see page 38) involved such an accusation. In 1928, in Massena, New York, the blood libel came to the United States.

Massena is a community in New York State close to the Canadian border. A small group of Jews lived among its total population of about ten thousand. In September 1928, two days before Yom Kippur ("Day of Atonement"), a mother sent her four-year-old daughter into some nearby woods to look for her older brother. The boy made it home; the little girl did not. Search parties were unable to find her. One of Massena's citizens recalled a story he had heard from his European grandmother about how, when she was a child, the Jews had come to her village the night before Easter and murdered a little boy to obtain his blood. Some of Massena's people thought that the possibility of Jewish involvement deserved further investigation. A state policeman was sent to the home of Massena's rabbi to bring him in for questioning. The rabbi felt that the trooper's manner was crude and insulting. At the police station the rabbi pointed out that Judaism forbids the consumption of any blood, whether human or animal; it does not even equate wine with blood in a symbolic sense, as do some Christian groups.

The next day a group of rescuers found the little girl, alive and well. She had gotten lost while trying to locate her brother and had wandered farther and farther from home. Massena's mayor issued a public apology to the town's Jews. The state trooper was reprimanded and transferred.

What magician delighted in exposing the fakery and frauds of other magicians and mind readers?

Harry Houdini (1874–1926; born Ehrich Weiss) came to New York in 1886 from Hungary with his father. Performing first as a trapeze artist, he later took up the art of illusion. During the 1890s he performed in American theaters and beer halls, but in 1900 he toured Europe for four years and returned with an international reputation as a master of escape from a variety of shackles, cells, and locked containers. Once he emerged free after being shackled in chains and locked in a box that was then submerged in New York's East River. Houdini had a particular antipathy toward mind readers, and mediums who claimed to communicate with the dead. Whenever possible he exposed their tricks to the public.

Before his death he promised family and friends that, if at all possible, he would find a way to contact them from the other world. Houdini died on Halloween. His devotees for years kept watch on Halloween at his tomb in a New York Jewish cemetery. Houdini has still not been heard from.

What did the phrase "near churches" mean in real estate ads during the first half of the twentieth century?

During the first half of the twentieth century, classified ads for real estate, both sales and rentals, often conveyed the information that the property being advertised was "near churches" or, occasionally, "near Catholic and Protestant churches." This was coded language letting Jews know that they would not be welcome in certain neighborhoods, and letting non-Jews know that they did not have to fear the presence of Jews. (No ads ever said "near churches and synagogues.")

Sometimes there were even written stipulations in deeds of sale that the buyer could not sell the property to Jews, or "restrictive covenants," in which homeowners in a certain area pledged among themselves not to sell or rent to Jews. (Similar devices were used to keep out other racial or ethnic groups from specific neighborhoods.) Practices such as these were particularly vexatious to Jews seeking to move from crowded cities to the numerous suburban developments opening up after World War II. Luckily, however, many states and localities in the 1950s passed legislation prohibiting these practices. Now the American ideal of equal opportunity, unbounded by race, religion, or ethnicity, at least from the stand-point of the law, is available to all.

What Jewish groups settled in the United States after immigration restrictions were imposed in 1924?

Nothing like the overwhelming mass of Eastern European Jews who came to the country between 1880 and 1924 was to be seen again, but other Jews have continued to adopt America as their home. Between 1900 and 1924 approximately thirty-seven thousand Sephardic Jews came, from Turkey, the Balkan countries, Greece, and Syria. Most settled in New York City, but some went to other areas, joining family members or fellow townspeople who had preceded them. By 1912 Seattle had become, after New York, the city with the largest Sephardic community in the country; most of its members were from Turkey.

During the 1930s some refugees from Nazi Germany were admitted. Many more would have come had it not been for the quota restrictions. Most of those who could not reach America were swept away in the Holocaust. After the Second World War the quota system was modified to permit the entry of some of the displaced persons, survivors of the Nazi death and labor camps. Eastern Europeans came, and formed the basis of much of the more rigidly Orthodox community, including the Hasidim, in the country today. In the 1950s and 1960s, during the turmoil in Arab countries protesting the founding of the state of Israel, Jews fled to America from Egypt and Morocco.

During the 1970s and 1980s many Jews wished to leave the Soviet Union, but the policy of that government prevented most of them from fulfilling their wish. Early in 1975 the U.S. Congress passed the Jackson-Vanik amendment, making certain trading privileges dependent upon the Soviets' willingness to allow Jewish emigration; this was very effective in opening doors that would otherwise have remained closed.

Soviet Jews in large numbers immigrated to both Israel and the United States. (Some American Zionists wished the U.S. to bar America's doors to these people, so that they would be forced to go to Israel. The majority of America's Jews, however, would not have approved of such action, nor would it have been possible under American law.) The many thousands of Soviet Jews who settled in the United States during the past thirty years were, for the most part, unlike the Russian Jews who came at the beginning of the twentieth century. They had grown up under the Communist regime and knew very little about Jewish religion or culture. Their native tongue was Russian rather than Yiddish. Many Soviet Jews began the reclamation of their Jewish heritage when they came to the United States, some by joining synagogues and other organizations that led them into religious observance. Others, however, did not take to the religious aspect of being Jewish. Like the nonreligious Jews who came to America in the early twentieth century, they seek to preserve a Russian Jewish ethnic heritage through Russian language, Russian restaurants, and Russian clubs. Brighton Beach in Brooklyn has become a major center of Russian, particularly Russian Jewish, life. Sometimes called "Little Odessa," it has the feel and atmosphere of the land its people have left behind.

There is a large contingent of Israelis who have settled in the United States. Some of them feel a twinge of guilt about having left Israel for the "fleshpots" of America, but most nonetheless remain in the U.S., living and working in all of the major cities in the country. The great majority, however, travel to Israel frequently and retain Israeli citizenship, even if they also become citizens of the United States.

There is also a group of Iranian Jews who have come to America after the revolution in 1979 made Iran into a Muslim theocracy. These people, many of whom settled in southern California, retain affectionate memories of the land and the culture that they left behind, but want no link to the repressive regime from which they have escaped.

How have Jewish Americans influenced American music?

According to some, without the contributions of Jewish Americans there would be little American popular music to speak of from perhaps the 1920s to the beginning of the rock era.

Irving Berlin (1888–1989), born Israel Baline, a cantor's son, arrived in America from Russia at the age of five. He had no formal musical education, but he could create memorable melodies and lyrics with the greatest of ease. He worked for a time as a singing waiter, then as a saloon composer and staff lyricist for a music publisher, turning out on occasion parodies in Yinglish (fractured Yiddish-English). His first great success was "Alexander's Ragtime Band," which sold a million copies in sheet music within three months. After serving in the army during World War I, he wrote songs for vaudeville and the *Ziegfield Follies*. Besides Broadway musicals, he composed "White Christmas," "Easter Parade," and "God Bless America."

George Gershwin (1898–1937) was the son of Russian Jewish immigrants. His parents paid for piano lessons, and Gershwin left high school to work as a piano player and eventually as staff composer for a music publisher. At age twenty he composed his first Broadway musical, *La La Lucille,* and continued composing for many more. His brother, **Ira Gershwin**, wrote the lyrics. In 1924, at the commission of orchestra leader Paul Whiteman, he composed a modern jazz concerto, *Rhapsody in Blue,* followed by some other serious works. He continued composing for Broadway and Hollywood, capping his career two years before his untimely death with his great folk opera *Porgy and Bess.*

In the area of classical music and opera, numerous widely acclaimed Jewish-American conductors, violinists, pianists, and singers have performed before audiences throughout the world. **Aaron Copland** (1900–1990) was known as a prolific composer of "serious" music with an American theme, such as *Appalachian Spring, Billy the Kid,* and *Fanfare for the Common Man.* Broadway musical theater could not have been what it was during the twentieth century without the creative contribution of Jewish Americans. **Oscar Hammerstein II** (1895–1960), grandson of Oscar Hammerstein, the theater builder and theatrical producer of the late nineteenth century, realized during the early 1920s that he was not meant for a career in law but, rather, in theater. He wrote the lyrics for Sigmund Romberg's *Desert Song* and **Jerome Kern**'s *Show Boat* (based on Edna Ferber's novel of the same name). In 1943 he joined forces with **Richard Rodgers**, who in earlier years had worked on musicals with **Lorenz Hart**, to bring into being one of the great achievements of the American stage, *Oklahoma!* Rodgers and Hammerstein later produced *Carousel* and *The Sound of Music.* During the 1960s the team of **Alan Jay Lerner** and **Frederick Loewe** lit up Broadway with their work, as did **Stephen Sondheim**, one of the few composers who wrote his own lyrics, during the 1960s, 1970s and 1980s.

In a class by himself was **Leonard Bernstein**, classical pianist, composer, conductor, and music educator, who also composed for Broadway. In 1958 he was appointed musical director of the New York Philharmonic. His classical works, some with a Jewish theme, include *Jeremiah, The Age of Anxiety, Kaddish,* and *Chichester Psalms.* For musical theater he wrote *On the Town, Wonderful Town, Candide,* and, in 1957, the great, never-to-be-forgotten *West Side Story.* In historian Howard Sachar's evaluation, "In whatever role, as conductor or composer, writer of classical or popular music, champion of Jewish music or pioneer guest conductor of the Israel Philharmonic, Bernstein, until his death in 1990 at the age of seventy-two, blazed across the firmament as possibly the most renowned musical figure of the late twentieth century."

What was so funny about the Marx Brothers?

The **Marx Brothers** (most often three of them—Groucho, Chico, and Harpo) were born in New York, Chico, the eldest, in 1887. Minnie, their mother, the sister of Al Shean of the vaudeville duo Gallagher and Shean, channeled her sons into comic entertainment, in vaudeville and on Broadway. From 1929 to 1960 they made movies. In Irving Howe's analysis, "The Marx Brothers split open the conventions of stage entertainment into extremes of social satire and chaotic farce; they were no longer so obsessed as earlier Jewish entertainers had been with simply pleasing the audience; they sought, instead, to spin it helplessly, dizzily away from standard expectations of coherence. . . . In their films the disassembled world is treated with total disrespect. The gleeful nihilism of the Marx Brothers made a shamble of things, reducing their field of operations to approximately what a certain sort of East Side skeptic had always thought the world to be: ashes and dust."

Here is one of the Brothers' early vaudeville routines:

GROUCHO: Why were you late?

HARPO: My mother lost the lid off the stove, and I had to sit on it to keep the smoke in.

GROUCHO: If you had ten apples and you wanted to divide them among six people, what would you do?

GUMMO: Make applesauce.

GROUCHO: What is the shape of the world?

HARPO: I don't know.

GROUCHO: Well, what shape are my cuff links?

HARPO: Square.

GROUCHO: Not my weekday cuff links, the ones I wear on Sundays.

HARPO: Oh, round.

GROUCHO: All right, what is the shape of the world?

HARPO: Square on weekdays, round on Sundays.

GROUCHO: What are the principal parts of a cat?

GUMMO: Eyes, ears, neck, tail, feet, etc.

GROUCHO: You've forgotten the most important. What does a cat have that you don't have?

GUMMO: Kittens.

SOME OF THE JEWISH COMEDIANS, COMIC WRITERS, AND THEATER PEOPLE OF THE PAST SIXTY YEARS

Woody Allen	Sam Levenson
Jack Benny	Jerry Lewis
Milton Berle	Groucho Marx
Fanny Brice	Jackie Mason
Mel Brooks	Zero Mostel
Lenny Bruce	S. J. Perelman
George Burns	Roseanne
Sid Caesar	Mort Sahl
Eddie Cantor	Jerry Seinfeld
Sammy Davis, Jr.	Elizabeth Taylor
Danny Kaye	Henny Youngman

Who were the first Jewish feminists?

Beginning in the 1880s middle-class Jewish women, like others in the society at large, began to organize women's clubs devoted to the amelioration of urban social problems. These women sought to devote a major part of their free time to working as volunteers, in such places as orphanages, training schools, settlement houses, and homes for juvenile delinquents. They could no longer accept the popular maxim that "woman's place is [solely] in the home." Reflecting these aims and ideals, the National Council of Jewish Women was formed in 1893.

The council was initiated by vote of the First Congress of Jewish Women, meeting in 1893 as part of the Parliament of Religions at the Chicago World's Fair. Originally, the women had been invited to "cooperate" with the men, but, upon seeing that they were to have no roles in the programs prepared by the men, they withdrew and, under the leadership of **Hannah G. Solomon**, set up their own meeting. Speakers at the women's congress included **Henrietta Szold**, **Josephine Lazarus** (noted essayist and sister of **Emma Lazarus**), and **Rebekah Kohut**, the widow of a distinguished rabbi and scholar at the Jewish Theological Seminary in New York and a Jewish scholar in her own right. By 1896 the National Council of Jewish Women had established sections in over fifty American cities and towns. It set up study groups for its own members, and Sabbath or Sunday schools for children. It lobbied state legislatures for laws to improve living conditions among the poor, and established facilities to aid immigrant women and children. In 1911 a total of 7,466 home visits were made by council volunteers to new immigrants in New York, Boston, Baltimore, and Philadelphia.

Kohut, president of the council's New York section, declared, "The idea existed that women had inherent incapacity for convictions and cooperation. Women could never work together, so it was said. It cannot be said now. Jewish women can work together, and working, can achieve definite results." She also said, "We refuse as women to be used merely to raise money and to act as figureheads in the management of sewing societies and ladies' auxiliaries. We have earned the title to larger responsibilities than this. It is now that woman can show for all time that she is able to meet the greater demands, not only in the social spheres, but in the productive fields of work as well."

Sadie American, a longtime officer of the council (her family name had been adopted by her immigrant father as a gesture of love for his new land), insisted that "we claim that for a woman to give in words and publicly of her enthusiasm or of the wisdom of her experience to make life fuller and better for others, is quite as womanly as to sing operatic arias in a parlor voice, to execute sonatas, or to imitate poor actresses—all of which meet with general approval." American, a committed feminist and suffragette, was sent by the council as its representative to the International Council of Women meeting in Rome in 1914. The National Council of Jewish Women took a strong interest in the problem of "white slavery" among the immigrant population (women and girls tricked or forced into prostitution). Sadie American was sent as the American delegate to the Jewish International Conference on the Suppression of Traffic in Girls and Women, held in London in 1910, and to the International White Slave Traffic Conference in Madrid that same year. American's conviction was, "There are forces in girls as in men, sexual forces which are stronger than they are; and there are girls who cannot help themselves and will become prostitutes and for them nothing can be done until the world treats the whole question of prostitution differently from what it has; if we recognize this we will not always condemn the woman of the streets."

What dedicated feminist was also active in the anti-suffrage movement (which opposed granting women the right to vote)?

Annie Nathan Meyer was born in 1867 in New York to Sephardic parents of distinguished lineage, related to such worthies as **Gershom Mendes Seixas**, the rabbi of the Spanish-Portuguese Synagogue who participated in George Washington's inauguration, **Emma Lazarus** the poet, and U.S. Supreme Court justice **Benjamin Cardozo**. At age nineteen she married Dr. Alfred Meyer, a physician. They had both been members of the Piano Club, a group that met weekly for the reading of music at sight. She had asked him to serve as a member of the program committee; his response was, "I don't see, Miss Nathan, that the work calls for any special intellectual ability." She replied, "Maybe that was the reason I asked you." Shortly thereafter he asked her to become his wife.

About a year before her marriage, Annie Nathan had told her father that, after secretly studying for them, she had passed the examinations for admission into the Collegiate Course for women at Columbia College. His immediate response was, "You will never be married. Men hate intelligent wives." Dr. Meyer, however, did not share Mr. Nathan's opinions, and was a constant support to his wife in her multifarious endeavors during more than sixty years of marriage.

The Collegiate Course for women did not require students to attend the professors' lectures. They were, in fact, prohibited from attending them. Female students were, instead, granted two interviews a year with professors, who would assign chapters in books for the students to read. At the end of each term the women would take the same examinations as the male students, who had attended the professors' lectures given at the college. These examinations were based upon the lectures, rather than upon the textbook material. It was, therefore, a rarity for a woman to pass one of these exams, and even rarer for her to earn an undergraduate degree from Columbia. When Annie Nathan discovered how the Collegiate Course for women operated, she withdrew from the program.

Annie Nathan Meyer did not completely sever her connection with Columbia. Since she wished to be a writer, she frequently used the college's library where Melvil Dewey, the inventor of the Dewey decimal system of cataloging, was librarian. He and Meyer agreed on the absurdity inherent in the Collegiate Course for women, and he encouraged her to take the lead in starting a college for women. Thus it was that Meyer, at the age of twenty, with no college degree herself, "the wife of a physician comfortably enough off," embarked upon this adventure. She set five tasks for herself: to learn which colleges in the country were open to women, and on what basis; to personally contact every man and woman in the New York vicinity who might support the establishment of a women's college, either financially or in an advisory capacity; to build up public opinion in favor of such a college by personal talks, interviews, letters, and editorials in the daily papers; to win over, individually and collectively, the trustees of Columbia College in favor of a women's college affiliated with Columbia; and "to build up a body of men and women who would command the confidence of the public and would undertake to direct this college." This was a very tall order, but Meyer did it. Barnard College, Columbia's affiliate for women, opened its doors on October 7, 1889. It was named to honor Frederick Barnard, Columbia's president, who had died a few months previously. Within its walls Columbia professors taught women! Meyer of course served as an active and interested trustee of Barnard College during the ensuing years of her long life. She wrote a number of well-received plays, novels, and articles about women in the working world, and was instrumental in acquiring a major private collection of materials about colonial New York for the New York Public Library. She also came to be recognized as an important commentator upon American art.

In light of all this, it is surprising to note that Annie Nathan Meyer was also an active opponent of the women's suffrage movement. In her autobiography she explains why. She writes that the suffragists were unsympathetic because they exuded "a distinct flavor of sex hatred" (i.e., a hatred or disdain for men) that she herself did not share. Also, she was disgusted by the claims "that were made as to the results that were certain to happen" if women were granted the right to vote.

The pages of my scrapbooks are full of the most fantastic claims: it would do away with prostitutes, with children killed in the streets, with graft in politics, with liquor, with war! An amusing story is told of Susan B. Anthony arguing before the New York State Legislature for the right of women to vote. Said she: "Why, the effect of woman voting is nothing short of marvelous. Do you gentlemen know that at the moment there is not a single prisoner in jail in Nevada, where women have had the vote for years?"

"Does Miss Anthony know," queried one of the legislators, "that Nevada has no jail at the present moment, but is temporarily using that of its neighboring state, Idaho?"

"Yes," snapped Susan B., "I know it, but I didn't think any of you men knew it!"

In spite of Annie Nathan Meyer's efforts to the contrary, the right of women to vote was incorporated into the U.S. Constitution by amendment in 1920.

Is The New York Times *a "Jewish" paper?*

The New York Times began publication in 1851. Its role as "the newspaper of record" in the United States was assumed, though, in 1896, when it was taken over by Adolph Ochs. Ochs, the son of German-born Jewish parents, had grown up in Cincinnati and Tennessee and gravitated to newspaper work. He married the daughter of Rabbi Isaac Mayer Wise. Ochs purchased the Chattanooga *Times* and turned it into a respected regional paper. In 1896, upon learning that the New York paper was about to enter into bankruptcy, he borrowed funds to buy it as well. He originated the paper's slogan, "All the News That's Fit to Print," as a way of distinguishing it from some of the other papers of the day that were noted for their sensationalist, "yellow" journalism. He resolved, as he said, to operate a "high standards newspaper, clean, dignified and trustworthy." Ochs's descendants continue to play a major role in managing the paper to this day, remaining true to the ideals that he established. The

Times specializes in complete, unprejudiced coverage of all genuine news, in all areas of human culture and endeavor.

Is the *Times* a "Jewish" paper? According to anti-Semites, it is, but to some tenacious Zionists it is sometimes an "anti-Jewish" paper. It strives to be as fair to Jews as it is to everybody else.

JOURNALISTS

Ann Landers	Born Esther Friedman, Landers has been for many years a widely syndicated columnist in newspapers throughout the United States and elsewhere, offering advice and a platform for expression to the many people whose significant (and insignificant) personal and social problems would otherwise go unheard.
Abigail Van Buren	Born Pauline Friedman, she is the twin sister of Ann Landers and author of a competing advice column ("Dear Abby") syndicated to many newspapers.
Barbara Walters	One of the leading TV news journalists, an indefatigable interviewer of important people and newsmakers throughout the world
Larry King	Anyone who seeks to play a major role in U.S. politics has to be interviewed on TV at least once by Larry King (on CNN).

Norman Cousins	Editor of the *Saturday Review* during the 1950s and 1960s
Victor Navasky	Publisher and editorial director of *The Nation*
Martin Peretz	Editor in chief of the *New Republic*
Norman Pearlstine and Walter Isaacson	Editor in chief and managing editor, respectively, of *Time*
Anthony Lewis, A. M. Rosenthal, and William Safire	Columnists for *The New York Times*, concentrating on political and social issues (Safire also contributes columns on contemporary developments in the English language)

SPORTS JOURNALISTS

Howard Cosell	The best-known and most controversial TV sportscaster in the country during his years with ABC, 1956–85. A regular on "Monday Night Football."
Mel Allen	"The voice of the Yankees" on radio and TV from 1939 to 1964
Marv Albert	NBC sportscaster

Are Hollywood movies a Jewish industry?

Anti-Semites have always maintained that there is too much Jewish influence or control in all the important institutions of society. **Charles Lindbergh**, for instance, when he had been co-opted by the America First Committee to head its agitation against the possibility of American entry into the Second World War, said in 1941 that the Jews' "greatest danger to this country lies in their large ownership and influence in our motion pictures, our press, our radio, and our government." When Lindbergh made this comment there was very little Jewish influence in the press, radio, or government; he was just plain wrong. But there was indeed considerable Jewish "ownership and influence" in the movie industry.

Beginning in the early years of the twentieth century, Jews began to gravitate to the movie industry. This did not reflect any concerted effort to "take over" or "control" it, any more than the large percentage of Irish in big-city police departments reflects an organized effort on the part of the Irish to "control" police forces. In both situations we find that individuals who are happy in an enterprise or employment are apt to recommend to relatives and friends that they follow them into that enterprise or employment. If they are in positions of leadership, they may hire relatives and friends, provided they have proper qualifications, to work for them, or they may recommend to those who do the hiring that particular relatives or friends be hired. People who have gone to schools or colleges together often behave in the same way: they often hire each other or recommend that others hire them. This is normal human behavior, and this is how a number of Jews got into the movie industry. Nowadays many Jews with an interest in writing, directing, or acting enroll in film programs offered at various universities and proceed to Hollywood as a consequence of their studies.

The first Jews in the industry were European immigrants who had been, like **Adolph Zukor**, in the fur business or, like **Carl Laemmle**, the manager of a clothing store. Zukor later became the head of Paramount Pictures, and Laemmle the head of Universal Studios. They began their involvement with moving pictures early in the 1900s, after observing how working people would flock in large numbers to the nick-elodeons or peep shows that, for the price of admission of a few pennies, exhibited short scenes of comedy or mayhem. (Moving-picture cameras and projectors had been developed by Thomas Edison and others during the 1890s.) Zukor in New York, Laemmle in Chicago, and others decided to beau-tify the settings in which these presentations were shown, and introduce seats for the spectators. Thus was a new industry born, one which provided the major source of entertainment for perhaps the majority of Americans for many years (and still does so today, through the related technology of tele-vision). **Louis B. Mayer**, later the head of Metro-Goldwyn-Mayer, was the son of an immigrant scrap-metal collector who had settled in New Brunswick, Canada. Mayer himself moved to Boston at age nineteen and in 1907 took over a ramshackle burlesque house in a suburb. He renovated it and began a "new family-oriented policy that won the confidence of the better element and held it with good, clean pictures and plays." As time went on, he came to operate four theaters in the town, then joined with some other distributors and exhibitors to finance production, and moved to Boston. In 1915 he won the New England distribution rights to D. W. Griffith's film *The Birth of a Nation*, the first "movie block-buster." Mayer made a great deal of money from it and subse-quently moved to New York.

Neal Gabler, chronicler of the progress of the movie industry's Jews, noted that by the end of the First World War "it seemed all the Hollywood Jews had moved from exhibition to distribution to production, as Laemmle, Zukor and Mayer had." Zukor in particular was interested in raising the quality of the material being exhibited, and wanted to introduce, on film, great plays with famous actors. Thomas Edison, with some partners, had attempted to control distribution and production of all films made in the United States and was not particularly interested in producing such elevated, and ele-vating, materials. Distributors could get films from Europe, but there was not enough available for the American market. In a sense, Zukor, Laemmle, Mayer, and others were pushed by circumstance into expanding their role into actual movie production. Though most had started out in New York, by 1918 there were over seventy production companies in Los Angeles, including Hollywood, and over 80 percent of the world's movies were being made there. Not only was the weather ideal for filming and the Edison Trust far away, but the Los Angeles area had little established social structure, and the movie Jews could be part of its "aristocracy."

Each studio developed its own particular style. Gabler writes, "Paramount pictures were decidedly nonegalitarian. They didn't ennoble the audience; they whisked them away to a world of sheen and sex where people spoke in innuendo, acted with abandon, and doubted the rewards of virtue. Paramount's was a universe of Marlene Dietrich's smoky come-ons, of Chevalier's eyebrows arched in the boulevardier's worldliness, of Mae West's double entendres sliding out of the corner of her mouth, of Gary Cooper's esthetized handsomeness, of the Marx Brothers' leveling chaos."

L. B. Mayer's MGM, on the other hand, was the bastion of uninhibited Americanism. Mayer himself had appropriated the Fourth of July as his birthday, since there were no records to indicate when he had actually been born. Each year he sponsored a gala celebration on the studio grounds commemorating both Independence Day and his birthday. Anyone who wished to remain in his good graces was sure to attend. Billy Wilder recalls another day when "we looked out the window because there was screaming going on, and Louis B. Mayer held Mickey Rooney by the lapel. [Rooney was the juvenile star of the Andy Hardy movies.] He said, 'You're Andy Hardy! You're the United States! You're the Stars and Stripes. Behave yourself. You're a symbol!' "

Among other Jewish film "tycoons" were the **Warner brothers**, who started out in the Pittsburgh-Youngstown area, and **Harry Cohn**, head of Columbia Pictures. Lest one think that Hollywood was entirely a Jewish industry, mention should be made of the **Walt Disney** studio, established in the 1920s. Disney did not like Jews, and did not like to hire them. Now, however, in the closing years of the twentieth century, some of the top executives and largest stockholders of the Walt Disney Company are Jews.

In 1996 the noted actor Marlon Brando said in an interview, "Per capita, Jews have contributed more to American culture than any other single group. If it weren't for the Jews, we wouldn't have music, we wouldn't have art, we wouldn't have much theater." But he went on to offend Jewish sensibilities by saying: "Hollywood is run by Jews. It is owned by Jews, and they should have a greater sensitivity about the issue of people who are suffering. We've seen the chink. We've seen the slit-eyed dangerous Jap. We have seen the wily Filipino. But we never saw the kike because they knew perfectly well that that's where you draw the wagons around."

Brando has been known throughout his career as a tireless defender of the civil rights, and public image, of even the most obscure ethnic communities. He sought in these comments not to defame Jews but, in his own heavy-handed way, to challenge those in the movie industry to reach toward the high standards of interethnic and interreligious concord to which he himself is devoted. He said in the same interview, "Thank God for the Jews. The Jews are amazing people."

Which studio produced the first feature film with spoken dialogue?

Jack and Harry Warner, the two brothers most involved in the affairs of the Warner Brothers studio, hated each other. Jack was considered, even by some of his dearest friends, to be "crude, vulgar, shallow, flashy and galling." When Albert Einstein visited the studio, he told him, "You know, I have a theory about relatives, too—don't hire them." Once, attending a banquet for Madame Chiang Kai-shek and noticing the large number of Asian guests, he said, "Holy cow, I forgot to pick up my laundry." Harry, on the other hand, was sober, conservative, concerned not to offend, and severely moralistic.

Movie sound was introduced to the industry by Warner Brothers. In 1925 engineers at Bell Labs had succeeded in synchronizing sound with film. Warner Brothers heard of this and obtained the first rights to the process. At first it was thought that the process, called Vitaphone, would be used exclusively for a musical track to be added to feature films. In 1926 this was done with *Don Juan*, starring John Barrymore. But in 1927 Warner Brothers put out the first feature film with both music and spoken dialogue: *The Jazz Singer*, starring Al Jolson. The story centered on the son of an Orthodox Jewish cantor who wanted to go into show business, rather than succeed his father in the synagogue. Jolson, himself the son of a cantor, felt that it very much reflected the tensions in his own life. October 6, 1927, when *The Jazz Singer* premiered, is a date writ large in motion-picture history. **Sam Warner**, the brother most involved in the movie's development at the studio, died the day before its opening.

Some people objected to various Warner Brothers films because they portrayed antisocial behavior without explicitly condemning such behavior. Harry Warner's reply to these critics was, "The motion picture presents right and wrong, as the Bible does. By showing both right and wrong, we teach the right." Neal Gabler describes Warner Brothers films this way: "They came to form a powerful, enduring mythology of urban Depression America with which dispossessed Americans could identify. Warner Brothers films certainly didn't provide the security that Columbia's or MGM's did, that pervasive sense of American decency that served as a shield in times of distress. Warners heroes are faintly disreputable and uprooted; they draw less on American traditions than on themselves. (One can think immediately of Cagney or

Bogart.) But because they ennoble energy and because they are low born, cocky, and self-sufficient, they demonstrate what one can accomplish against all the odds and outside the traditions. They exalt the small rather than the outsized, the people at the margins rather than those at the center."

Who was the most hated man in the movie industry?

Harry Cohn, head of Columbia Pictures, was without doubt the most hated man in Hollywood. He thought he had an image to protect, "that of the toughest, least cultivated man" in the industry, and he succeeded in doing so. He was, unless thousands of people were wrong, "profane, vulgar, cruel, rapacious, and philandering." When he died in 1958, his funeral was held at a Columbia soundstage with seating for over a thousand people. The comedian Red Skelton, seeing that all the seats were taken, observed, "If you give the people what they want, they'll come." Once, when Cohn was asked for a contribution to a Jewish relief fund, he screamed, "Relief *for* the Jews? What about relief *from* the Jews? All the trouble in the world is caused by Jews and Irishmen."

Cohn, however, did have his moments of kindness. He once arranged for a rare medicine to be flown in from New York for a dying screenwriter who had testified against him in a legal matter. When the writer thanked him, he responded, "Don't tell anybody. I don't want to lose my reputation." On another occasion a group of women asked him during World War II for a contribution from Columbia profits to a war relief fund. He refused, saying the profits belonged to Columbia stockholders. Then he wrote them a check for ten thousand dollars from his personal funds.

Was there major Jewish involvement in the growth of radio and television?

David Sarnoff came to America from Russia as a young child and grew up on New York's Lower East Side. He dropped out of school in the eighth grade and worked first as a newsboy, then as a messenger. In his spare time he took courses in telegraphy at the Educational Alliance, and at age fifteen became a junior operator for the Marconi Wireless Company. Three years later he became the chief wireless operator of the company. He toyed with the idea that if wireless radio can communicate with one person with a receiver, why can't it communicate just as well with many thousands of people? In a 1914 memorandum to his company's management, he suggested that radio could transmit music, and that "events of national importance can be simultaneously announced and received. Baseball scores can be transmitted in the air by the use of one set installed at the baseball park. Farmers and others living in outlying districts could enjoy concerts, lectures, music recitals, etc." It was he who suggested that revenue could be earned through the sale of advertising to sponsors of radio broadcasts. Wisely, his company's executives did not ignore young Sarnoff's suggestions. In 1919 the Marconi organization and General Electric established the Radio Corporation of America (RCA) with Sarnoff as one of its leading active figures.

RCA began its spectacular growth during the 1920s. In 1926 it began the manufacture of its own "radio music boxes" and established its network, the National Broadcasting Company (NBC). Even while radio was in its infancy, Sarnoff was already thinking of what he knew would surely come in the future—television. In 1929 he hired **Vladimir Zworykin**, the Russian Jewish scientist who supervised the development of the kinescope, the cathode-ray tube that is in the television receiver. Television technology was available, theoretically, for general public use in 1939, but World War II intervened. For its duration, RCA was converted totally to defense production. Sarnoff volunteered to serve in the military, and in 1944 he organized the entire system of radio communication for the Allied forces fighting in Western Europe. He was commissioned a brigadier general. In 1945 RCA produced its first television sets, and the "age of television" had begun. Radio and television broadcasting on a nationwide scale can be credited, in large measure, to David Sarnoff's energy and administrative skills, and to his undeviating faith in what the future was bound to bring.

In 1928 **William Paley** purchased a group of sixteen radio stations and became the head of the Columbia Broadcasting System (CBS), remaining in that position for sixty years. In the 1950s, under the chairmanship of **Leonard Goldenson**, a group of stations that had been spun off from NBC began to flourish as another independent network, the American Broadcasting Company (ABC).

Who was Stephen Wise?

Stephen Wise, during most of the years of his career, was the most important rabbi in America. Born the son of a rabbi in Budapest in 1874, he came to New York as a small child, attended the City College of New York and earned a doctorate in Semitics at Columbia. He obtained his rabbinic ordination in Europe. After serving Congregation Bnai Jeshurun in New York for a few years, Wise accepted a call from the Reform temple in Portland, Oregon. There he plunged with enthusiasm into all aspects of community life, fighting liquor interests and gambling and political corruption. His reputation grew so that, even from the far-off West, he was invited to Temple Emanu-El in New York to discuss his possible call to that august pulpit. Wise asked the temple's president, Louis Marshall, if he, as rabbi, would be guaranteed freedom of the pulpit, to speak on whatever subject, in whatever manner he chose. Marshall replied that on sensitive issues, matters that might affect the good name of the Jewish community, he, like all previous rabbis of the temple, would have to consult the board for guidance. Wise immediately closed his discussions with Emanu-El. Instead, he returned to New York in 1906 to form the Free Synagogue, its name advertising the fact that its rabbi was free to preach without interference. Until the congregation obtained its own building, it met for several years at Carnegie Hall.

. Wise incorporated a "social service division" into the structure of his congregation. It provided activities for patients at city hospitals and endowed a child-adoption center. For a time nearly half the temple's budget went to social services. Wise preached often about decent conditions of employment and the right of workers to unionize. When steelworkers went on strike in 1919, Wise denounced the chairman of United States Steel as "the most prolific breeder of Bolshevism in America because of his union-busting." He was also instrumental in driving New York mayor **Jimmy Walker** from office. **Fiorello La Guardia**, New York's reform mayor in the 1930s, whom Wise helped to elect, noted, "When Rabbi Wise talks about mayors, there is usually a run on steamship accommodations." Wise was also a confidant of presidents, particularly Woodrow Wilson and Franklin Roosevelt. A passionate Zionist, Wise resented the non-Zionist orientation of the Hebrew Union College's faculty. He thereupon opened his own seminary, the Jewish Institute of Religion, in 1922. In 1950, shortly after Wise's death, the institute united with the college.

Though Wise's religious orientation could be styled "classic Reform" (little use of Hebrew, no great emphasis on Jewish ritual practice), and though his studied, impressively rehearsed oratory appealed more to Central European than to Eastern European Jews, he nonetheless made the welfare and advancement of the Eastern European Jewish masses, in Europe, the United States, and Palestine, a central concern of his career. For this reason he and some supporters created the American Jewish Congress in 1922 as a permanently existing body, devoted to vigorous advocacy of civil rights for all Americans and fearless advocacy of Jewish rights the world over. Wise was its president. The congress's membership was largely lower middle class Eastern European, in contrast to the older American Jewish Committee's wealthier Central European membership. In Wise's estimation, the committee stood for an "undemocratic, un-American, un-Jewish method of dictation from above, however well meaning in intent, however soft spoken in manner." In March 1933, after the consolidation of Nazi power in Germany, Wise and the congress sponsored a mass protest rally at Madison Square Garden. Twenty-two thousand were crowded into the Garden, with another thirty thousand outside. Similar meetings and rallies took place in other cities. To those who complained that Wise's tactics would harm German Jews, who were seeking some sort of accommodation with the Nazis, he replied, "The time for caution and prudence is past. We must speak up like men. How can we ask our Christian friends to lift their voices in protest if we keep silent?" During the following weeks the congress helped organize the Non-Sectarian Anti-Nazi League, which set up a partially effective boycott of German goods in response to the boycott of Jewish goods taking place in Germany. The league's publications during the 1930s played an important role in keeping Americans aware of the crimes and cruelties of the Nazis.

Wise was also instrumental in setting up the World Jewish Congress in 1936. From its headquarters in Switzerland in 1942 came the first confirmed word of the systematic slaughter of Europe's Jews by the Nazis. Wise received this information and immediately brought it to the State Department in Washington. To President Franklin Roosevelt he said, "I beg you, Mr. President, as the recognized leader of the forces of democracy and humanity, to initiate the action which may yet save the Jewish people from utter extinction."

Roosevelt's reply assured Wise of the government's desire to help victims of persecution, insofar as "the burden of war permits." As we know, little was done until World War II ended.

Stephen Wise died in 1949. His life continues to inspire all who are interested in social justice, and all who seek to serve the Jewish cause. Though the American Jewish Committee and the American Jewish Congress continue to exist as distinct organizations, there is no longer any noticeable social or demographic difference between their respective membership bodies.

THREE

From the Second World War to the Present

What was the Jewish role in
the development of atomic energy?

Who were the Hollywood Ten?

Who were Julius and Ethel Rosenberg?

Who was Abba Hillel Silver?

How did Eddie Jacobson influence relations between
the United States and the newborn State of Israel?

*What Jewish-American woman became
Prime Minister of Israel?*

*How did Jewish Americans participate in
Israel's war for independence?*

Who was Meir Kahane?

What is the significance of Levittown, New York?

*What is the link between
Joseph Goldberger and Jonas Salk?*

Was Meyer Lansky a criminal or a nice guy?

*Were Southern rabbis involved in the
civil rights struggle?*

*Though Southern Jews, because of
their circumstances, found it difficult to play
a prominent role in the civil rights struggle,
what about Northern Jews?*

*What instigated black-Jewish tensions
during the 1960s?*

What was unique about Arthur Goldberg?

*How is Henry Kissinger different from all other
Jews who had served before him in the
United States government?*

Have Jewish women been active in the contemporary feminist movement?

When was the first woman ordained a rabbi?

Why was Isaac Bashevis Singer awarded the Nobel Prize in literature in 1978?

Were any Jews involved in the Wall Street scandals of the 1980s?

Why did Elie Wiesel win the Nobel Peace Prize in 1986?

Who was Jonathan Pollard and what did he do to upset Jewish Americans?

Who is the outstanding filmmaker of the 1990s?

Why was Ruth Bader Ginsburg President Bill Clinton's nominee for the United States Supreme Court in 1993?

Who, during the 1990s, was judged to be the largest single charitable donor in the world?

What was the Jewish role in the development of atomic energy?

Albert Einstein, author of the theory of relativity and one of the great scientific thinkers of all time, had sufficient foresight to leave Europe and come to America soon after the Nazis assumed power in Germany in 1933. Between 1933 and 1938 several European scientists made discoveries demonstrating the possibility of atomic fission, the process that would release the energy bound within the nucleus of the atom. This research had great significance for those interested in the development of new weapons of war. One of the scientists who had participated in this research was **Leo Szilard**, a Hungarian Jew who took refuge in the United States. Szilard and others approached Einstein in 1939 to discuss the implications of these matters and the importance of developing a program of atomic research in the United States which, they hoped, could anticipate the discoveries that might be made in Nazi Germany. A letter was prepared, under Einstein's signature, and presented to President **Franklin Roosevelt**. It stated, "This new phenomenon would also lead to the construction of bombs, and it is conceivable—though much less certain—that extremely powerful bombs of a new type may thus be constructed."

Roosevelt immediately appointed an Advisory Committee on Uranium, the material being used in atomic research. Later this group became part of the National Defense Research Committee. In early 1942, after America's entry into World War II, Roosevelt ordered that even greater resources be put into this work, now known by the code name "Manhattan Project." Appointed as the scientific director of the project was **J. Robert Oppenheimer** of the University of California, the son of German Jews from New York. He directed the Los Alamos laboratory in New Mexico, where the atomic bomb was to be built. Working with him were some of the greatest physicists in the world, most of them Jewish refugees from Europe. One of them was **Eugene Wigner**, who was to be awarded the Nobel Prize in physics in 1963 "for his contribution to the theory of the atomic nucleus and the elementary particles, particularly through the discovery and application of fundamental symmetry principles."

By early 1945 it was already apparent that Germany would be defeated with conventional weapons. Japan was also likely, it seemed, to give up without it being necessary to drop an atomic bomb on the country. Einstein and Szilard once again decided to approach President Roosevelt, advising that "the use of an atomic weapon against Japanese civilians would represent both a military superfluity and a moral defeat for the United States." Szilard was granted an appointment with the President in May 1945. Roosevelt, however, died on April 12 of that year. President **Harry Truman** was uninterested in what Szilard and Einstein had to say, and on August 6 the atomic bomb was dropped on Hiroshima.

Who were the Hollywood Ten?

While most movie studio heads were very conservative politically, and active Republicans, a large number of screenwriters (the writers were about two-thirds Jewish) were active in liberal and leftist causes. Some were even members of the Communist party. During the anti-Communist hysteria that gripped the country after the Second World War, the House Committee on Un-American Activities initiated hearings attempting to uncover Communist influence in Hollywood. There was a strong anti-Semitic undertone to this inquiry. Studio heads were frantic with fear that their deep-seated American loyalties would come into question. The screenwriters knew that if they refused to cooperate with the committee, their jobs would be in jeopardy. Ten of the screenwriters refused to answer the committee's questions, and on November 24, 1947, were voted in contempt of Congress by the House of Representatives. The majority of the Ten were Jews. The Hollywood Jewish community was racked by dissension over these developments. A committee representing the studio heads adopted a statement deploring "the action of the ten Hollywood men who have been cited for contempt. Their actions have been a disservice to their employers and have impaired their usefulness to the industry." The signatories to the statement agreed to discharge the Ten until they had purged themselves of contempt or renounced Communism under oath. They also agreed that they would not knowingly employ a Communist.

Others in Hollywood, and throughout the country, objected to this abrogation of the First Amendment rights of people who were not accused of any crime. Lillian Hellman commented, "I don't think the heads of movie companies, and the men they appointed to run the studios, had ever thought of themselves as American citizens with inherited rights and obligations. Many of them had been born in foreign lands and inherited foreign fears." The Hollywood Ten were deprived of the right to pursue their livelihood because of the political opinions they held. Some of them served time in prison for contempt of Congress. Some of them were able to write for studios under assumed names, but the principle of the "blacklist" remained in force.

Eventually people in Hollywood and elsewhere in the country came to realize the injustice that had been done to these people, and to others who had been called before the House committee and hounded to answer the question "Are you now, or have you ever been, a member of the Communist party?," and then asked to give the names of others whom they knew or suspected were Communists. The House Committee on Un-American Activities is, thankfully, no longer in existence.

Who were Julius and Ethel Rosenberg?

Julius Rosenberg grew up in the 1920s and 1930s in a poor Eastern European Jewish family in New York. He studied electrical engineering at City College, where he became a member of the Young Communist League. He moved on to become a Communist party member and married **Ethel Greenglass**, who was also devoted to the Communist cause.

The party held meetings in their apartment. In attendance at these meetings, and caught up in the cause, was Ethel's brother David, a machine-tool maker. Julius worked as a civilian engineer for the U.S. Army Signal Corps; David Greenglass was drafted into the army and in 1944 was assigned to work on implosion lenses at Los Alamos, New Mexico, the top secret Manhattan Project to produce the atomic bomb. Beginning in 1943 Julius had been copying secret information about radio tubes, fuses, and a bombsight for transmission to Soviet Russian consulate officials in New York. In 1945, on a furlough in New York, Greenglass delivered drawings of the atom bomb implosion lenses to Rosenberg. Later a courier picked up additional information on these lenses from Greenglass in New Mexico. All of this, of course, was delivered to Soviet scientists who were seeking to develop an atomic bomb for their country.

In 1949 the Soviets detonated the atom bomb; shortly thereafter the FBI was able to decipher a Soviet code book that led its agents to understand that secret atomic information from Los Alamos had reached the Soviets in 1944 and 1945. Through diligent investigative work the FBI uncovered Julius Rosenberg and David Greenglass as the sources from which this material had come. Greenglass immediately confessed everything and cooperated with the government, implicating not only Julius but his own sister Ethel. They were indicted for conspiracy to commit espionage. The prosecuting attorney was a Jew who delighted in convicting Communists; the judge was a Jew who wished to send the message that Jews were not soft on Communists, not even Jewish ones. Both Julius and Ethel were convicted by the jury; the judge sentenced them both to death, in spite of the fact that "conspiracy to commit espionage" had not been punished by death before, and that, though much evidence had been amassed against Julius, there was little or no evidence that Ethel had taken an active part in any conspiracy.

Appeals on behalf of the Rosenbergs were turned down.

Their case became a cause célèbre in European countries, particularly in France and Italy with their huge Communist parties, and mass demonstrations were held to "Save the Rosenbergs." In this country, on the other hand, there was hardly anyone willing to take to the streets in their behalf, and only a few more who were willing to write letters to the editor, or to the White House, advocating a commutation of the death sentence. Julius and Ethel Rosenberg each went to their deaths in the electric chair on June 18, 1953. Their two young sons were given up for adoption.

Who was Abba Hillel Silver?

Born in Lithuania, **Abba Hillel Silver** was brought to America as an infant in 1894 and grew up on New York's Lower East Side. He was ordained a rabbi at the Hebrew Union College and assumed leadership of The Temple—Tifereth Israel ("Splendor of Israel") in Cleveland. An orator of great power and skill, he is said to have "overwhelmed his listeners when he was not intimidating them." Though it was his older colleague, **Stephen Wise**, who introduced him to the leadership circle of American Zionism, Silver gravitated to the more militant element that, even in the midst of World War II, demanded that Great Britain withdraw from Palestine as soon as the war was over to allow for an independent Jewish state. Wise stood with the group that was willing to wait for the war to end before challenging Britain over this issue. At the American Jewish Conference held in 1943 Silver castigated Wise, declaring, "If the overwhelming majority of American Jews believe in the upbuilding of a Jewish Commonwealth, they should have the right to say so and to make their demand upon the world. There is but one solution for national homelessness. That is a national home!" Wise once told a friend that he would begin to tremble whenever he saw Silver enter a meeting hall.

After Roosevelt's death in April 1945, there was a clamor

among American Zionists calling for Wise to share the power of the Zionist leadership with Silver. Wise, a Democrat, had been close to Roosevelt; Silver was a Republican. It was Silver and Wise who came together to confer with President **Harry Truman** when Palestine was to be discussed. At the end of 1946, though, Silver and his partisans achieved total victory over Wise and the "moderates." Truman came to dislike the militant Zionists intensely. Silver he could not stand at all. After Silver pounded on Truman's desk in 1946, he was banished from the White House.

Abba Hillel Silver remained as rabbi of his temple in Cleveland, and a respected world Zionist leader, until his death in 1963.

How did Eddie Jacobson influence relations between the United States and the newborn State of Israel?

In November 1947 the United Nations voted to partition Palestine between Arabs and Jews upon the expiration of the British mandate. Britain set the date for that consummation—May 15, 1948. American Zionists, since they had deeply alienated President **Harry Truman**, could only reach him indirectly. One of these contacts was through **Eddie Jacobson**, Truman's old friend from Kansas City with whom he had once been in the haberdashery business. Jacobson had been in touch with Truman seeking his support for unlimited Jewish immigration to Palestine, but in February 1948 the Zionist leadership asked him to set up a presidential appointment with **Chaim Weizmann**, the leader of world Zionism (and, upon the birth of the Jewish state, its first President). Jacobson visited Truman in March 1948 and got around to mentioning a Weizmann visit. Truman was not receptive. Jacobson recalled the meeting this way: "The President replied how disrespectful and mean certain Jewish leaders had been to him. I suddenly found myself thinking that my dear friend was at that moment as close to being an anti-Semite as a man could possibly be. I then found myself saying this to the President, almost word for word: 'Harry, all your life you have had a hero. You are probably the best read man in America on the life of Andrew Jackson. Well, Harry, I too have a hero, a man I never met but who is, I think, the greatest Jew who ever lived. I am talking about Chaim Weizmann. He is an old man and a sick man, and he has come all the way to America to see you. Now you refuse to see him because you were insulted by some American Jewish leaders. It doesn't sound like you, Harry.' " Truman, of course, could not resist this appeal, and he consented to see him. When Israel's statehood was proclaimed on May 14, 1948, Harry Truman announced America's recognition of its government; he was the first world leader to do so.

What Jewish-American woman became Prime Minister of Israel?

Born in Kiev, Ukraine, in 1898, Golda Mabovitch moved to Milwaukee, Wisconsin, in 1906 with her family. There she attended high school and continued her studies at the Milwaukee Normal School for Teachers. Becoming a member of the Labor Zionist movement in 1915, she early on won notice as a gifted orator in both English and Yiddish. In 1921 she and her husband, Morris Myerson, immigrated to Palestine, settling on a kibbutz (agricultural cooperative). By 1928 she had risen to become executive secretary of the Labor Zionist group Moetzet haPoalot, and served as its emissary to its affiliate in the United States from 1932 to 1934. Under her married name, Golda Myerson, she became prominent in Zionist circles the world over, becoming a member of the executive committee of the Histadrut (the Jewish labor organization in Palestine) in 1934, then head of its political department. From 1946 until the establishment of the State of Israel, she served as head of the political department of the Jewish Agency (the world body that coordinated Jewish investment in Palestine). During the exciting months of 1948 that preceded the proclamation of Israel's independence on May 14 of that year, she visited the United States to enlist the aid of Jewish Americans in the struggle that was to come, and went secretly to meet with King Abdullah in Jordan, hoping to convince him not to join other Arab nations in attacking the Jewish state.

Hebraizing her name to **Golda Meir**, upon the birth of the state, she served as its first ambassador to the Soviet Union until April 1949. She was then elected to the Israeli Knesset (Parliament) and appointed Minister of Labor. From 1956 to 1965 she served as Israel's Foreign Minister, visiting the United States frequently to speak at the United Nations and meeting often with American officials in Washington. She was named secretary-general of Mapai (the largest Israeli labor party) in 1965, and became the fourth Prime Minister of the state in 1969. She served in that office until 1974 and died in 1978.

How did Jewish Americans participate in Israel's war for independence?

Realizing that the Jewish state would most likely come into being as a result of blood and struggle, **David Ben-Gurion**, the chairman of the Jewish Agency who would be named Israel's first Prime Minister when the state's independence was declared on May 14, 1948, had quietly visited the United States just as World War II was drawing to its close in 1945. His purpose was to set up an organization, manned by sympathizers of the Jewish national cause, which would be able to procure some of the surplus arms that would be available and ship them to the Haganah, the Jewish defense forces, in Palestine. **Rudolf Sonneborn**, a wealthy German Jewish industrialist from New York, created the Sonneborn Institute, whose task it was to buy machinery, blueprints, scrap metal, and weapons for transshipment to Palestine. **Adolf Schwimmer**, who had been a wartime ferry command pilot, set up the Schwimmer Air Freight Company, which bought mothballed military transport planes and recruited pilots and mechanics. The institute set up a shipping company in Panama that bought surplus warships and freighters. Crews for these vessels were recruited by organizations with names like the "Palestine Vocational Service" and "Service Airways." Not only did these ships and planes bring munitions to the Haganah; they also transported some fifteen thousand illegal immigrants from the DP (displaced persons) camps of Europe to Palestine, evading, when possible, the British blockade set up to prevent such Jewish immigration.

As war with Arab armies broke out in 1948, the Sonneborn Institute, and other groups, recruited American Jewish volunteers to join with the Israelis of the Haganah, and volunteers from other countries, in the struggle. The Americans numbered only about seventeen hundred, less than 4 percent of the total Israeli forces, but many of the pilots in Israel's newborn air force were from the United States. The best known U.S. volunteer was Col. **David ("Mickey") Marcus**, a graduate of West Point who had given up his commission to study law. He rejoined the U.S. Army when America neared entry into the Second World War, and parachuted into France on D-Day, June 6, 1944. In February 1948 he arrived in Palestine and was immediately utilized by the Haganah leadership to help mold their men into a disciplined military force. In May 1948 he helped set up a system of road convoys bypassing the Arabs who controlled the main highway to Jerusalem. In June, however, he was accidentally killed by "friendly fire" from an Israeli sentry.

Besides the fighters who came to the aid of Israel in 1948, another American was important in Israel's early history. **Golda Meir**, Israel's fourth Prime Minister, born in Ukraine in 1898, came with her family to the United States at the age of eight. Somewhat similar is the story of **Moshe Arens**. Born in Lithuania in 1925, he came to the United States and received his higher education there, concentrating on aircraft engineering. He served in the U.S. Army Corps of Engineers and took degrees at the Massachusetts Institute of Technology and the California Institute of Technology. Settling in Israel, he became active in **Menachem Begin**'s conservative Likud party and served as both his Minister of Defense and Foreign Minister.

In 1996 **Benjamin ("Bibi") Netanyahu**, another Likud stalwart, was elected Prime Minister of Israel. Though born in Israel, he lived as a young man and studied extensively in the United States. His brother Yonatan, the hero killed while leading the spectacular Israeli mission to rescue hijacked airline passengers at Entebbe, Uganda, in 1976, had also lived and studied in the U.S.

Who was Meir Kahane?

Meir Kahane (1932–1990), an Orthodox rabbi in Brooklyn, founded the Jewish Defense League in 1968. A militant from his teenage years, Kahane rejected the role of the Jew as "victim." In U.S. cities, he declaimed, Jews must not be afraid of becoming vigilantes in their own neighborhoods; they must, in fact, be ready to meet violence with violence if black elements, a population that lived cheek by jowl with Jews in sections of Brooklyn and other urban areas, committed criminal acts against Jews. In Israel and the areas of Judea and Samaria under Israeli control, Arabs, according to Kahane, could never be trusted to live peaceably with Jews. They must be transferred, either voluntarily or by force, to live in Arab countries.

According to Kahane's obituary in *The New York Times*, the Jewish Defense League "mounted anti-mugger patrols in neighborhoods bordered by black areas. They escorted Jewish teachers through black neighborhoods with baseball bats, taught rifle and karate to rabbinical students, and invaded Soviet diplomatic offices to protest the treatment of

Jews in the Soviet Union." Kahane was sentenced to a year in jail for conspiring to make bombs. In 1971 he and his family moved to Israel, where he founded a small party dedicated to his teachings. He was elected to the Israeli Knesset (Parliament) in 1984, but in 1988 his party was banned from putting up candidates again because it was "Nazi-like," "racist," and "undemocratic."

Kahane's views and activities were denounced by Reform, Conservative, and the majority of Orthodox Jews while he was still active in the United States. In Israel his views were rejected by the overwhelming majority of the population. While speaking to a group of his followers in a New York hotel, Kahane was shot to death by an Arab in 1990.

In 1994 **Baruch Goldstein**, one of Kahane's followers, a Jewish-American physician who had grown up in Brooklyn and settled in Israel, achieved gruesome fame by massacring over thirty Muslims in the Abraham Mosque at Hebron before being killed himself.

What is the significance of Levittown, New York?

There have been a number of major Jewish real estate developers in various parts of the country, but it was **William Levitt**, during the late 1940s and early 1950s, who erected "the first mass-produced town that put affordable housing within the range of middle-income and even low-income Americans." Levitt, building "Levittown" on New York's Long Island, used cut-rate mass-production techniques to erect seventeen thousand single-family homes for World War II veterans. The development included village greens or commons, athletic fields, swimming pools, and spaces left open for schools and places of worship. Later Levitt put up similar developments in other parts of the country.

What is the link between Joseph Goldberger and Jonas Salk?

Joseph Goldberger (1874–1929) and **Jonas Salk** (1914–1995) probably never met each other (Salk was fifteen years old when Goldberger died). Both devoted their lives to researching ways in which dreaded diseases could be overcome and human life not only lengthened but also ennobled. Goldberger was a physician with the U.S. Public Health Service who worked in preventive medicine and the development of antitoxins for yellow fever, dengue fever, measles, typhus, cholera, diphtheria, and pellagra. This last is a disease caused by a lack of niacin in the diet which used to afflict many poor and undernourished people in the Southern United States. Goldberger's work was instrumental in eliminating it as a major health problem. Goldberger died relatively young, debilitated by contact with some of the infectious agents he dealt with in his work.

Salk lived to a good age. In his career he participated in developing vaccines against the flu, but the accomplishment for which he is best known throughout the world is the creation of a vaccine against polio. The Salk vaccine, released for use in 1954, utilized killed polio virus and was administered by injection; its competition was a vaccine developed by **Albert Sabin** (another Jewish-American researcher), a drug using live but attenuated virus which is taken orally. During his later years Salk founded and headed the Salk Institute for Biological Studies in La Jolla, California. He had hoped that his institute would find an agent that could prevent AIDS.

Was Meyer Lansky a criminal or a nice guy?

According to police records, **Meyer Lansky** was an active participant in the bootleg liquor industry during the time that the Eighteenth Amendment to the Constitution (prohibiting the manufacture and distribution of alcoholic beverages except for sacramental purposes) was in force. After 1933, when the amendment was repealed, he and his associate, **Benjamin ("Bugsy") Siegel**, turned to gambling as a gainful employment. They moved into Hot Springs (Arkansas), New Orleans, and several spots in Florida and opened highly profitable casinos (all of them illegal, but the police in these communities had better things to do with their time). During World War II Lansky and his associates profited greatly, since the effects of the 1930s depression were over. They opened operations in Havana, paying off the corrupt Batista regime, and then set up some operations in Los Angeles. Bugsy Siegel became intrigued with the possibilities of opening up in Las Vegas, where gambling was legal. The national gambling syndicates gave him money to put up a spectacular casino, the Flamingo. Opening just as the new year of 1947 began, the operation did not clear as much as had been expected, so Lansky appointed a local Los Angeles mobster, Mickey Cohen, to keep an eye on Siegel. The Flamingo began to make huge profits, but matters still did not appear quite right; Bugsy, the higher-ups thought, was skimming money off the top. Sadly, Lansky gave his consent for Siegel to be done away with (he was shot while in his mistress's home in Los Angeles), and casino profits surged. It should be noted that Lansky himself did not engage in physical violence. He functioned as the brains and the financial wizard advising other top-level mobsters. Over the years Lansky's group opened additional hotel casinos in Las Vegas and its environs.

Though customers did not complain that they had been cheated at the casinos, the federal government did. To save on taxes, cash was skimmed each day and deposited in various bank accounts in the United States and Switzerland. Lansky and some associates were indicted in 1972. They fled to Israel, where that country's Law of Return welcomed all Jews who wished to settle there. The Israeli government, however, not wishing to offend the U.S. government by giving sanctuary to someone as notorious as Lansky, extradited him for trial in the United States. A jury in Miami Beach found Lansky innocent of all charges. Meyer Lansky lived the rest of his days quietly and comfortably in Florida. He gave generously to the United Jewish Appeal and other charities.

Were Southern rabbis involved in the civil rights struggle?

A number of rabbis in Southern communities were active in the efforts to bring about compliance with the 1954 U.S. Supreme Court decision outlawing racial segregation in public schools, but perhaps a larger number chose to remain silent. The reasoning of this latter group was that if they were to take a strong stand favoring desegregation, they would accomplish nothing more than the encouragement of anti-Semitism within the general white community; others, particularly some Orthodox rabbis, felt that it was not their duty to become involved in issues not specifically Jewish in nature.

Of the Southern rabbis who chose to publicly proclaim their support for school desegregation, and in favor of the civil rights struggle as a whole, two names stand out. One is **Jacob M. Rothschild** of Atlanta. In 1948, two years after his arrival in the city, Rothschild affirmed his shame at "the growing race hatred that threatens the South," and urged his people to "be among those who are willing to do something" about it. Ten years later he advised his fellow members of the Rotary Club that blacks had every right to resent the white community's lack of interest in racial progress. A short time later Rothschild's temple was dynamited, causing extensive damage, one of five incidents of violence against Jewish buildings in Southern cities that year. In an interview Rothschild was asked why his synagogue was targeted: "I suppose that part of it was because I was so obviously identified with the civil rights movement. What happened was a small group of so-called Nazis took advantage of the atmosphere of violence.

They used the atmosphere to bomb a synagogue, because they were specifically anti-Semitic. But they misread the attitudes of the community. The bombing created a reaction of such outrage that it backfired, and as a result of the bombing of the Temple, it now, for perhaps the first time in Atlanta, became possible to speak out." Rothschild felt that it was this episode that prevented Atlanta from becoming the kind of closed society that some other Southern communities became for a time.

Rothschild often spoke at black churches, and black clergy came to his temple. In 1965 it was primarily through his efforts that the black and white communities of the city came together to sponsor a testimonial dinner honoring Dr. **Martin Luther King, Jr.**, winner of the Nobel Peace Prize. In Rothschild's estimation, this event was "the most significant meeting that Atlanta ever had."

The second Southern rabbi whose courageous approach to civil rights became an example and a byword during the years of struggle was **Charles Mantinband** of Hattiesburg, Mississippi. Hattiesburg was a small community in which the Ku Klux Klan was active; its Jewish population was about 175. Mantinband stated that

from the very beginning I had to make up my mind to two things as to what I would do. The first thing was that the pigmentation of a person's skin would make no difference to me in my relationship to him. I would judge a man, if I would judge him at all, in terms of his merit, his worth. That means that Negroes came to my home, through the front door, sat at my table, all the time, and that was my private affair. The second thing was much harder. I vowed that I would never sit in the presence of bigotry and hear it uttered, that I would not fail to voice a contrary opinion and make my opposition felt. I wouldn't try to make a speech, I would just register what my religion compels me to think, and feel, and be, and how it makes me behave. And when they would say to me, "God is a segregationist, because the Bible is full of it," I always ripped out a Bible, and I would open it to where the opposite is stated and say, "Do you mean here? Or do you mean there? Or do you mean the other place?" And then they would say, "You're too smart for your pants."

After the Atlanta bombing, a former mayor of Hattiesburg approached Rabbi Mantinband and warned him that bombings of buildings were really not necessary; he could see to it that Mantinband himself would be personally harmed. The rabbi, however, never changed his behavior or his mode of speaking. An editorial from 1962 praised him as follows: "It is possible in the South for a man to be what he is, speak what he believes and stand up to segregationist hatred, as our rabbi, Charles Mantinband, has stoutly demonstrated for fifteen or sixteen years in darkest Alabama and Mississippi."

Though Southern Jews, because of their circumstances, found it difficult to play a prominent role in the civil rights struggle, what about Northern Jews?

The National Association for the Advancement of Colored People was formed in New York in 1910. Among those drawn to join or support this organization were a number of German Jews eager to improve all aspects of society. In 1914 **Joel Springarn**, a professor at Columbia University, became chairman of the NAACP and brought **Jacob Schiff** and **Stephen Wise** to its board. Since then many Jews, not just Germans but Eastern Europeans as well, have been supporters of the cause of black rights and the NAACP. Jews were also among the first to support the Urban League, founded in New York in 1911 to help blacks migrating from the South to Northern cities. National Jewish religious bodies, as well as the American Jewish Committee, the Anti-Defamation League, and the American Jewish Congress, have a long history of advocating black rights. All three of these organizations submitted amicus curiae briefs to the U.S. Supreme Court, advocating an end to legally imposed school segregation, in advance of the Court's 1954 *Brown vs. Board of Education* ruling. Jewish involvement in the struggle for black civil rights was well known throughout the nation, and Jews, generally speaking, were known to be opposed to racial segregation.

It was not surprising, therefore, that during the 1960s, when personal involvement on the part of those who believed in the cause of racial equality was called for in the South, many Jews from the North responded. A black leader in Mississippi observed that "as many as ninety percent of the civil rights lawyers in Mississippi were Jews," and it has been estimated that Jews, mostly college students, "made up at least thirty percent of the white volunteers who rode freedom buses to the South, registered black voters, and picketed segregated establishments." Perhaps thirty Reform rabbis, and some Conservatives, marched with demonstrators in Selma and Birmingham. Several were arrested, and one, **Arthur Lelyveld** of Cleveland, was severely beaten in Hattiesburg, Mississippi.

The Jewish martyrs to the cause of black liberation were New Yorkers **Mickey Schwerner** and **Andrew Goodman**, who were killed in Meridian, Mississippi, together with a black colleague from the town, **James Chaney**. Schwerner, twenty-four years old, went to Meridian with his wife, Rita, to work with the black community. In April 1964 Schwerner tried to persuade a local variety store to hire a black salesclerk. When the owner refused, Schwerner organized a successful boycott of the store, and a black clerk was hired. The local Klansmen decided to kill Schwerner. On June 21 Schwerner's station wagon was stopped by the sheriff in Philadelphia, Mississippi. With him were Chaney and twenty-year-old Goodman, who had been in the state only one night. The three of them were arrested and held in the local jail while the Klan deliberated. At 10:30 that night the three young men were released by the sheriff. They drove off into the hands of the waiting lynch mob. All three were shot; their bodies were not found for forty-four days, until the FBI, through vigorous interrogation, was able to learn their location and the identity of the killers.

What instigated black-Jewish tensions during the 1960s?

Many Jewish Americans have been dismayed by the fact that, in their judgment, black Americans have not always shown sufficient gratitude to Jews for all that they did for them during the civil rights struggle. One factor that kept blacks and Jews from participating in an uninterrupted love-feast is that many blacks knew individual Jews only as landlords, storekeepers, and employers of domestic help. Even if they share the same skin color and religion, not everyone is fond of his or her landlord and/or neighborhood merchant, particularly if he does not live in the community where he makes his profits. Another factor is that a number of blacks, including those associated with the Muslim community, were developing feelings of kinship with dark-skinned peoples over the world, including Palestinian Arabs. Jews for the most part are white, and felt a kinship with Israeli Jews, who were locked in a struggle with Palestinian Arabs. Related to this is a kind of condescension shown by some Jews, on some occasions, when discussing Middle East issues. In 1979 Israel's delegate to the United Nations met with some leaders of the Southern Christian Leadership Conference, a black civil rights group, and chastised them for their support of a Palestinian state. He added this comment: "Understandably, you are less knowledgeable about the Middle East conflict than other parties." Such a comment was not likely to engender good feeling between blacks and Jews.

Roberta Strauss Feuerlicht characterizes the teachers' strikes in New York City in the 1960s as a "manic demonstration of the national breakdown" between blacks and Jews. "During the long dispute, there was only one indisputable fact—black children were not being educated by the public schools. The dropout rate was high and the test scores were low. On one side of the issue were teachers, most of them Jewish, who were worried about their jobs. On the other side were parents, most of them black, who were worried about their children and wanted to make school 'the agent for transforming the ghetto into a community.' " Under New York's system of community control, a group of parents in Ocean Hill–Brownsville, in Brooklyn, took over as the district school board and in 1967 appointed a district administrator. In 1968 he transferred thirteen teachers and six supervisory personnel for not cooperating with the community-control experiment. The teachers' union insisted that these people had been fired without due process, and went out on strike. An examiner ruled that the district board had to take back ten of the transferred teachers; the board refused, and the teachers' union called a city-wide strike. The union and the city's Board of Education agreed that the ten teachers would be taken back. The district board said that it would not prevent them from returning, but when they appeared, they were refused classroom assignments. A second strike was called. After another agreement that the ten teachers be allowed to return, upon doing so they were "harassed, jeered, and threatened by armed blacks." The union struck a third time, this time demanding that the Ocean Hill–Brownsville district be declared a failure and closed down.

According to Feuerlicht,

There was no suppressing the black-Jewish nature of the confrontation, but there was no need to exploit it. Yet to divert the public from the weakness of its case—teachers were regularly transferred without incident—the union made the issue not community control but anti-Semitism. The union maliciously and deliberately publicized every anti-Jewish slur to make it appear that Ocean Hill–Brownsville was prelude to a coming pogrom. The racial antagonisms unleashed by the strike made it the most racially polarizing event in the city's history. Several pieces of anti-Semitic literature surfaced during the strike. Instead of throwing them in the garbage where they belonged, the union printed and distributed 500,000 copies of one of the leaflets, along with a letter from the chairman of a fictitious committee demanding black control of black schools.

A report issued by the New York Civil Liberties Union accused the union of fanning the flames by using "code words": "Nazis," "vigilantes," "black militants," "black racists." "By incessant use of such words, by the fraudulent leaflets, and by the whole tone and tenor of the campaign, the union did what no one else has ever before been able to do in this city. It legitimized liberal racism." What was forgotten in all the abuse was that the Ocean Hill–Brownsville board had denounced both the leaflets and anti-Semitism.

The teachers' strikes were followed in subsequent years by other neighborhood incidents in which black and Jewish interests clashed. On a national level, however, as well as in many communities, black and Jewish leaders realize that it is important to keep alive the cooperative links that have benefited both groups for so many years. Just as Jews, by and large, are able to live out "the American dream," so now it is the turn of black Americans to reach for their share of that dream. Jews, as well as many other Americans, will seek to be with them as they do so.

What was unique about Arthur Goldberg?

Arthur Goldberg (1908–1990) was born in Chicago and became a noted attorney specializing in labor law. He served as a union attorney and played an important role in arranging the merger of the AFL (American Federation of Labor) and the CIO (Congress of Industrial Organizations) into a unified labor union movement.

His career in government service was unique for the

number of significant positions to which he was appointed during a relatively short span of years. He served as President **John F. Kennedy**'s Secretary of Labor from 1961 to 1962 and as a justice on the U.S. Supreme Court from 1962 to 1965. President Lyndon Johnson insisted that he become the permanent representative of the United States to the United Nations, so he served in that capacity from 1965 to 1968.

How is Henry Kissinger different from all other Jews who had served before him in the United States government?

Born in 1923 in Bavaria, **Henry Kissinger** came with his family to New York in 1938, settling in the Manhattan neighborhood favored by German Jewish refugees. Kissinger attended City College before entering the U.S. Army, and saw action in Germany during the closing days of World War II. Upon his return to America he was awarded a scholarship to Harvard, and he remained there until completing his doctorate in the field of international relations. Thereafter he worked at the Council on Foreign Relations and the Rockefeller Brothers Fund until Harvard called him back to teach in its political science department. He wrote several admired books about U.S. foreign policy. In 1969 President **Richard Nixon** appointed Kissinger his national security adviser, and, in 1973, Secretary of State. Kissinger was heavily involved with the peace negotiations with North Vietnam (for which he shared the Nobel Peace Prize in 1973), with Nixon's dramatic visit and opening of relations to China, and with "shuttle diplomacy" between Israel and its Arab antagonists during the Yom Kippur War of 1973. He remained Secretary of State until President **Gerald Ford** left office at the beginning of 1977.

How was Henry Kissinger different? In his day Jews in high positions in the United States government were no longer a novelty. They had served as cabinet secretaries, senators, and Supreme Court justices so often that even some of the most chauvinistic Jews no longer paid attention to the phenomenon. (Fervent anti-Semites, of course, continue to catalogue the names and numbers of Jews in government, as they seek to solidify "proof" bolstering their conviction that Jews are out to take over and control everything.) What was different about Kissinger was that, as historian Howard Sachar observed, by the end of the Ford administration "this Jewish ex-refugee had become the single most renowned figure in the United States government."

Have Jewish women been active in the contemporary feminist movement?

American Jewish women have not only been active in all aspects of contemporary feminism; they were among the first to formulate and promote feminist ideas that have opened up employment opportunities to women in all areas, as well as egalitarian concepts that have taken hold in aspects of family structure. (Some of these "subversive" notions include the principle that only those women who wish to bear children should do so, and that men should take on as many of the responsibilities associated with rearing children as women.) **Betty Friedan**'s 1963 book, *The Feminine Mystique*, is considered the seminal publication that ignited contemporary feminism. Friedan affirmed: "We can no longer ignore that voice within women that says: 'I want something more than my husband and my children and my home.'"

Friedan was one of the organizers of the National Organization for Women, the foremost feminist activist group in the country. The feminist magazine *Ms.* was founded and edited in its first years by **Gloria Steinem**. Her immigrant grandmother had, years earlier, been president of the Ohio Women's Suffrage Association.

When was the first woman ordained a rabbi?

Sally Priesand was ordained a rabbi in 1972, upon the completion of her studies at Reform Judaism's Hebrew Union College in Cincinnati. Not long thereafter the Reconstructionist Rabbinical College ordained its first woman. Several years thereafter, following a more vigorous debate than had engaged the other two groups, the Conservative movement's Jewish Theological Seminary ordained its first woman. Once the sex barrier was broken, female students entered in large numbers into all three of these seminaries and, upon completion of their studies, received ordination. At least 50 percent of each class is now made up of women.

At Orthodox rabbinic schools the percentage of women enrolled remains at zero, since Orthodoxy does not permit women to serve as rabbis.

Why was Isaac Bashevis Singer awarded the Nobel Prize in Literature in 1978?

Isaac Bashevis Singer (1904–1991) lived in Poland until his settlement in New York in 1935, but he was awarded, as an American, the Nobel Prize in Literature in 1978, "for his impassioned narrative art which, with roots in a Polish-Jewish cultural tradition, brings universal human conditions to life." He composed his stories and novels in Yiddish but participated actively, with others, in their translation into English.

Singer's father had been a rabbinic judge in Poland. Young Singer spent many hours observing the give-and-take that went on in his father's chambers; much of this is recorded in his autobiographical *In My Father's Court*. After settling in New York, like his brother Israel Joshua Singer he decided upon a career devoted to writing about the life of the Jews in the Poland he had forsaken, with emphasis upon some of its more exotic aspects. He became a writer for the

Jewish Daily Forward, in which much of his work was serialized in Yiddish before publication in English.

In 1953 his story "Gimpel the Fool," as translated by **Saul Bellow**, was published in the important literary and intellectual journal *Partisan Review,* and his reputation began to grow. Among his acclaimed story collections are *Gimpel the Fool, The Spinoza of Market Street, The Séance, A Friend of Kafka,* and *A Crown of Feathers.* Novels include *The Family Moskat, Satan in Goray, The Magician of Lublin,* and *Enemies: A Love Story.* In all of his works Singer uses fable, folktale, and sermon to explore the meaning of faith. His characters question the acceptance of family, community, and universe. They ask about the nature of evil and God. Like Gimpel, all of his characters seem to declare, "In the first place, everything is possible."

JEWISH-AMERICAN NOVELISTS AND SHORT STORY WRITERS, WITH THE NAME OF A NOTED WORK BY EACH

Saul Bellow	*Henderson the Rain King*
E. L. Doctorow	*Ragtime*
Erica Jong	*Fear of Flying*
Norman Mailer	*The Naked and the Dead*
Bernard Malamud	*The Assistant*
Tillie Olsen	*Tell Me a Riddle*
Cynthia Ozick	*The Pagan Rabbi and Other Stories*
Grace Paley	*Enormous Changes at the Last Minute*
Henry Roth	*Call It Sleep*
Philip Roth	*Goodbye, Columbus*
Delmore Schwartz	*The World Is a Wedding*
Nathanael West	*The Day of the Locust*
Anzia Yezierska	*Hungry Hearts*

PLAYWRIGHTS AND A POET

Tony Kushner	*Angels in America*
Arthur Miller	*The Crucible*
Neil Simon	*Biloxi Blues*
Wendy Wasserstein	*The Heidi Chronicles*
Allen Ginsberg	*Howl!*

Were any Jews involved in the Wall Street scandals of the 1980s?

During the earlier years of the twentieth century **Lepke Buchalter** and others took advantage of the various opportunities that arose to extort funds from truckers, clothing manufacturers, and unions, and they were not averse to physical violence and even murder when dealing with people who refused to cooperate with them. By the end of the century, however, Jewish criminals had become, by and large, a kinder and gentler breed. Great amounts of money were available to be made on Wall Street during the high-flying 1980s, but it was no longer necessary to resort to anything as crude as violence, or even the threat thereof, to get what one wanted. In the era of mergers and acquisitions, if one knew ahead of time that a company was about to be acquired, one could make a lot of money by buying up available stock of that company before news of the acquisition became public. That was what **Ivan Boesky** did. He paid **Dennis Levine**, employed at one of the investment banking firms, to inform him in advance of what was developing, and he made hundreds of millions of dollars through possession of this inside information. Boesky, Levine, and others served prison sentences and paid fines, and the firm of Drexel Burnham Lambert had to go out of business. Government supervision of the financial markets paid off, and the public interest, in this instance at least, was protected.

Why did Elie Wiesel win the Nobel Peace Prize in 1986?

Elie Wiesel was born in 1928 in Sighet, a Hungarian-speaking city that was then within Romania. In 1944, during the Second World War, the Jews of Sighet were rounded up for transport to the death camps. Wiesel and his family were imprisoned at Auschwitz and then Buchenwald, where his parents and a younger sister died. After the war he made his way to Paris, where he served in 1947 as the chief correspondent for an Israeli newspaper and, from 1948 to 1951, studied at the Sorbonne. He moved to New York in 1956, joining the staff of the *Jewish Daily Forward* in 1957 and becoming a United States citizen in 1963. From 1972 to 1976 he taught Judaic studies at the City University of New York, and since 1976 has held a professorship in the humanities at Boston University.

Wiesel has achieved worldwide fame as a novelist and lecturer, and as an eloquent spokesman for those who survived the Holocaust. In his writing he makes frequent use of biblical imagery and mystical symbolism. Though a master stylist in English, he composes most of his works in French. In 1983 he was awarded the International Literary Prize for Peace for his novels *The Testament* and *Words from Strangers*, and in 1985 the Congressional Gold Medal of Achievement (the highest nonmilitary award issued by the government of the United States). Important works by Wiesel, many of them set during the Holocaust, include *Night*, *The Gates of the Forest*, *Dawn*, *The Accident*, *The Jews of Silence*, and *A Beggar in Jerusalem*.

Wiesel's career, it would seem, could have steered him toward a Nobel Prize in literature. Why, instead, was he awarded the Peace Prize in 1986? During the 1970s and 1980s Wiesel played an important role as a spokesman for peace between Israelis and Palestinians, as well as other groups whose animosities disturbed world order. As chairman of the President's Commission on the Holocaust (which oversaw the construction of Washington's Holocaust Museum), he pleaded that, just as the world must not forget what happened to the Jews during the Second World War, so must it not forget the genocide directed against the Armenians during the First World War. During the 1990s he decried the genocidal conflicts raging between tribal groups in Africa and the religious strife in Bosnia. Serving as an adviser to American presidents, his remains a voice that cries out for peace and understanding among all peoples.

Who was Jonathan Pollard and what did he do to upset Jewish Americans?

Since the birth of the Jewish state in 1948, the relationship between Israel and the United States has always been especially close. Israel relied on the United States for military and financial aid; the United States relied on Israel as an ally whose territory would be available, if need be, in case the "cold war" with the Soviet Union should ever escalate into a military conflict. Thus many Jews were astonished to learn that on November 21, 1985, an American by the name of Jonathan Pollard had been arrested in Washington for turning over secret U.S. military materials to Israel. If two countries are friendly allies, why would one have to spy on the other? This, of course, is a naive question. All countries spy on one another, even when they are friends.

The real question is, Why would Pollard wish to spy for Israel? He had grown up in Indiana in a viscerally Zionist family, one in which "the centrality of Israel was with me every waking moment." While a thirty-one-year-old civilian employee of the U.S. Naval Intelligence Service, he became convinced that the United States was not sharing enough of its intelligence information with Israel. In his words, "I watched the threats to Israel's existence grow and grow, and gradually came to the conclusion that I had to do something." Meeting a visiting Israeli military official in Washington, Pollard offered to transmit to Israel intelligence data that he came across in his work. After some consultation this offer was accepted. In Howard Sachar's words, "During the next year the material comprised several hundred classified publications: messages and cables providing estimates, graphs, satellite photographs, and other details of Middle East weapons systems, among them the location of Syrian air defense batteries and of Iraqi nuclear and chemical warfare production and storage facilities." There was also information on Pakistan's atomic bomb project. In sending on material of this type, Pollard did not look upon himself as being disloyal to, or endangering, the United States. He was merely sharing with Israel information that it needed for its own defense capabilities.

Be that as it may, Pollard's Israeli contacts insisted upon giving him money so that the bond between them would be strengthened. Pollard's extravagant use of this money is what gave him away. He was placed under surveillance and was discovered removing classified documents. He and his wife fled for sanctuary to the Israeli embassy, but he was turned away. Instead they were arrested by the FBI. Anne Pollard served a five-year prison sentence. Jonathan Pollard remains in prison, serving a life sentence.

Who is the outstanding filmmaker of the 1990s?

There will never be universal agreement about the identity of the greatest filmmaker of any decade, least of all in Hollywood, but **Steven Spielberg** would certainly be selected by a large plurality for that honor. An innovative and painstaking director, he was responsible for *E.T.* ("extraterrestrial"), released in 1982, and *Jurassic Park*, released in 1993. These two movies are, to date, the two highest-grossing films of all time.

In 1993 Spielberg released a second film, an adaptation of a book telling a true story of the Holocaust—that of Oskar Schindler, a German businessman well positioned with the Nazis who was able to save the many Jews who worked at his factory from the death camps. *Schindler's List* is one of the great artistic triumphs of American film. Spielberg said the following about *Schindler's List*: "I came to realize the reason I came to make the movie, is that I have never in my life told the truth in a movie. My effort as a moviemaker has been to create something that couldn't possibly happen. So people could leave their lives and have an adventure and then come back to earth and drive home. That was one of the things I thought: if I'm going to tell the truth for the first time, it should be about this subject." The result is one of the most affecting and memorable treatments of the Holocaust ever seen on film.

A SELECTION OF SOME OF THE ACCLAIMED JEWISH-AMERICAN PAINTERS AND SCULPTORS OF THE PAST CENTURY

Ben Shahn
Leonard Baskin
Louise Nevelson
Robert Rauschenberg
Mark Rothko

Moses and Raphael Soyer
William Zorach
Jack Levine
Sir Jacob Epstein

Why was Ruth Bader Ginsburg President Bill Clinton's nominee to the United States Supreme Court in 1993?

President Clinton, during his time in office, was very interested in choosing people for high federal office who were as diverse as the nation itself—racially, ethnically, religiously, including a noticeable number of women. So it is possible that he chose Ruth Bader Ginsburg to be a justice of the Supreme Court because she is Jewish (the first Jew to serve on the court in twenty-four years) and because she is a woman (joining Sandra Day O'Connor, the first woman in history to serve on the court). It is more likely, though, that of even greater importance to the president than her religion or her gender were Ginsburg's views and judicial temperament. She was a person who could be counted on to gravitate to "centrist" positions on many of the issues that the court takes up, and it could be assumed that she, as she has throughout her career, would be able to maintain a collegial friendship not only with those justices on the court who support her views but with the others as well. If this is what the president was looking for, then he should be very pleased, for this is what he got.

Ginsburg (the name she acquired from her husband, a prominent tax lawyer) grew up in New York and was sixty years old when nominated to the Supreme Court. Though she had graduated first in her class from the law school of Columbia University, she got no invitations from major New York law firms; they were not yet ready, it seems, for women to join their ranks. Instead, she clerked for a federal district court judge in New York and then went on to teach at the law school of Rutgers University in New Jersey. In 1971 she taught at Harvard, and a year later was selected for a tenured position at her alma mater, Columbia. While teaching she also litigated, achieving a national reputation for the sex discrimination cases she took on, some of them on behalf of men. She argued six women's rights cases before the Supreme Court and won five. She also served as counsel to the American Civil Liberties Union. In 1980 she was appointed by President Jimmy Carter to the United States Circuit Court of Appeals in Washington, D.C. Noted for devotion to principle and a clear, incisive manner of expression, it was from this position that she ascended to the nation's highest court.

Who, during the 1990s, was judged to be the largest single charitable donor in the world?

George Soros as a Jewish teenager in Hungary escaped arrest by the Nazis in Budapest during the mid-1940s. In 1956 he immigrated to the United States and, over the years, has amassed a net worth of some $2 billion through international currency trading and other market transactions. His annual giving to various political and charitable causes approximates $350 million. He has established this pattern because, as he says, "I can't take it with me." In the estimation of those who track major philanthropic donations, "Soros is the only American who rivals the great philanthropists of the 1890s— John D. Rockefeller, Andrew Carnegie and Julius Rosenwald." If his dispensed gifts are compared to his income, he is "the world's single largest donor, individual or foundation."

During the early 1990s Soros poured over $1 billion into efforts to transform the former Communist nations of Eastern Europe into capitalist democracies. In the latter part of the 1990s he has expanded his attention to social problems within the United States. He was the major financial supporter of ballot initiatives in California and Arizona that authorized the use of marijuana for medicinal purposes, and he is ready to support similar efforts in other states. He insists that the nation's drug policy should be one of "saving our jails for violent criminals and predatory drug dealers, not nonviolent drug addicts willing to undergo treatment or the occasional marijuana smoker."

In addition to his continued support for groups seeking to reform drug policy, Soros plans at present to subvention legal immigrants to the United States who have lost various rights and financial assistance due to recent congressional legislation. He will also support the Project on Death in America, enhancing "the comfort, dignity, care and relief from pain for the dying"; the Algebra Project, seeking to improve mathematics skills of both rural and inner-city young people; and the Center on Crime, Communities and Culture, devoted to research on crime and prisons. Future projects that Soros wishes to fund will concentrate on teen pregnancy, political campaign finance reform, and professional standards applicable to law, medicine and journalism. He is convinced that, today, "market values and excessive individualism" permeate these professions, turning them into businesses rather than callings. Many of these causes are not tax-deductible, but Soros, convinced of their social utility, will underwrite them nonetheless.

FOUR

Some Aspects of Jewish-American Life

Are there still restrictions on the number of Jews allowed into certain professions?

Do Jews still face discrimination in the upper ranks of corporate America?

How did Jewish Americans, generally speaking, come to identify with the Democratic party?

What is the Conference of Presidents of Major American Jewish Organizations?

*Why are Jewish Americans noted for
lavish bar mitzvah celebrations?*

Are bagels Jewish?

What is Jewish delicatessen?

Do Jews have too much power in America?

*Some Orthodox synagogues have "Young Israel"
as part of their name. Does this mean that people
over a certain age are not eligible to participate?*

*Why are there so many Chinese restaurants in
Jewish neighborhoods?*

How do Jewish charities raise their funds?

*Why did so many children of Eastern European
immigrants become intellectuals?*

Is there anything unique about Jewish humor?

What is Orthodox Judaism?

What is Reform Judaism?

What is Conservative Judaism?

What are Hasidim?

Is there a Chief Rabbi of the United States?
Is there a Chief Rabbi of the world?

Do Jews seek to convert non-Jews to Judaism?
Are there any racial distinctions in Judaism?

What has been styled the "civil religion"
of Jewish Americans?

What is the likely consequence of the high rate of
intermarriage for Jewish Americans?

Are there still restrictions on the number of
Jews allowed into certain professions?

Jewish Americans who grew up during the earlier years of the twentieth century remember quite well that many private colleges and universities restricted the percentage of Jews granted admission to the student body (10 percent or thereabouts was what many admissions offices aimed for). Quotas were even more rigidly enforced in many graduate and professional schools. Very few Jews, for instance, were admitted to engineering programs prior to the 1960s. Architectural programs were also stingy in welcoming Jews. **Louis I. Kahn** was the best known and most admired architect among Jews practicing the profession for much of the century.

During the later years of the century, however, numerous American Jews took degrees in architecture and many of them have achieved renown for their work. Among them are **Frank Gehry**, **Richard Meier**, **Peter Eisenman**, **Denise Scott Brown**, **James Ingo Freed**, **Stanley Tigerman**, **Robert A. M. Stern**, and **Eric Owen Moss**. Meier in 1996 won the commission offered by the Roman Catholic Church (the Vatican) to design a Church for the Year 2000.

Law schools up to mid-century often adhered to a 10 percent Jewish quota. In the 1950s this policy largely disappeared, and by 1960 the number of Jews in the student bodies of many law schools exceeded 40 percent. Many Jews also wanted to be doctors. A large number of medical schools, prior to the 1960s, believed they had a responsibility to hold down the number of Jewish physicians being released into the labor force; untold numbers of Jewish applicants were turned down because of this policy. Change at last came to the medical schools, and by 1986 the number of Jews in medical school student bodies had reached 39 percent.

The widespread interest of Jews in the medical profession underlies the following joke: "According to Catholics, a fetus becomes a person at the moment of conception. According to Jews, a fetus remains a fetus until it graduates from medical school."

Do Jews still face discrimination in the upper ranks of corporate America?

During most of the twentieth century the "conventional wisdom" held that Jews (as well as members of various other racial and ethnic groups) were not welcome in the highest ranks of corporate leadership. Jews might be acceptable in certain professional and technical capacities, but not as presidents, department heads, and the like. Even today there remain a great many corporate addresses in which this is still the case.

By the 1970s, though, a vast number of opportunities had opened up for Jewish leadership in many industries, including airlines, oil, automobiles, and the newer communications and computer industries. In 1974 **Irving Shapiro** was named chairman and chief executive officer of the Du Pont Corporation. Shapiro had grown up in Minneapolis during the 1930s depression and gone into law. He found a position in the antitrust division of the U.S. Justice Department. There he came to know Du Pont representatives who were negotiating various antitrust issues with the division over several years. Du Pont hired Shapiro away from the Justice Department to serve on its legal staff; he then moved up the ranks to the corporate chairmanship.

In the automotive industry **Gerald Greenwald** moved from executive positions with Ford to serve as chairman or vice chairman in the Chrysler organization from 1979 to 1990. In 1990 he became chief executive officer of the United Employee Acquisition Corporation. When this group succeeded in assuming a major ownership stake in United Air Lines, Greenwald became chairman and chief executive of the company.

How did Jewish Americans, generally speaking, come to identify with the Democratic party?

The political ties of most German Jews in the United States, from the 1860s to the 1930s, were largely to the Republican party. While some Eastern European Jews on the Lower East Side voted for the Democratic candidates of Tammany Hall, a larger number either stayed away from politics altogether (this would have been true of some of the Orthodox) or were attached to the Socialist party. These long-standing patterns began to change around 1912, when **Woodrow Wilson** ran for President on the Democratic ticket. German Jews who had formerly been pillars of the Republican establishment, like **Henry Morgenthau** (who had served as America's ambassador to Turkey) and the banker **Jacob Schiff**, now supported Wilson and contributed funds to his campaign. Morgenthau saw in him "a man of lofty idealism and a knightly spirit," as did many other American liberals and intellectuals. When Wilson ran for his second term in 1916, he received a majority of the Jewish vote. Influencing some of the Eastern Europeans was the fact that **Louis Brandeis** was one of his closest advisers. Brandeis was a noted attorney devoted to the rights of laboring people and their unions. In 1916 Wilson appointed him to the Supreme Court; he was the first Jew to serve as a justice of that august body.

Among the Jews of the Lower East Side the emergence of **Al Smith** as a major Democratic figure was of great importance. Smith was an Irishman who worked his way through the ranks of Tammany, but he was different from the typical Tammany politician. Having grown up poor himself, he identified with the poor Jews who were his neighbors. He served as assemblyman and governor of New York, combining support for social reform with party loyalty. In Irving Howe's words, "He made the people of the slums—Irish, Jewish, Italian— feel that they too had begun to count for something in the world." Social workers, lawyers, others dedicated to a more just society, supported his runs for office, including his campaign as the Democratic (and the first Catholic) nominee for President in 1928. Many of these people were Jews who became his closest advisers. Some of his old Tammany buddies lamented that since he had "moved uptown and deserted the Fourth Ward, Al had surrounded himself with Jews."

Symbolic of the greater rapport linking German to Eastern European Jews was the election in 1932 of **Herbert Lehman** as governor of New York. Lehman was a German Jewish banker of great wealth who, in 1926, after the disastrous strike of the cloak makers, lent the ILGWU fifty thousand dollars. In 1928 Lehman was elected lieutenant governor of New York, under Governor **Franklin Roosevelt**. When Roosevelt accepted nomination as the Democratic candidate for President in 1932, Lehman replaced him as the party's candidate for governor. He was a beloved figure on the Lower East Side, and its citizens voted overwhelmingly in his favor. He served in the office for ten years, resigning it when President Roosevelt asked him to head the federal Office of Foreign Relief and Rehabilitation, organized to meet the needs of the liberated areas of

Europe during World War II. In 1943 he was chosen to be the director-general of the United Nations Relief and Rehabilitation Administration. Though Lehman later served as a senator from New York, he said toward the close of his life, "My service with UNRRA during the war years was, bar nothing, the greatest experience of my life. Our work undoubtedly saved millions of lives and set scores of millions more on the road to recovery. There is no doubt we saved much of Europe from Communism."

Social analyst Nathan Glazer evaluated Herbert Lehman's career in 1963, while he was still alive, calling it a near-perfect embodiment of the high standards of philanthropy advocated and practiced by many of the German Jewish banking and mercantile families. He noted that "sixty-five years after his first visit to the Lower East Side, Lehman sits on the board of the Henry Street Settlement, is active in the affairs of the Jewish Theological Seminary and the American Jewish Committee; and visits the new zoo in Central Park that he and his wife have given to the children of the city."

Franklin Roosevelt's assumption of the nation's presidency in 1933, and the social legislation promoted by his New Deal administration, cemented the ties of the majority of America's Jews to the Democratic party. Many of Roosevelt's confidants and advisers were Jews. **Henry Morgenthau, Jr.** was his Secretary of the Treasury. Though today the number of Jewish Republicans is considerable, it is to the Democratic party that the majority still feels a link.

Robert Strauss, a lawyer from Dallas and active in its Jewish community, was elected Democratic national chairman in 1976.

What is the Conference of Presidents of Major American Jewish Organizations?

Late in 1953 some of the people in the U.S. State Department noted that a number of Jewish organizations routinely sought to advise the department about various issues involving the State of Israel. They thereupon suggested to some of the Jewish leaders of the day that it might be helpful if these organizations could consult among themselves and then send a single representative to the department to express their concerns. This was the inspiration for the establishment of the Conference of Presidents of Major American Jewish Organizations. **Philip Klutznick**, at the time the national president of Bnai Brith, was a major force in setting up this conference.

Klutznick, a son of immigrants, had grown up in Omaha. A lawyer, he served under Presidents **Franklin Roosevelt** and **Harry Truman** as federal housing administrator. Then he became a developer of suburban housing. Under President **Jimmy Carter** he served as Secretary of Commerce from 1979 to 1981. During the 1956 Suez crisis he played an important role as the spokesman for the Presidents' Conference on behalf of the organized American Jewish community. Complementing the efforts of the Presidents' Conference was the work of the American Israel Public Affairs Committee (AIPAC), a registered lobbying group representing the interests of Israel. AIPAC had been set up in 1949 to work on behalf of Israel among U.S. senators and congressmen. It continues to this day to achieve recognition as one of the most effective lobbying groups working in Washington. One of AIPAC's greatest challenges has been its obligation to work with and support whatever Israeli government may be in power at a particular time. When the conservative Likud regime is in power, AIPAC has to speak in its behalf; when the Labor alliance takes over, AIPAC has to change over to a liberal tone almost overnight.

Among the members of the Conference of Presidents of Major American Jewish Organizations are the various Zionist groups (including AIPAC), and bodies associated with Reform, Conservative, Orthodox, and Reconstructionist Judaism. Other member groups include the American Jewish Congress, the American Jewish Committee, Bnai Brith, Jewish

War Veterans of the USA, the National Jewish Community Relations Advisory Council, the National Jewish Welfare Board, and the National Council of Jewish Women. The Jewish Labor Committee is also a member. This group was organized in 1934 as a loose association linking the Jewish garment unions, the Workmen's Circle (a socialist-oriented fraternal order advocating the preservation of Yiddish language and culture), and the Farband (a similar group with a more Zionist orientation).

In 1996 there were fifty-three national Jewish bodies affiliated with the Presidents' Conference.

Why are Jewish Americans noted for lavish bar mitzvah celebrations?

In Jewish tradition a boy becomes a "man," religiously speaking, on his thirteenth birthday. (The corresponding age of religious majority for a girl is twelve and a half.) This means, theoretically, that the young man is responsible for his behavior, both ethical and ritual, and that he is eligible to be counted in the quorum of ten necessary for public Jewish prayer (minyan) and even lead such public prayers. In Jewish communities overseas a young man's attainment of his thirteenth year was traditionally commemorated by his participation, in a public way, in a synagogue service, and perhaps his presentation of a discourse to the congregation. A modest repast was then presented by the boy's family to the congregants present, and other relatives and invited guests. The boy was now (by virtue of his thirteenth birthday, not his participation in the synagogue service or the celebratory repast) a *bar mitzvah*, a "son of commandment," obligated to live by the commandments of the Torah and the rabbinic tradition.

In America the synagogue ritual commemorating a young man's attainment of the status of "bar mitzvah" is observed by large numbers of American Jews of all varieties (even though there is no religious obligation or "commandment" to do so). What is unique about America, however, is that the "modest repast" that, in other lands, often followed the prayer service has been transformed into a lavish spectacle of food, drink, and entertainment rivaling many a wedding. As the expression goes, emphasis at these celebrations is more on "bar" than on "mitzvah." America has also created a *bat mitzvah* ("daughter of commandment") celebration for girls. The first such ritual observance took place at a New York Conservative synagogue in 1922. Conservative and Reform congregations commemorate the attainment of bat mitzvah status with the identical ritual procedures utilized at a bar mitzvah commemoration; Orthodox synagogues, however, differentiate between the readings assigned to girls and those assigned to boys, since in Orthodoxy the ritual obligations of women differ from those of men.

Rabbis of all schools have inveighed for years against the excess of expense and display at bar mitzvah celebrations (and nowadays at some bat mitzvah celebrations as well). But perhaps it is not too terrible for families who take pride in their children to want to celebrate their coming of age in a way that their guests will likely remember (for a while at least). No one should go into debt for such an occasion, but if people can afford it, why not? It contributes to the livelihoods of caterers, waiters, musicians, photographers, and florists. According to Jenna Weissman Joselit, the folk wisdom of American Jews made of bar mitzvah "a good time, a socially justifiable occasion for sentiment, camaraderie, and high spirits. Fashioned in the people's image of what it meant to be Jewish in modern America, glittering occasions and red-letter rituals like bar mitzvah and bat mitzvah bring pleasure to thousands of grandmas and grandpas, mothers and fathers, sons and daughters, eager to dramatize their Jewishness."

In recent years it has become customary for many American Jews, when celebrating a bar or bat mitzvah or a wedding of a son or daughter, to contribute a percentage of the amount they spend on the event to organizations serving the hungry and homeless.

Are bagels Jewish?

The term "bagel" is a variant of the German word *Beugel,* used in Austria to refer to a croissant or twisted roll. It is shaped like a doughnut and made with malt (rather than sugar) and high-gluten processed flour. It is boiled before it is baked, so as to give it a crisp outer crust and a chewy inside. Bagels are associated with the cuisine of Eastern European Jews, but in the closing years of the twentieth century they have spread throughout the country and are happily consumed by people of all ethnic and religious backgrounds.

Are bagels Jewish? Moses never ate a bagel, nor did other Jews eat them during the first two and a half millennia of their history. It may be said that in more recent times Jews as a group seem to like bagels, especially since various flavored varieties have become available.

What is Jewish delicatessen?

Shops dispensing kosher or kosher-style beef salami, beef hot dogs, corned beef, tongue, and hot pastrami, along with accoutrements like potato knishes and potato pancakes, are known far and wide as "Jewish delicatessens," and the food they purvey is "Jewish delicatessen." A taste for such meats is widespread in Central and Eastern Europe, but it took the massive Jewish immigration from these areas to popularize these items in many parts of the United States. (Pastrami was brought in by Romanian Jews; the term comes from the Turkish word *basdirma,* referring to meat flavored with spices and garlic and cured under pressure.) Jewish delis are identified primarily with New York, where in the 1930s there were about five thousand of them, but they also play an important part in the culinary and social life of cities like

Baltimore, Richmond, Memphis, Chicago, Minneapolis, and Los Angeles. Orson Welles wrote, "We get a good deal of Jewish delicatessen in Hollywood. Without pastrami sandwiches there could be no picture-making."

Another Jewish culinary phenomenon, at least in New York, is the "appetizing store." (No one seems to know how this term originated.) An "appetizing" features dozens of smoked and dried fishes (at least ten kinds of herring, whitefish, several varieties of salmon or lox), salads, cheeses, bulk candy, and all kinds of nuts. One observer noted, "Although people of every nationality patronize the retail appetizing stores, the Jewish people are by far the greatest customers."

Do Jews have too much power in America?

Early in 1996 an article in *New York Magazine* by Philip Weiss, a Jewish writer, raised the interesting question of whether it isn't time for Jewish Americans to stop looking upon themselves as "victims," accused by envious non-Jews of possessing a disproportionate share of wealth, power, and control. The writer argued that Jews, who comprise under 3 percent of the country's population, *do* possess a much greater fraction of wealth, power, and control than a mere 3 percent, and that Jews should be willing, collectively, to admit this fact to themselves and to others. He presented the following statistics to support his argument: there are ten Jewish senators and over thirty Jewish congressmen; Jews have become presidents of Harvard, Yale, and Princeton universities; Jews make up 26 percent of reporters, editors, and executives at major print and broadcast media; they comprise 59 percent of the writers, producers, and directors of the fifty top-grossing movies and 40 percent of the partners in leading New York and Washington law firms; there are sixteen Jews among the top forty on the "*Forbes* 400" list of leading businesspeople, and Jews comprise 23 percent of the total list; they make up 7.5 percent of the senior executives of the nation's largest businesses, and 13 percent of the executives under age forty; Jews contribute a quarter to a third of all political contributions made to the Democratic and Republican parties (added together). Weiss derives from all this the conclusion that "Jews have entered fully into the elite, and are in powerful positions that had heretofore been barred to us. The formerly narrow power elite is much more broadly distributed, and, like it or not, Jews are one of the groups that compose it." Jews in America are, in other words, "players and not victims."

It is difficult for Jews to willingly recognize that any of their number are indeed part of the power elite, because the myth of a "world-wide Jewish conspiracy" has long been part of anti-Semitic doctrine. During the nineteenth century "international Jewish bankers" supposedly manipulated the banking systems of European countries. The rise of Communism in Russia in the twentieth century was alleged to have been engineered by Jews. The Nazis wedded "international Jewish bankers" to "Jewish Bolshevism," maintaining that both groups sought, in concert, to subvert Western societies and cultures so that Jews could control all of the world's wealth. Jews of course knew that both parts of this conspiracy theory were lies; except for a handful of Jews in Western Europe and the Soviet Union who had formed their own personal ties to the respective "power elites" in those countries, most Jews were desperately poor and had neither the opportunity nor the qualifications to "control" anything. Many European Christians, however, and even some in America, influenced by the strain of anti-Judaism in much Christian teaching in those days, subscribed to the anti-Semitic conspiracy theories promulgated by the Nazis. The Holocaust of European Jewry during the Second World War was the result. For these reasons many Jews today still prefer to look upon the group to which they belong as "victims" rather than as part of the power elite. It is safer to do so.

In fact, however, many American Jews have moved into the ranks of the power elite. They certainly did not "conspire" to do so. Their rise from poverty to economic and political significance has been through the normal workings of the democratic political system, and the free-market economic system, in which we live. Jews, generally speaking, value education and are willing to delay immediate gratification of desires they may have. Thus they believe in saving and investing their money, and are likely to even risk some money when a promising, well-researched opportunity comes along. For this reason many Jewish Americans, whose families were desperately poor at the beginning of the twentieth century, are now prominent and well remunerated in business, the professions, the arts, and the sciences. Jews, like many others, have benefited from the political and economic system that enlivens this country. As a general rule, such people realize that they have an obligation to the American system that has treated them so well. They wish it to continue to confer its benefits, not only upon their own descendants but upon others, of all racial, religious, and ethnic backgrounds, who "play by the rules" that promote the welfare and prosperity of all.

Some Orthodox synagogues have "Young Israel" as part of their name. Does this mean that people over a certain age are not eligible to participate?

"Young Israel" was organized in 1912 on the Lower East Side by second-generation, English-speaking Jews. It first sponsored lectures on Friday nights. (Orthodox services take place on Fridays at sunset to welcome the Sabbath, after which men go home to eat the Sabbath meal. These lectures were presented later in the evening, sometimes featuring speakers like **Judah Magnes**, **Israel Friedlander** of the Jewish Theological Seminary, or **Mordecai Kaplan** before he was drummed out of Orthodoxy.) Later on Young Israel synagogues developed; these were Orthodox in practice and preaching but welcomed people who shaved their beards, dressed in modern style, and listened to English sermons. Such synagogues still exist, in New York and other cities throughout the country.

Many Young Israel members today are in their eighties and nineties.

Why are there so many Chinese restaurants in Jewish neighborhoods?

In 1903 the *Jewish Daily Forward* noticed that a new word had entered the American Yiddish vocabulary: *ausessen*, "eating out," a custom unknown in Europe or, in earlier years, among Eastern European immigrants in America. Chances are most immigrants were not yet "eating out" in Chinese restaurants in 1903, but it was not too long before they would be doing so. Chinese food was usually very cheap, compared to other cuisines, and was often the preferred choice of people without too much money. Chinese food was not kosher, but many Jews wished to give up at least some of the strictures of the Jewish dietary laws. The first step in doing so was to eat Chinese food. It might not be kosher, but it really didn't "look" not kosher the way a ham or a pork chop does. (The pork in Chinese dishes is usually scraped into strings, so it is not as noticeably "porky" to people moving away from a strictly kosher diet. Some people who keep kosher homes not only eat Chinese food when dining out but even bring it home, taking care to eat it off disposable paper plates.) Chinese restaurateurs have set up shop in Jewish neighborhoods because they know that what they have to offer is very much appreciated by the people who live there.

It should be noted, of course, that nowadays some Chinese restaurants are very expensive, and that some are strictly kosher.

How do Jewish charities raise their funds?

Jewish Americans are noted for their generous gifts to worthy causes, whether it be general charities like the United Way and its constituent organizations; the arts, including museums, music, and drama; educational institutions; and specifically Jewish charities. In 1939 the United Jewish Appeal was organized to raise funds on a national level in a combined campaign for the benefit of the United Palestine Appeal (to support causes in Israel), the Joint Distribution Committee (for needy Jews in Europe and around the world), and the Hebrew Immigrant Aid Society (for needy Jews settling in the United States). In 1948 the United Palestine Appeal changed its name, as might be expected, to the United Israel Appeal. In many Jewish communities local Jewish causes, such as social service agencies and community centers, have combined their appeals for funds with the annual campaign of the United Jewish Appeal. New York City was one of the last places to do this. It was not until 1974 that the United Jewish Appeal and the Federation of Jewish Philanthropies combined their fund-raising efforts.

Fund-raising professionals have frequently been envious of the success that often crowns the efforts of the United Jewish Appeal to raise "real money." One reason for its success is the innate generosity of many donors. Another reason is that other donors are sometimes shamed into contributing more than they might initially wish to give. The UJA, as a tactic, often organizes local community gatherings of affinity groups based on business or profession. At these gatherings people are asked to publicly declare how much they plan to give to the campaign. Sometimes booklets are published in which these amounts are listed. It is not unusual, in situations like this, for gifts to be jogged upward a notch or two, to the benefit of the causes that the campaign is set up to serve.

As the twentieth century draws to its end, a diminution in the massive amounts that earlier were being given to the UJA seems to be taking place. In 1990 the UJA stood in first place on the *Chronicle of Philanthropy*'s list of top charities. In 1994 it slipped to fourth place. The reason, in all likelihood, is attributable to the "peace process" in which Israel and the Arab states are engaged. Donors give a lot of money when there is a crisis or a sense of urgency to motivate them to do so; the crisis atmosphere surrounding the State of Israel has considerably lessened, so contributions have gone down. There are two other reasons for the drop in gifts to the UJA. Some Jews who still have a great interest in Israel-centered giving prefer to donate directly to smaller, more specific causes or groups, and thereby achieve a sense of personal participation in the work that their money underwrites. With other Jews, their growing assimilation into American society has weakened the feeling of obligation to contribute to Israel-centered causes.

Why did so many children of Eastern European immigrants become intellectuals?

The mastery of the Bible in its original Hebrew and a knowledge of the commentaries upon the Bible as well as the Talmud and other rabbinic texts have always been the ideal held aloft by traditional Jewish religion. A male Jew, if he had the capacity, was expected to immerse himself in this learned tradition all the days of his life. Among those who departed from strict Orthodoxy, both in Europe and in American immigrant communities, this compulsion to learn was expanded to encompass the wide horizons of secular culture as well. In Irving Howe's words, "All through the late nineteenth and early twentieth century, learning came to seem an almost magical solution for the Jews, a people that has always placed an enormous faith in the sheer power of words. Learning in its own right, learning for the sake of future generations, learning for the social revolution, learning in behalf of Jewish renewal—all melted into one upsurge of self-discovery."

As early as 1903, Abraham Cahan advised his readers in the *Jewish Daily Forward*: "In America a worker can sometimes even go to college and get an education. But it takes a long time. You must try to be an intellectual, not just a doctor or a lawyer." Another *Forward* columnist wrote, "We know workers have little time or strength to read after a day in the shop. But a half hour of serious reading every day for several years can provide an excellent education."

SOME OF THE "NEW YORK INTELLECTUALS"

Irving Howe
Lionel Trilling
Philip Rahv
Paul Goodman
Harold Rosenberg
Sidney Hook
Alfred Kazin
Norman Podhoretz
Midge Decter
Irving Kristol

Several of these people have been professors of literature, philosophy, or politics, and over the last forty years all of them have written extensively (books and articles) in the fields of politics and literary criticism. Many were associated with the journal *Partisan Review.* All of them took a liberal, social democratic, and vigorously anti-Stalinist stance. Beginning in the late 1950s and continuing into the 1960s, though, Podhoretz (the editor of *Commentary*), his wife (Decter), and Kristol developed what came to be called "neoconservatism," questioning various liberal values. These ideas were influential, to an extent, during the Nixon and Reagan administrations.

Is there anything unique about Jewish humor?

It is, of course, well known that Jewish comedians and comic writers have been a mainstay of American entertainment, but why has this been the case? Is there some special Jewish propensity for comedy? There is humor in the Bible and in rabbinic texts, but does this spill over into the way of life of ordinary people pursuing secular occupations? One writer, Henry Spalding, maintains that "the true Jewish joke mirrors the history of the Jewish people. It is a reflection of their joy and anguish, their aspirations and discouragements, their all too brief periods of social and economic well-being. It expresses their age-old yearning for a world in which justice, mercy, understanding and equality will prevail—not only for themselves but for all people. It portrays their quest for eternal truths."

This characterization may not apply to all Jewish humor, but it certainly captures the quality of some of it. Jewish humor also encompasses a self-critical quality, sometimes directed at Jews as a whole but more often at particular character types within the community. Here is a joke aimed at the ubiquitous Jewish mother:

> An elderly Jewish woman says to her two friends: "My son is so good to me that last year for my birthday he gave me an all-expense-paid cruise around the world."
>
> Her friend says: "My son is even better. For my birthday he catered an affair for me, and paid the money to fly in a planeload of my friends from California."
>
> The second friend responds: "That's nothing. My son goes three times a week to a psychiatrist, and pays him a hundred twenty dollars an hour. And what does he talk about the whole time? Me!"

Not all jokes are about Jewish mothers. Here is one about a Jewish son:

A mother goes into her son's room, shakes him, and says, "You have to get up for school, Bernie."

Bernie answers, "I don't want to go to school."

"You have to go," his mother says.

"I don't want to. The teachers don't like me, and all the children make fun of me. Give me one good reason why I should go to school."

"You're fifty-two years old and you're the principal."

And not to be forgotten is this ancient witticism from the early 1900s:

What does R.S.V.P. mean?
Remember to Send Vedding Present.

What is Orthodox Judaism?

In Jewish teaching the Jewish people constitute a unity as descendants of the revered patriarchs whose sagas are told in the Hebrew Scriptures. Many Jews do not think of themselves as "Orthodox" or "Conservative" or "Reform"; they think of themselves simply as Jews. The Orthodox regard their practices and teachings as the only ones that are truly Jewish, but they do not deny the Jewish identity of most of the people who participate in the other groups. Marriage across denominational lines within Judaism is quite common; this in itself presents no problem unless there was a conversion to Judaism in someone's ancestry that could be questioned by Orthodoxy. It may be said that, viewed from a strictly logical perspective, there is probably more that divides the non-Orthodox Jew from the Orthodox than the teachings that they share. From an emotional standpoint, however, many Jews place an emphasis on what they have in common.

The group called "Orthodox" is that body of Jews that remains faithful to the *halaka*—classical Jewish law as derived from the written Torah (the Hebrew Scriptures) and the enactments of the rabbinic sages (the oral Torah, contained in the Talmud and later writings). Orthodox Judaism remains committed to the idea that the first five books of the Bible were dictated by God verbatim to Moses and that the oral Torah is divinely inspired, all its teachings being implicit in the Torah of Moses and unfolding from generation to generation in the enactments and interpretations of the authentic (Orthodox) teachers of Torah. According to Orthodox belief, when the Jewish people as a whole truly repents and commences to live in accordance with a proper understanding of the Torah, the Messiah will appear, the exile of the Jews from their homeland will end, and the Temple will be rebuilt on the holy mount in Jerusalem. It is understandable, given these commitments, that Orthodox Judaism is loath to permit changes in accepted religious practice. One such practice is the custom of Jewish men to keep their heads covered (with a skullcap or other type of hat) at all times. This is a practice so tenaciously cherished by Orthodox Judaism, and even by many non-Orthodox Jews when they are praying or performing religious acts, that in popular thinking it has become inseparable from Judaism.

The rules governing the observance of the Sabbath (Friday night and all of Saturday until sundown) are more rigorous in Orthodox Judaism than in the other groups. Not only is work forbidden, but also many other acts that most people would not categorize as work, such as writing or telephoning. Travel by either animal or motor vehicle is forbidden, nor may electricity be either switched on or turned off for the duration of the Sabbath. Buying and selling, or any handling of money, is forbidden. The purpose of these regulations is not to burden the people, but rather to set the Sabbath apart as a unique and holy day, one in which the joy of worship and study, as well as the sharing of hearty meals and religious song, will not be disturbed by the intrusion of everyday concerns. All of the Sabbath prohibitions are to be suspended when the saving of human life is involved. Besides the rules of the Sabbath, Orthodoxy is very concerned with promoting the observance of the dietary rules of the Torah among Jews. These include the prohibition of pork and shell-fish, and the prohibition of serving milk products with meat products at the same meal. Any meat eaten by a Jew (except if the saving of a life is involved) must come from an animal that has been slaughtered in the ritually correct manner.

Worship services in Orthodox synagogues are in Hebrew, though sermons and supplementary readings might be in any language that the community understands. No organ or other instrumental music may be played at a liturgical service. The prayer leader may be a layman or a cantor with musical training. The leader is always male, as are the occasional choirs that may be found in Orthodox synagogues. Women do not have leadership roles in the worship service because they are not obligated to recite the statutory prayers in the same way that men are, and only one who has an obligation to do something can, according to *halaka*, discharge that obligation for others. The reason women are not obligated to recite the prayers is that they have many responsibilities at home, particularly relating to the care of children. Women are seated in Orthodox synagogues in a section separate from the men, either in a balcony area or on the same level as the men if a partition divides them. Women are expected to dress modestly, and married women must cover their hair when out in public or at gatherings where men not related to them are present.

Orthodox Jews are united in regarding homosexual behavior as sinful, in rejecting the legitimacy of a marriage between a Jew and a non-Jew who has not converted to Judaism, and in insisting that Jewish identity can be trans-mitted to a child only through its mother. (A person whose mother was not Jewish at the time of his or her birth must undergo a ritual of conversion to Judaism in order to become part of the Jewish people.) Contemporary feminism has of course affected Orthodox Jewish women who pursue secular occupations, but it has had little influence upon their religious life. Orthodoxy is the only Jewish group that refuses to ordain women as rabbis.

What is Reform Judaism?

In the early years of the nineteenth century Reform Judaism grew up in Germany and Central Europe in opposition to Orthodoxy. After the French Revolution the armies of Napoleon carried the ideals of the Enlightenment into these regions, and it was not long thereafter that a number of Jews decided that in the new world that was coming into being, a "reform" of some Jewish practices was in order. The movement first began by advocating slight changes in the worship services (for example, the elimination of the repetition of identical liturgical passages within the same service), but ideological changes were not far behind as rabbinic scholars who had also been trained in scientific historical studies became involved. The aim of Reform Judaism is to retain as Jews people who seek a more scientific and rationalistic approach than Orthodoxy evinces in some of its teachings. Large numbers of Jews came from Germany and contiguous areas to the United States during the mid-nineteenth century; many of them found the spirit of Reform congenial to their needs. Thus it was that Reform Judaism came to be the dominant expression of the faith in many American communities for quite some time. Its seminary, the Hebrew Union College in Cincinnati, was established in 1875; it now has additional branches in New York, Los Angeles, and Jerusalem.

The Reform movement eliminated separate seating for men and women at the synagogue services, shortened the prayers, and authorized that many of the readings be done in the vernacular rather than in Hebrew. Mixed choirs of men and women, as well as the organ and other musical instruments, are utilized at services. The need for Jewish men to wear the skullcap or other head covering was eliminated, as well as the dietary restrictions. The rules governing the Sabbath were relaxed, so that the use of electricity and automobiles on that day became legitimate. The Reformers changed the expectation of a messianic king of the line of David who would come at the end of days to a hope that a "messianic age" will come to fruition, when peace and universal brotherhood will prevail. Although some of the early Reformers believed that the Torah of Moses had come from the mouth of God, modern biblical study soon became part of the Reform rabbinic curriculum, and the doctrine of "progressive revelation" came to replace the belief that God had revealed himself for all time to Moses. The doctrine of the "mission of Israel," the idea that the Jews had been sent to the far corners of the earth to share the concept of ethical monotheism with all peoples, replaced the traditional conviction that they had been exiled from their ancient homeland because of sin. Many an American Reform rabbi, and laypeople as well, have equated the democratic and egalitarian ideals of the Declaration of Independence, the Constitution, and the Bill of Rights with the teachings of Reform Judaism.

Reform Jews are often rather secular people whose way of life differs from that of committed Orthodox Jews. They may even be indistinguishable from other decent, moral people who have no formal religious affiliation at all. In spite of this, however, the dedicated Reform Jew is conscious and proud of his ties to the past of his people and seeks, through learning and good works, to transmit this heritage to his children. He feels that Reform Judaism, more so than any other segment of the religious community, best preserves the heritage of the biblical prophets. That is to say, like the prophets, it emphasizes the primacy of ethics and the responsibility of humanity to form a wholesome and equitable society. Purely ritualistic behavior is of decidedly secondary importance in the face of this moral imperative.

In response to contemporary feminism, Reform Judaism

has opened its seminaries to women; the first woman was ordained a rabbi in 1972. In recent years the movement has gone on record to rescind the ancient stigma attached to homosexuality; both membership in Reform congregations and the rabbinate itself are now open to homosexuals. Though the movement is on record as discouraging intermarriage between Jews and non-Jews who do not seek conversion to Judaism, many Reform rabbis refuse to conform to this dictum and are willing to officiate at such marriages. In response to the high rate of intermarriage in today's United States, Reform Judaism affirms the Jewish identity of all children whose parents have provided them with Jewish religious schooling. This contrasts with the stand of Orthodoxy and the Conservative movement, which insists that such children undergo a ceremony of conversion to Judaism unless the mother was Jewish at the time of their birth.

What is Conservative Judaism?

Conservative Judaism may well be the largest of the organized Jewish religious groups in the United States (though the number of Jews who are unaffiliated with any synagogue may be the largest of all). It derives its name from the conviction of its early leaders that while "reform" of traditional Judaism was indeed necessary, many of the "reformers" had gone too far: what was needed was a more "conservative" approach, one that retained more of the ritual and the traditions that were dear to many Jews. Its great national center was and still is the Jewish Theological Seminary in New York. Conservative Judaism appealed to American Jews of East European descent, while Reform Judaism satisfied more Jews of German descent. Nowadays the great mass of American Jews are of East European descent, even in the Reform temples. And it is accurate to say that nowadays in many communities there is very little that distinguishes the liturgies offered in the Conservative synagogue from those offered in the Reform one.

In its early days Conservative Judaism advocated nothing that contravened *halaka*; it functioned, rather, as an "Americanized" version of Orthodoxy, with an English sermon as part of all Sabbath and holy day services, unison and responsive readings by the congregation, and unison singing of hymns. (These elements are not necessarily part of Orthodox worship; some Orthodox people regard them as too "churchlike" for truly Jewish worship.) A major break with Orthodoxy occurred, however, when the Conservative movement advocated the mixed seating of men and women in its synagogues. This is now the norm in all Conservative congregations. In addition, as time went on women came to be counted as part of the necessary quorum for public prayer; they were granted the right to lead services and read from the Torah scroll, and at last, in 1985, the first woman was ordained a Conservative rabbi. Sabbath prohibitions were modified to allow Conservative Jews to drive automobiles to and from the synagogue for services, and allowing families to turn on the radio or television to listen to or watch programs that might enhance the spirit of Sabbath holiness. Orthodoxy, of course, could not countenance these decisions by the Conservative authorities. To many Orthodox rabbis Conservatism is even worse than Reform, since it appears to preserve traditional Jewish practice while actually doing away with much that Orthodoxy considers of vital importance. One traditional element that Conservative Judaism holds on to tenaciously is the requirement that men wear the skullcap while attending a synagogue service. Even non-Jewish visitors are expected to do this.

In recent years a fourth grouping within American Judaism has achieved recognition in the religious community, though its synagogues serve a relatively small percentage of people. This is the Reconstructionist movement, founded by **Mordecai Kaplan** in the 1920s to serve not as an independent "denomination" but as an organization that might influence all the branches of American Judaism. It sought to appeal to people who were not too attached to supernaturalism but who at the same time nurtured a warm feeling for Jewish tradition and "peoplehood," the Hebrew language, and classical Jewish texts. Kaplan angered Orthodoxy by excising all references to the Jews as a "chosen people" from the prayer book that he edited. To this day many people look upon Reconstructionism as "left-wing Conservatism," allowing individuals to believe in whatever "God-idea" they find meaningful while cherishing the forms of Jewish worship. The movement's seminary was established in Philadelphia in 1968.

What are Hasidim?

The Hasidim (plural of the Hebrew word *hasid*, meaning "pious") are a subset within Orthodox Judaism. Hasidism began in eighteenth-century Poland as a movement among the poor. It emphasizes the need for joy and enthusiasm in worship, and brings elements of Jewish mystical teaching into popular religion. Hasidic men often take pride in growing beards and side-curls, believing that there is a biblical commandment to do so. They dress modestly, often in black, and on Sabbaths and holy days they put on the type of festive garments worn by their ancestors two hundred or more years ago. In this way they show their love and reverence for their ancestors. Hasidic women are very concerned with exhibiting modest and chaste behavior at all times. Hasidim ordinarily attach themselves to charismatic teachers called "rebbes" (from *rabbi*), who are leaders of particular sects. A Hasid seeks to be in the presence of his rebbe whenever possible, for he believes that the rebbe is close to God and can transmit some of the power and holiness that he possesses to those who love and follow him. (During the early 1990s many in the Lubavitcher sect of Hasidim, whose rebbe, Menachem Mendel Schneerson, lived in Brooklyn, were swept up in the belief that their rebbe was in fact the promised Messiah of the entire Jewish people. His death has dampened that conviction, though some remain convinced that had this generation of Jews been worthy, his messianic identity would have been revealed to all.)

Hasidim have increased in both numbers and significance in some Jewish communities during the latter years of the twentieth century because they, as well as other Orthodox Jews, often have a high birth rate, following closely the biblical commandment "to be fruitful and multiply." In this way they seek to make up for, in some measure, the millions of Jews who perished during the Holocaust of World War II.

Is there a Chief Rabbi of the United States? Is there a Chief Rabbi of the world?

Non-Orthodox Judaisms, by their very nature, would not be expected to possess "chief rabbis," since these groups grant to their rabbis, and even to their laypeople, the right to interpret and practice their religion as they see fit, even if on occasion they deviate from previous tradition. Orthodoxy, however, could be expected to have chief rabbis, since within Orthodoxy the accepted decisions of recognized rabbinic authorities on matters of religious practice are determinative. Israel has two chief rabbis, one for the Sephardic community and one for the Ashkenazi. There is a "Chief Rabbi of the British Empire," a position created in the nineteenth century so that British Jews would have a counterpart to the Anglican Church's Archbishop of Canterbury. (The non-Orthodox do not recognize him, just as he does not recognize them, and some of the "right-wing" Orthodox ignore him as not being sufficiently Orthodox from their perspective.)

The United States, however, has never had a Chief Rabbi, even for the Orthodox, and most other countries have not had chief rabbis either. What Orthodoxy possesses, rather than a Pope-like figure who can speak with unimpeachable authority, is a written tradition that itself speaks with authority. When asked to research a question of religious practice, the Orthodox rabbi turns to the texts that have been written over the centuries. If he himself cannot render an informed opinion, he turns to an Orthodox scholar of recognized intellectual reputation, who will send him a written analysis of the question at issue with, in most instances, a solution. If the analysis and proposed solution are not convincing, the rabbi who raised the question can turn to rabbis of even greater intellectual reputation anywhere in the world and await their written replies. Eventually one of "the great ones of the generation" will provide a satisfactory solution. In a system such as this, there is no need for "chief rabbis" who adjudicate over specific territories. The written tradition itself adjudicates. Those who interpret it do so on the basis of intellectual reputation alone; they need not hold any professional position at all.

Just as most countries do not possess "chief rabbis," there has never been a Chief Rabbi of the world either. If there were to be such an office, its seat could be only in Jerusalem. In the unlikely event that the government and legal system in Israel should ever be taken over completely by Jewish Orthodoxy, there might be an attempt to establish a rabbinic office of this type, seeking to exert a measure of control over Orthodox Judaism the world over. It would, of course, be a highly controversial move.

Do Jews seek to convert non-Jews to Judaism? Are there any racial distinctions in Judaism?

According to traditional Judaism, it is only those who are descended, through the maternal line, from the biblical patriarch Jacob (also known as Israel) who are *obligated* to accept the Jewish religion and live in accordance with its practices. Others, who do not lay claim to this line of descent, have no need to embrace Judaism. From ancient days, however, they have been welcome to do so if their spiritual studies lead them to the conviction that the Hebrew Scriptures and the rabbinic texts contain an authentic revelation of God and his will. Non-Jews who do not become proselytes to Judaism are regarded by the tradition as righteous in the sight of God and worthy of his fullest blessing if they live by the "seven precepts commanded to the sons of Noah: to establish courts of justice and to refrain from blasphemy, idolatry, adultery, murder, robbery, and from eating flesh that has been cut from a living animal." This includes earnest practitioners of most of the world's great religions, as well as a goodly number of agnostics and atheists.

Besides instruction in Jewish beliefs and practices, the process of conversion to Judaism includes immersion in a ritual bath and, for males, the rite of circumcision (unless this is not possible for medical reasons). Orthodox rabbis, generally speaking, do not accept the validity of conversions to Judaism that have been presided over by non-Orthodox rabbis. Within American Judaism, as elsewhere, the Orthodox will not accept anyone for conversion who seems influenced by some material motive, such as a desire to marry a Jew. Reform Judaism, however, as well as some rabbis from other non-Orthodox groups, regard an impending marriage to a Jew as an eminently suitable motive for conversion (provided, of course, that the proselyte is sincere in his or her undertaking to adopt Jewish beliefs and practices). No significant American Jewish group has ever attempted an organized effort to proselytize among groups of non-Jews; those who are interested are expected to initiate contact with a rabbi to discuss the matter. Reform, Reconstructionist, and Conservative groups have, however, established "outreach" programs to publicize the possibility of conversion among non-Jews already married to Jews.

All the groups within American Judaism include in their number people of every racial extraction. The black Jews of Ethiopia are an ancient branch of the Jewish people. Several groups of Jews, physically indistinguishable from their neighbors, existed in India for centuries, as did one in China. It would be the gravest of sins for a rabbi, or any other Jew, to discourage anyone from seeking conversion to Judaism for racial reasons.

Besides the black Jews who are affiliated with established Jewish-American institutions, there is also an unknown number of black Jews who participate in independent synagogues that, in general, remain apart from the Jewish community. Some participants in these groups are Ethiopian Jews who have settled in the United States. Others are descendants of American blacks who adopted Judaism years ago, perhaps prior to the Civil War. Yet others are descendants of those who adopted Judaism during this past century as an alternative to Christianity, which some American blacks came to regard as the "slave religion" imposed upon them by their masters. Some of these synagogues combine a Jewish liturgy with the spirit and enthusiasm of many black churches.

What has been styled the "civil religion" of Jewish Americans?

In Judaism Israel's slavery in Egypt is recalled not only on Passover but on every sacred occasion, followed by thanks for God's redemption of his people. Some observers feel that among many American Jews, this genuine and ancient linkage between bondage and redemption has been transmuted into a new "civil religion," one concentrating upon the Holocaust of the Jews of Europe during World War II and the subsequent founding of the State of Israel in 1948 (as well as Israel's occupation of Jerusalem's sacred sites in 1967). There is nothing inherently wrong with equating Israel's slavery in Egypt with the Holocaust, and the Exodus to the promised land with the founding of the State of Israel. Some, however, think that this gives leave to those who want to ignore the tradition as a whole and instead carry out their Jewish responsibilities by visiting or endowing Holocaust memorials and museums, and/or supporting Israeli and Zionist causes. As time goes on, we will see if these concerns are well founded.

Jewish-American consciousness of the Holocaust is reflected in the many Holocaust museums and courses of study that have been established, even at secular schools and universities. A major undertaking, the Holocaust Museum in Washington, D.C., was opened in 1993. It stands on land donated by the U.S. government, but the cost of building and operating it is paid for by private donations.

While it is true that the Holocaust and the State of Israel have come to dominate the religious consciousness of many Jews who maintain an intense attachment to their ethnic background, there is another type of "civil religion" that has become dominant among many other Jews, particularly the younger generation, who lack this intensity of ethnic memory. It is quite similar, in fact, to the "civil religion" that is found among many people with Christian roots who reject the certainties of religious fundamentalism. It revolves around the conviction, or perhaps the feeling, that there is a God who is related to the world and humanity, and that this God is more forgiving than judgmental. God loves all people and reveals to us that we should love one another. In this type of "civil religion" the ethical ideals of the Judeo-Christian tradition are often identified with the ideals of American democracy.

What is the likely consequence of the high rate of intermarriage for Jewish Americans?

As the twentieth century draws to its close, the intermarriage rate of Jewish Americans with people of other religions, for the most part Christians, has been estimated at about 50 percent. Most rabbis, and others professionally involved with Jewish life, lament this. They fear a decline in the size of the community and a deterioration of interest and emotional attachment to things Jewish on the part of those who intermarry, and among their children. To lament intermarriage, however, is to lament a natural and inevitable consequence of a democratic society. The fairly low rate of intermarriage that used to characterize American Jewish life was based not only upon the fact that most Jews did not feel comfortable in close relationships with Christians, but also upon the reciprocal fact that most Christians did not desire a close association with Jews. Even people who respected and admired those who adhered to another religion thought of the Jewish community as a discrete group unto itself, particularly where family relationships and social life were concerned. To cross the lines of demarcation was considered "unnatural," on both sides.

In the last quarter of the century there are no longer large numbers of people who think along these lines. Among both Orthodox Jews and fundamentalist Christians intermarriage across religious lines is still regarded either as a sin or a major shortcoming (unless one of the parties to the marriage converts to the religion of the other), so people who are sincere adherents of either of these groups will not intermarry (or, if they are tempted to do so, they *should* not intermarry). The majority of American Jews, however, are not Orthodox, and the majority of American Catholics and Protestants, are not fundamentalists. Jews and Christians go to school together; they work together and participate in recreation together; for the most part they do not feel foreign or uncomfortable in each other's company. Many Jews share more with Christians whom they know than with their fellow Jews, and the same can be said for many Christians. So, quite naturally, the intermarriage rate among non-Orthodox Jews and non-fundamentalist Christians will continue to remain very high.

How will this affect Jewish Americans and Judaism? Of course, no one can predict with any degree of accuracy what will happen many years hence, but there is a strong possibility that the central Jewish belief that Jews are united by a common biological descent from the biblical patriarchs, and that it is for this reason that they share a common faith, will become attenuated. Judaism, for many who intermarry and for descendants of those who intermarry, may become a matter of personal choice rather than a family obligation. It may, in other words, become for some people a religious "denomination" rather than an ethnic culture expressing itself in religious terms. We may even find families or individuals who, when living in a specific neighborhood, will find the Jewish temple a congenial place with which to affiliate, but who, when relocating to another neighborhood, will prefer affiliation with one of the local Christian churches. Americans of all backgrounds are increasingly demanding that religion satisfy personal, individual needs; they are no longer content when religion seeks only to transmit ancient doctrine. This factor, along with the high rate of intermarriage, means that as the years unfold, Jewish institutions will likely have to compete with other institutions to capture and retain the interest of those who, in past generations, would never have thought to seek spiritual inspiration outside the Jewish fold.

What are "Jews for Jesus"?

Evangelical Christians have sought to proselytize among Jews since America's early days, with relatively little success. During the sixties and seventies some of them began a new approach— they organized groups that mingled Christian theology with various Jewish rites and customs (e.g., Hebrew prayers, Yiddish terminology, some kosher dietary rules, an emotional attachment to Zionism and the State of Israel), and set out with renewed vigor to "save" Jews. Those active in these evangelical efforts may be Jews who have already embraced Christianity, or they may be people of non-Jewish ancestry who feel a need to bring Jews to Jesus. The group Jews for Jesus, headquartered in San Francisco, is noted for its pamphlets handed out on street corners and its prominent newspaper advertisements. Often the term "Jews for Jesus" is used in a generic sense, to refer to any group that seeks to evangelize Jews through similar tactics.

The few Jews who have been attracted to "Jews for Jesus" groups are, typically, people afflicted with a strong consciousness of sin. They seek the assurance of forgiveness that comes from commitment to a Savior who died on their behalf. Judaism, on the other hand, teaches that forgiveness comes from repentance directed to God, the Father in heaven.

Official Judaism does not recognize "Jews for Jesus" as belonging to the Jewish fellowship. Some of its members may be of ethnic Jewish ancestry but, if they take on a belief that redemption from sin can come only through a commitment to Jesus as the Anointed Son of God and Savior, then they are no longer Jews but Christians. They have a right to adopt this commitment, but it is incompatible with Judaism as most people understand it.

Sources

Adamson, Joe. *Groucho, Harpo, Chico and Sometimes Zeppo.* New York: Simon & Schuster, 1973.

The American Rabbinate: A Century of Continuity and Change. Edited by J. R. Marcus and A. J. Peck. Hoboken, N.J.: Ktav, 1985.

Ansen, David. "Spielberg's Obsession." *Newsweek,* December 20, 1993.

Appel, John J. "The *Trefa* Banquet." *Commentary,* February 1966.

Baum, C. P. Hyman, and S. Michel. *The Jewish Woman in America.* New York: Dial, 1976.

Berkow, Ira. *Maxwell Street: Survival in a Bazaar.* Garden City, N.Y.: Doubleday, 1977.

Birmingham, Stephen. *Our Crowd.* New York: Harper & Row, 1967.

Carlson, Margaret. "The Law According to Ruth." *Time Magazine,* June 28, 1993.

"Chronicle: Brando Angers Jewish Groups." *New York Times,* April 9, 1996.

Davis, David Brion. "The Slave Trade and the Jews." *New York Review of Books,* December 22, 1994, and March 2, 1995.

"Donations to a Jewish Philanthropy Ebb." *New York Times,* December 27, 1995.

Eichhorn, David Max. *Jewish Folklore in America.* Middle Village, N.Y.: Jonathan David, 1996.

The Encyclopedia of New York City. Edited by K. T. Jackson. New Haven: Yale University Press, 1995.

Epstein, Melech. *Profiles of Eleven.* Detroit: Wayne State University Press, 1965.

Feuerlicht, Roberta Strauss. *The Fate of the Jews.* New York: Times Books, 1983.

Gabler, Neal. *An Empire of Their Own: How the Jews Invented Hollywood.* New York: Crown, 1988.

"Georgia Pardons Victim 70 Years After Lynching." *New York Times,* March 12, 1986.

Glazer, Nathan. "Herbert H. Lehman of New York." *Commentary,* May 1963.

Gompers, Samuel. *Seventy Years of Life and Labor.* New York: Dutton, 1925.

Goren, Arthur. *New York Jews and the Quest for Community.* New York: Columbia University Press, 1970.

Grant, James. *Bernard Baruch: The Adventures of a Wall Street Legend.* New York: Simon & Schuster, 1983.

Hapgood, Hutchins. *The Spirit of the Ghetto.* New York: Funk & Wagnalls, 1965.

Howe, Irving. *World of Our Fathers.* New York: Harcourt Brace Jovanovich, 1976.

The Jewish Question: A Selection of the Articles Published by Mr. Henry Ford's Paper. Paris: Editions R.I.S.S., 1931.

Jews in the South. Edited by L. Dinnerstein and M. D. Palsson. Baton Rouge: Louisiana State University Press, 1973.

Joselit, Jenna Weissman. *The Wonders of America: Reinventing Jewish Culture, 1880–1950.* New York: Hill & Wang, 1994.

Katcher, Leo. *The Big Bankroll: The Life and Times of Arnold Rothstein.* New York: Harper, 1958.

Koppman, L., and B. Postal. *Guess Who's Jewish in American History.* New York: Shapolsky, 1986.

Korn, Bertram W. *The Early Jews of New Orleans.* Waltham, Mass.: American Jewish Historical Society, 1969.

Learsi, Rufus. *The Jews in America.* Cleveland: World, 1954.

Levine, Peter. *Ellis Island to Ebbets Field.* New York: Oxford University Press, 1992.

Levinson, Nancy Smiler. *I Lift My Lamp: Emma Lazarus and the Statue of Liberty.* New York: Dutton, 1986.

Like All the Nations? The Life and Legacy of Judah L. Magnes. Edited by W. M. Brinner and M. Rischin. Albany: State University of New York Press, 1987.

Logan, Andy. *Against the Evidence.* New York: McCall, 1970.

Marcus, Jacob Rader. *Early American Jewry.* 2 volumes. Philadelphia: Jewish Publication Society, 1951, 1953.

———. *Memoirs of American Jews.* 3 volumes. Philadelphia: Jewish Publication Society, 1955.

Mason, A. T. *Brandeis: A Free Man's Life.* New York: Viking, 1946.

"Meir Kahane, 58, Militant and Founder of the Jewish Defense League." *New York Times,* November 6, 1990.

Meyer, Annie Nathan. *It's Been Fun.* New York: Henry Schuman, 1951.

Riis, Jacob. *How the Other Half Lives.* New York: Scribner, 1890.

Rosenberg, Roy A. *The Concise Guide to Judaism.* New York: Meridian, 1994.

Sachar, Howard M. *A History of the Jews in America.* New York: Knopf, 1992.

Sanders, Ronald. *The Downtown Jews.* New York: Harper & Row, 1969.

"A Sensation at Saratoga—New Rules for the Grand Union." *New York Times,* June 19, 1877.

Spalding, Henry. *Encyclopedia of Jewish Humor*. New York: Jonathan David, 1969.

Telushkin, Joseph. *Jewish Humor*. New York: Morrow, 1992.

Vorspan, Albert. *Giants of Justice*. New York: Union of American Hebrew Congregations, 1960.

Wald, Lillian. *House on Henry Street*. New York: Holt, 1915.

Weiss, Philip. "Letting Go." *New York Magazine*, January 29, 1996.

Wexler, Alice. *Emma Goldman: An Intimate Life*. New York: Pantheon, 1984.

Winter, William. *The Life of David Belasco*. New York: Moffat, Yard, 1918.

"With Big Money and Brash Ideas, a Billionaire Redefines Charity." *New York Times*, December 17, 1996.

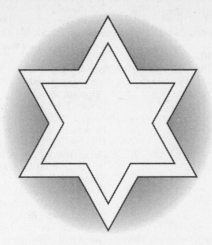

Index

ABC, 173
Abdullah, King of Jordan, 187
Abolitionists, 21, 50
Abraham and Straus, 147
Adler, Cyrus, 119
Adler, Felix, 63
Advisory Committee on Uranium, 180
AFL, 71, 102, 104, 199
AFL-CIO, 104, 199
Aguilar Free Library Society, 87
Albert, Marv, 165
Alcott, Amy, 93
Alexander, Moses, 127
Algebra Project, 211
Allen, Mel, 165
Allen, Woody, 158
Altman, Sidney, 133
Altman's, 147
Amalgamated Clothing Workers, 104, 105, 140–41, 143
Amalgamated Meat Cutters, 142

America First Committee, 166
American, Sadie, 159–60
American Broadcasting System (ABC), 173
American Civil Liberties Union, 210
American Federation of Labor (AFL), 71, 102, 104, 199
American Israel Public Affairs Committee (AIPAC), 219
American Jew as Patriot, Soldier and Citizen, The (Wolf), 58
American Jewish Committee, 75, 116–18, 120–21, 122, 175, 176, 195–96, 218, 219
American Jewish Conference, 184
American Jewish Congress, 175, 176, 195–96, 219
American Jewish Relief Committee, 122
American Labor party, 98
American Smelting and Refining Company, 113–14

Anarchists, 82, 96
Anshe Emeth (Albany), 34
Anthony, Susan B., 163
Anti-Defamation League, 116, 135, 195–96
Anti-Semitism, 92, 107, 118, 148–51, 153, 165–66, 181, 193, 201
  "blood libel," 38–39, 150–51
  during Civil War, 51–54, 57
  in Europe, 38–39, 68, 74, 77, 116–17
  myth of world-wide Jewish conspiracy, 224
  restricted facilities, 60–64
Appetizing stores, 223
"Ararat," 27–28
Architects, 214–15
Arens, Moshe, 188–89
Artists, 87, 208
Asch, Sholem, 97
Ashkenazic Jews and Judaism, 4, 239
  first American congregation, 32
  see also names of individuals and congregations
Athletes, *see individual sports and athletes;* Sports
Atlanta, Georgia, 134–35, 193–94
Atomic energy, 132, 179–81
Atomic weapons, 180–81
  the Rosenbergs and, 182–84
A. T. Stewart and Company, *see* Stewart and Company, A. T.
Auerbach, Red, 90

Bache, 73
Baer, Max, 89
Balaban, Barney, 145
Balfour Declaration, 111
Bamberger, Simon, 127
Bankers, 53, 58–61, 63, 73–76, 224
Bar mitvah celebrations, 220–22
Barnard College, 162
Barsimson, Jacob, 10–11
Bartholdi, Frédéric Auguste, 69
Baruch, Bernard, 130–32
Baruch, Simon, 129
Baruch College of the City University of New York, 134
Baruch Plan, 132
Baseball, 90–91, 93
Basketball, 89–90

Baskin, Leonard, 208
Bat mitvah, 221
Begin, Menachem, 189
Belasco, David, 76–77
Bellow, Saul, 133, 203
Benderly, Samson, 122
Ben-Gurion, David, 187
Benjamin, Judah P., 52–54
Benjamin on Sales, 54
Benny, Jack, 158
Berger, Victor, 88, 108
Berkman, Alexander, 82
Berkow, Ira, 144–45
Berle, Milton, 158
Berlin, Irving (né Israel Baline), 155
Bernstein, Leonard, 156
Beth El, Congregation (Albany), 33–34
Beth Elohim (Charleston), 18
Beth Shalom (Richmond), 15
Bingham, Theodore, 120
"Bintl Brief," 98–99
"Black Death" in Europe, 68
Blacks:
  civil rights movement, 193–97
  -Jewish tensions in 1960s, 197–99
  as Jews, 241, 242
  slavery, *see* Slavery
"Blood libel," 38–39, 150–51
Bloomingdale's, 147
Bnai Brith, 58, 115–16, 134, 135, 219
Bnai Jeshurun Synagogue (New York City), 39, 50
Board of Delegates of American Israelites, 38, 40, 51
Board of Delegates of Civil and Religious Rights, 58
Boesky, Ivan, 204
Boxing, 88–89, 145
Brandeis, Louis, 103, 135–37, 217
Brandeis University, 137
Brando, Marlon, 169
Brewster, Mary, 85
Brice, Fanny, 158
Brighton Beach, Brooklyn, 154
Britain:
  Chief Rabbi for, 239
  Palestine and, 184, 185, 188
Brit Shalom, 123
Broadcasting industry, 172–73
Brooks, Mel, 158
Brown, Denise Scott, 214

Brown University, 15–16
Brown vs. Board of Education, 196
Bruce, Lenny, 158
Bryant, William Cullen, 57
Buchalter, Louis ("Lepke"), 143, 204
Buchanan, James, 42
Buffalo Historical Society, 27
Burns, George, 158
Byrnes, James F., 105, 132

Cabinet secretaries, 72, 144, 200, 218, 219
Caesar, Sid, 158
Cahan, Abraham, 81, 95–98, 142, 228–29
California, 126, 154
   Gold Rush, 59, 146
Cantor, Eddie, 158
Capone, Al, criminal organization of, 144, 145–46
Cardozo, Benjamin, 67, 160
Carew, Rod, 93
Carter, Jimmy, 210, 219
Catholic Church, 40
CBS, 144, 173
Center on Crime, Communities and Culture, 211
Central Conference of American Rabbis, 35
Central Park zoo, 218
Central Relief Committee, 122
Chaney, James, 196–97
Charitable giving, *see* Philanthropy
Charities, *see* Philanthropy
Charleston, South Carolina, 12, 15–16, 18
Chicago, Illinois, 144–45
"Chief Rabbis," 83, 239–40
China, Jews of, 241
Chinese food, 226
Chrysler Corporation, 216
Church of England, 14, 24
CIO, 104, 199
Circumcision, 241
City College of New York (CCNY), 87, 130
City University of New York, 205
Civil and human rights, 2, 58, 175
"Civil religion," 242–43
Civil rights movement, 193–97
Civil War period, 49–58, 59

anti-Semitism during, 51–54, 57
   General Order No. 11, 55–56
   Jews in armed forces during, 58
   military chaplains during, 50–51
   secessionists, 41, 49, 50, 52–53
Cleveland, Grover, 72
Clinton, Bill, 209
Clubs, restricted, 60–61, 64
Cohen, Henry, 124–25
Cohen, Mickey, 192
Cohen, Morris Raphael, 87
Cohn, Harry, 168–69, 171
Colonial period, 5, 10–23
Colorado Smelting and Refining Company, 113–14
Columbia Broadcasting System (CBS), 144, 173
Columbia College, 18, 161, 162
Columbia Pictures, 168, 171
Columbia University, 209
Comedians, 157–58, 230–31
Commentary, 229
"Committee of Seventy," 63
Communists, 98, 140–42
   see also Soviet Union
Comstock Lode, Virginia, 127
Confederacy, 49, 51–54
Conference of Presidents of Major American Jewish Organizations, 219–20
Congress, U.S., 117
   lobbying groups on behalf of Israel, 219–20
   see also House of Representatives, U.S.; Senate, U.S.
Congressional Gold Medal of Achievement, 205
Congress of Industrial Organizations (CIO), 104, 199
Conley, Jim, 134, 135
Conservative Judaism, 75, 117, 118–19, 121, 202, 231, 236, 241
   defining beliefs and practices of, 236–38
Constitution, U.S., 23–24, 163
Continental Congress, 22, 23
Conversion to Judaism, 231, 233, 240–41
Copland, Aaron, 155–56
Corporate America, discrimination in, 214–15

Cosell, Howard, 165
Council of National Defense, Advisory Commission of the, 131
Cousins, Norman, 165
Craftsmen, 18
Crime and criminals, 120, 122, 142–43, 144, 145–46, 191–93, 204

Damascus Affair, 38–39, 151
Dance to Death, The (Lazarus), 68, 69
Davis, David Brion, 20
Davis, Jefferson, 49, 53, 54
Davis, Sammy, Jr., 158
Day of Atonement, *see* Yom Kippur
Dearborn Independent, 131, 148–49, 150
Debs, Eugene, 88, 96, 97, 106
Decter, Midge, 229
DeLeon, Daniel, 96, 102
Delicatessen, Jewish, 222–23
Democratic party, identification with, 216–18
Department stores, 146–47
Dewey, Melvil, 161
Diamond, Legs, mob lead by, 142
Diaspora, 2, 5
Dietary laws, 66–67, 83, 226, 233, 235
Doctorow, E. L., 203
Drexel Burnham Lambert, 204
Dubinsky, David, 97, 104, 141
Du Pont Corporation, 215–16

Eastern European Jews, 3, 87, 95–98, 153, 174, 195, 236
  cuisine of, 222
  immigration of, 5, 75, 77–79
  intellectual offspring of, 228–29
  political affiliation of, 216–17
  see also names of individuals
Edison, Thomas, 167
Education, 72–73, 86–88
  admission quotas of colleges and universities, 214
  religious, 121–22
  valuing of, 225, 228–29
  of women, 114–15, 161, 162
Educational Alliance, 72–73, 86–88, 172
Egyptian Jews, 2, 153
Einhorn, David, 50
Einstein, Albert, 169, 179–80, 181
Eisenman, Peter, 214

Emanu-El, Temple (New York City), 32, 60, 68, 117, 118, 121, 173–74
Emerson, Ralph Waldo, 68
Engineers, 214
England, Jews of, 2, 17
Entebbe rescue mission, 189
Epstein, Melech, 108–109, 110, 112
Epstein, Sir Jacob, 87, 208
Espionage, 183–84, 206–207
Espionage Act, 107–108
Ethical Culture Society, 63
Ethiopian Jews, 241, 242
Ethnic community, Jews as, 1–2
Exclusionary policies, *see* Restricted facilities

Farband, 220
FBI, 143, 183, 197, 207
Federal Reserve System, 74
Federation of American Zionists, 138–39
Federation of Jewish Philanthropies, 122, 227
Feinstein, Moshe, 84
Feminine Mystique, The (Friedan), 201
Feminism, 158–60, 201, 233–34, 235–36
Feuerlicht, Roberta Strauss, 197–99
Filene's, 147
Filmmakers, *see* Movie industry
First Congress of Jewish Women, 159
Flamingo Hotel, 192
Florida during Civil War, 52–53
Food:
  Chinese, 226
  Jewish, 222–23
Football, 91–92
Ford, Gerald, 200
Ford, Henry, 118, 131, 148–50
Frank, Leo, 116, 118, 134–35
Franks, David, 19–20
Franks, Jacob, 19
Freed, James Ingo, 214
Free Synagogue, 174
French and Indian War, 19
Frick, Henry Clay, 82
Friedan Betty, 201
Friedlander, Israel, 225
Friedman, Benny, 91
Fur traders, 20
Fur Workers Union, 141–42

Gabler, Neal, 167, 170–71
Galveston, Texas, 124–25
Gangsters, *see* Crime and criminals
Garment industry, 78–79, 113, 114, 136, 140–42, 143
Gehry, Frank, 214
George, Henry, 96
Georgia, 16
German Jews, 3, 51, 63, 73, 78, 87, 118, 119, 120, 124, 175, 195, 234, 236
    immigration of, 5, 31–32
    political affiliation, 216, 217
    in Western states, 127
    see also names of individuals
Gershwin, George, 155
Gershwin, Ira, 155
Gimbel's, 147
Ginsburg, Ruth Bader, 209–10
Glashow, Sheldon, 133
Glazer, Nathan, 218
Glickman, Marty, 92–93
Gold, Ben, 141–42
Goldberg, Arthur, 144, 199–200
Goldberg, Joseph, 144
Goldberg, Marshall, 91–92
Goldberger, Joseph, 191
Goldenson, Leonard, 173
Goldfogle, Henry, 106, 110, 111–12
Goldman, Emma, 81–82
Goldman, Sachs, 73
Gold Rush, 59, 146
Goldstein, Baruch, 190
Goldwater, Barry, 126
Goldwater, Michael, 126
Golf, 93
Gomez, Mordecai, 19
Gompers, Samuel, 71–72, 102
Goodman, A. V., 35
Goodman, Andrew, 196–97
Goodman, Benny, 145
Goodman, David, 144–45
Goodman, Paul, 229
Gordin, Jacob, 97
Gottheil, Gustav, 68
Governors, first Jewish, 127–28
Grand Island, 27
Grand Union Hotel, Saratoga Springs, 61–64
Grant, Ulysses S., 55–56, 59, 115–16
Gratz, Rebecca, 31
Greenberg, Hank, 90

Greenglass, David, 183
Greenglass, Ethel, *see* Rosenberg, Ethel
"Greenhorns," 77–78
Greenwald, Gerald, 216
Gross, Chaim, 87
Guggenheim, Daniel, 113–14
Guggenheim, Meyer, 113
Guggenheim family, 113–14, 119
Guggenheim Fund for the Promotion of Aeronautics, 114
Guggenheim Memorial Foundation, John Simon, 114
Guggenheim Museum, Solomon R., 114
Guzik, Jake "Greasy Thumb", 144, 145–46
Guzik, Max, 144

Hadassah, 139
Hadassah Hospital, Jerusalem, 139
Hadassah Study Circle, 139
Haganah, 187, 188
Halaka, 231–32, 233, 237
Hammerstein, Oscar, II, 156
Hapgood, Hutchins, 94–95, 96
Harding, Warren G., 108
Harlem, New York City, 106, 107
Har Sinai (Baltimore), 32, 50
Hart, Lorenz, 156
Hart, Schaffner and Marx, 104, 113
Hasidim, 153, 238–39
Hattiesburg, Mississippi, 194–95
Hays, Catherine, 24–25
Hays, Moses Michael, 24–25
Hebrew, 3
Hebrew Emigrant Aid Society, 68
Hebrew Free School Association, 87
Hebrew Immigrant Aid Society, 227
Hebrew Scriptures, 1917 translation of, 128–29
Hebrew Union College, 34–35, 65, 66, 118, 121, 128, 174, 184, 202, 234
Hebrew University, Jerusalem, 123
Hellman, Lillian, 182
Henry Street Settlement, 85–86, 218
Heschel, Abraham Joshua, 84
Hillel Foundation, 116
Hillman, Sidney, 97, 104–105, 132, 141, 143
Hillquit, Morris, 105–108, 111

Hilton, Henry, 61–63
Histadrut, 186
History of the Jews in America, The (Sachar), 6
Hollywood, *see* Movie industry
Hollywood Ten, 181–82
Holman, Nat, 89–90
Holocaust, 80, 153, 175–76, 205, 206, 208, 224, 239, 242–43
Holocaust Museum, 206, 243
Holzman, Red, 90
Homosexuality, beliefs about, 233, 236
Hook, Sidney, 229
Hotels and motels, exclusionary policies of, 61–64
Houdini, Harry (né Ehrich Weiss), 151–52
House of Representatives, U.S., 41, 72, 88, 108–12, 223
  Committee on Un-American Activities, 181, 182
Howe, Irving, 6, 141, 142, 157, 217, 228, 229
Howells, William Dean, 96
Human rights, 2, 58, 175
Humor, Jewish, 157–58, 230–31
Hyams, H. M., 53
Hylan, "Silent" John, 107

Idaho, 127
Ihud, 123
Immigrants and immigration, 5–6, 31–32, 58, 68–69, 75, 77–79, 80, 117, 153–54, 211
  advancement of immigrant women, 114–15
  "Americanization" of, 75, 87
  geographic dispersal of, 124–25
  1924 legislation restricting, 6, 58, 77, 153
  post-1924, 153–54
  social services for, 72–73, 80, 83–86, 159
  Western settlers, 126
India, Jews of, 241
In My Father's Court (Singer), 202
Inquisition, Spanish, 4–5
Intellectuals, 228–29
Intermarriage, 231, 236, 243–45
International Council of Women, 160

International Jew, The, 148–49
International Ladies Garment Workers Union (ILGWU), 102–103, 104, 105, 108, 141, 217
International Literary Prize for Peace, 205
International White Slave Traffic Conference, 160
Iranian Jews, 154
Irving, Washington, 31
Isaac Elchanan Yeshiva, 83
Isaacs, Isaiah, 18
Isaacson, Walter, 165
Israel, 153, 192–93, 197, 205, 242
  chief rabbis in, 239
  espionage and, 206–207
  establishment as state, 186–87
  Israelis settling in the United States, 154
  Knesset, 190
  Law of Return, 192
  lobbying groups in U.S. on behalf of, 219–20
  Soviet Jews emigrating to, 154
  war of independence, 187–89
  Yom Kippur War, 200
  see also Palestine
Israelite, 34
Ivanhoe (Scott), 30–31

Jackson, Andrew, 25
Jackson-Vanik amendment, 153
Jacobson, Eddie, 185–86
J. & W. Seligman and Company, *see* Seligman and Company, J. & W.
Japan:
  Hiroshima, 181
  Russo-Japanese War, 74
Japanese-Americans, 118
  during World War II, 56
Jazz Singer, The, 170
Jefferson, Thomas, 14, 29
Jerusalem, 25, 26
Jewish Agency, 186–87
Jewish Agency for Palestine, 118
Jewish-American life, aspects of, 214–45
Jewish Community Centers, 123
Jewish Daily Forward, 81, 96–100, 103, 110, 203, 205, 226, 228–29
  "Bintl Brief," 98–99

Jewish Defense League, 189–90
Jewish Encyclopedia, The, 128
Jewish identity, defining of, 231, 233, 236, 240
Jewish Institute of Religion, 174
Jewish International Conference on the Suppression of Traffic in Girls and Women, 160
Jewish Labor Committee, 220
Jewish Publication Society, 128–29, 138
Jewish state:
  Israel, *see* Israel
  Palestine, *see* Palestine
  plan to establish, within United States, 26–28
Jewish Territorial Organization, 124, 125
Jewish Theological Seminary, 75, 117–19, 128, 202, 218, 236
Jewish War Veterans of the USA, 219–20
Jewish Welfare Board, 122–23
Jewish Workers Association, 101–105
"Jews for Jesus", 245–46
Johnson, Lyndon B., 200
Joint Distribution Committee, 122, 227
Joint Distribution Committee of American Funds for Relief of Jewish War Sufferers, 75
Jong, Erica, 203
Joselit, Jenna Weissman, 221
Joseph, Rabbi Jacob, 83
Journalists, 164–65

Kahane, Meir, 189–90
Kahn, Louis I., 214
Kahn, Otto, 74
Kaplan, Mordecai, 121, 123, 225, 237–38
Kashrut, laws of, 3
Kaskel, Cesar, 56
Kaufmann, Jacob, 147
Kaufmann's, 147
Kaye, Danny, 158
Kazin, Alfred, 229
Kennedy, John F., 200
Kern, Jerome, 156
King, Larry, 164
King, Dr. Martin Luther, Jr., 194
King James Bible, 129

Kissinger, Henry, 200–201
Klutznick, Philip, 219
Know-Nothing party, 33
Knudsen, William, 132
Kohn, Abraham, 35–37
Kohut, Rebekah, 159
Kosher food, 66–67, 83, 226, 233
Koufax, Sandy, 91
Krickstein, Aaron, 93
Kristol, Irving, 229
Kuhn, Abraham, 73
Kuhn, Loeb and Company, 73–74
Ku Klux Klan, 194, 196–97
Kushner, Tony, 204

Labor unions, *see* Unions
Ladino, 3
Laemmle, Carl, 166–68
La Guardia, Fiorello, 174
Landers, Ann, 164
Landsmanschaften, 79–80
Languages spoken by Jews, 3
Lansky, Meyer, 191–93
Las Vegas casinos, 192
Law school quotas, 215
Lazarus, Emma, 67–70, 159, 160
Lazarus, Josephine, 159
Lee, Robert E., 54
Leeser, Isaac, 37–38, 39, 129
Legislators, *see* Politicians and legislators
Lehman, Herbert, 217–18
Lehman Brothers, 73
Lelyveld, Arthur, 196
Lemlich, Clara, 102, 103
Leonard, Benny, 88–89
Lerner, Alan Jay, 156
Levenson, Sam, 158
Levin, Lewis C., 32–33
Levine, Dennis, 204
Levine, Jack, 208
Levinsky, Abe ("Battling"), 88
Levi Strauss and Company, 146
Levitt, William, 190
Levittown, New York, 190
Levy, Asser, 10–11
Levy, Marv, 91
Levy, Uriah Phillips, 28–30
Lewis, Anthony, 165
Lewis, Jerry, 158
Liberal party, 98

Lieberman, Nancy, 90
Liebman, Joshua Loth, 84
Likud party, 189
Lincoln, Abraham, 37, 49, 51, 56
Lindbergh, Charles, 114, 166
Lindo, Moses, 15–16
"Little Odessa," 154
Lobbying groups, 219–20
Loeb, Carl M., 73
Loeb, Fanny Kuhn, 73
Loeb, Solomon, 73
Loeb, Therese, 73
Loeb, Rhodes and Company, 73
Loewe, Frederick, 156
London, Meyer, 108–12
Lopez, Aaron, 12, 19, 21
Los Alamos laboratory, 180, 183
Louisiana, 52–53, 54
Lowell, James Russell, 70
Lower East Side, New York City,
        77–79, 83–86, 87, 94–95, 106,
        112, 114–15, 122, 217
    Triangle Shirtwaist fire, 99–101
Lubavitcher sect of Hasidim, 238–39
Luckman, Sid, 92
Lumbrozo, Jacob, 18
Lynchings, 134–35

McCoy, Al (né Harry Rudolph), 88
McKinley, William, 125, see Unions,
        strikes
Macy department store, R. H., 72
Macy's, 147
Madison, James, 22, 23
Magicians, 151–52
Magnes, Judah, 121–23, 225
Mailer, Norman, 203
Maimonides College, 38
Malamud, Bernard, 203
Manhattan Project, 180, 183
Mann, Alonzo, 135
Mantinband, Charles, 194–95
Mapai (Israeli labor party), 187
Marcus, David ("Mickey"), 188
Marcus, Jacob R., 6, 23
Marriage:
    conversion and, 241
    intermarriage, 231, 236, 243–45
Marshall, Louis, 103, 117, 119, 120,
        173
Marx, Marcus, 113

Marx Brothers, 157–58
Maryland, 24, 50
Mason, A. T., 137
Mason, Jackie, 158
Massena, New York, "blood libel" in,
        151
Maxwell Street; Survival in a Bazaar
        (Berkow), 144
Mayer, Louis B., 167, 168
Medical school quotas, 215
Meier, Richard, 214–15
Meir, Golda, 186–87, 188
Merchants, 19–20, 55–56, 58–59, 63,
        126
    department stores, 146–47
    see also names of individuals
Messiah, coming of the, 235, 238–39
Metro-Goldwyn-Mayer (MGM), 167,
        168
Metropolitan Opera, 74
Meyer, Dr. Alfred, 160–61
Meyer, Annie Nathan, 160–63
Michelbacher, Maximilian J., 52
Michelson, Albert Abraham, 132–34
Mikveh Israel (Philadelphia), 18,
        22–23, 37, 40
Mikveh Israel (Savannah), 17–18
Miller, Arthur, 204
Mining, 113–14
    Gold Rush, 59, 146
Minis, Abigail, 19
Mission of Israel, doctrine of, 235
Mitchel, John, 107
Moetzet ha Poalot, 186
Monticello (Jefferson home), 29
Morais, Sabato, 118
Morgan, J. P., Sr., 74
Morgenthau, Henry, 216
Morgenthau, Henry, Jr., 218
Moroccan Jews, 153
Morris, Robert, 21, 22
Mortara case, 39–40
Moses, Hannah, 19
Moses, Robert, 143–44
Moss, Eric Owen, 214
Most, Johann, 82
Mostel, Zero, 158
Mothers, Jewish identity transmitted
        through, 233
Movie industry, 165–71, 207–208, 223
    Hollywood Ten, 181–82

Ms. magazine, 201
Muni, Paul, 145
"Murder Incorporated," 143
Musicians, 155–56
Myers, Myer, 18
Myerson, Morris, 186

NAACP, 118, 195
National Association for Public
    Health Nursing, 86
National Association for the
    Advancement of Colored People
    (NAACP), 118, 195
National Broadcasting Company
    (NBC), 172
National Council of Jewish Women,
    158–60, 220
National Defense Research
    Committee, 180
National Jewish Community Relations
    Advisory Council, 220
National Jewish Welfare Board, 220
National Organization for Women, 201
Nation of Islam, 20
Native American party, 32–33
Nativism, 32–33, 124
Navasky, Victor, 165
Navy, U.S., 28–30, 145
Nazi Germany, 92, 175, 181, 224
    refugees from, 153, 180
    see also Holocaust
NBC, 172
"Near churches" phrase in real estate
    advertisements, 152–53
Neoconservatism, 229
Netanyahu, Benjamin ("Bibi"), 189
Netanyahu, Yonatan, 189
Nevelson, Louise, 208
New Amsterdam, 5, 10–11
"New Colossus, The," 69–70
New Deal, *see* Roosevelt, Franklin D.,
    New Deal
New Orleans, Louisiana, 25, 64
Newport, Rhode Island, 11–15
    first synagogue in, *see* Yeshuat Israel
    (Newport)
New York City, New York, 12, 73, 125,
    129, 153
    Board of Education, 198
    "Chief Rabbi" of, 83
    "Committee of Seventy," 63

delicatessens and appetizing stores
    in, 222, 223
"Kehilla," 119–23
Lower East Side, *see* Lower East
    Side, New York City
mayoral races, 107, 174
public school system, 115
Tammany Hall, *see* Tammany Hall
teachers' strikes of 1960s, 197–99
urban renewal projects in, 143–44
*see also names of individual
    congregations*
New York Civil Liberties Union, 199
New York *Commercial Advertiser,* 96
New York *Evening Post,* 57
New York Magazine, 223
New York Public Library, 162
New York State, 24
    urban renewal projects in, 143–44
New York Times, The, 62, 163–64, 189
Nixon, Richard, 200
Noah, Mordecai Manuel, 26
Nobel Prize winners, 132–34, 180,
    200, 202–203, 205–206
Non-Sectarian Anti-Nazi League, 175
North Carolina, 24
Northern European Jews, *see*
    Ashkenazic Jews
Novelists, 202–203

Occident and American Jewish Advocate, 38
Occupations, 223–24
    during Colonial period, 18–20
    of Western settlers, 126
    see also specific occupations
Ocean Hill-Brownsville district school
    board, 198–99
Ochs, Adolph, 163
O'Connor, Sandra Day, 209
Office of Foreign Relief and
    Rehabilitation, 217–18
Oglethorpe, James, 16
Olsen, Tillie, 203
Olympics, 92, 93
Oppenheimer, J. Robert, 180
Orgen, Jacob ("Little Augie"), mob
    led by, 142
Orthodox Jews and Judaism, 3, 153,
    202, 216, 221, 225, 241
    defining beliefs and practices of,
    231–34

Oswald, Lee Harvey, 145
Ozick, Cynthia, 203

Palestine, 27, 123, 187–88
  Balfour Declaration, 111
  British control of, 184, 185
  Jewish settlement of, 118, 139–40
  United Nations vote to partition, 185
  see also Israel
Palestinians, 197, 205
Paley, Grace, 203
Paley, Samuel, 144
Paley, William, 144, 173
Panama, 61
Panama Canal, 61
Paramount Pictures, 145, 166, 168
Partisan Review, 203, 229
Pearlstine, Norman, 165
Peddlers, 35–37, 58, 78
Peixotto, Benjamin Franklin, 115–16
Pennsylvania, 23
People's Relief Committee, 122
Perelman, S. J., 158
Peretz, Martin, 165
Phagan, Mary, 134
Philadelphia, Pennsylvania, 12
  see also names of individual congregations
Philanthropy, 73, 75, 85, 114, 127, 210–11
  Jewish charities, fund raising by, 122–23, 226–28
Phillips, Eugenia Levy, 41
Phillips, Philip, 41–42
Pierce, Franklin, 54
Playwrights, 204
Podhoretz, Norman, 229
Poets, 67–70
Pogroms, 68
Polio vaccine, 191
Politicians and legislators, 17, 52–54, 72–73, 88, 104, 105–108, 127–28, 217–28, 223
  right to hold political office, 24
  see also names of legislative bodies and individuals
Pollard, Jonathan, 206–207
Polygamy, 4
Population, Jewish:
  of New York City, 80

power and wealth of, 223–25
  of United States, 5, 134, 223
  world, 27
Power elite, 223–25
Prayer books, 37–38, 238
Presidential advisers, 130, 174, 200–201
President's Commission on the Holocaust, 206
Priesand, Sally, 202
Privateering, 19
Professions, restrictions on entry into the, 214–15
Progressive revelation, doctrine of, 235
Prohibition, 145, 149, 191–92
Prostitution, 160
Protocols of the Elders of Zion, The, 148
Provident Loan Society, 75
Provisional Executive Committee for General Zionist Affairs, 136
Public accommodations, restrictive policies of, 60–64
Public health, 85–86, 129, 191
Pulitzer, Joseph, 69
Pushcarts, 78
Putting Farming on a Modern Business Basis, 131

Rabbinic seminaries, 34–35, 83, 202, 236
Rabbis:
  "Chief Rabbis," 83, 239–40
  civil rights movement and Southern, 193–95
  female, 202, 234, 236, 237
  prominent, 84, 173–76
Racial makeup of Jewish population, 241–42
Racketeers, *see* Crime and criminals
Radio, growth of, 172–73
Radio Corporation of America (RCA), 172, 173
Rahv, Philip, 229
Railroads, financing of the, 74
Raphall, Morris Jacob, 50
Rauschenberg, Robert, 208
RCA, 172, 173
Real estate advertisements, "near churches" phrase in, 152–53
Real estate developers, 190

Rebbes, 238
Reconstructionist movement, 123, 237–38, 241
Reconstructionist Rabbinical College, 202
Reformed Society of Israelites, 41
Reform Judaism, 34, 41, 66, 202, 221, 241
  defining beliefs and practices of, 234–36
  dietary laws and, 66–67, 235
  first American congregation, 32, 50
Religious freedom during Colonial period, 14–15, 23–24
Reminiscences (Wise), 33–34
Republican party, 216, 218
Restricted facilities, 60–64
Restrictive covenants, 153
Revolutionary War, 12, 19–20, 21–23
Rhode Island College (later Brown University), 15–16
Rice, Grantland, 91
Richmond, Virginia, 15
Rickover, Abraham, 144, 145
Rickover, Admiral Hyman G., 145
Riis, Jacob, 79, 86
Rise of David Levinsky, The (Cahan), 96
Rockefellers, 113–14
Rodef Shalom (Philadelphia), 32
Rodgers, Richard, 156
Rodriguez Rivera, Jacob, 12, 19, 21
Romanian Jews, 58, 116–17, 222
Romberg, Sigmund, 156
Roosevelt, Franklin D., 98, 104, 105, 131–32, 174, 180, 217, 219
  Holocaust and, 175–76
  New Deal, 88, 111, 218
Roosevelt, Theodore, 72, 74
Roseanne, 158
Rosenberg, Ethel, 182–84
Rosenberg, Harold, 229
Rosenberg, Julius, 182–84
Rosenfeld, Morris, 99–101
Rosenthal, A. M., 165
Rosenwald, Julius, 147
Ross, Barney, 89, 145
Roth, Henry, 203
Roth, Philip, 203
Rothko, Mark, 208
Rothschild, Jacob M., 193–94
Rothschild, Salomon de, 53

Rothschild banking house, 53
Rothstein, Arnold, 142
Ruby, Jack, 145
Russia, 72, 74, 116–17
  pogroms in, 68, 77, 116
  Russo-Japanese War, 74
  see also Soviet Union
Russian-American Treaty of Commerce and Navigation of 1832, 117
Russian Jews, 58, 68, 77, 80, 120, 154
  geographic dispersal of, efforts at, 124–25

Sabbath, rules of the, 232–33, 235, 237
Sabin, Albert, 191
Sachar, Howard, 6, 146–47, 156, 201, 207
Safire, William, 165
Sahl, Mort, 158
Salam, Abdus, 133
Salk, Jonas, 191
Salomon, Haym, 21–23, 64
Salomon, Louis J., 64
Salvador, Francis, 17, 18
Samuelson, Paul, 133
Sanders, Ronald, 80
Sarnoff, David, 172–73
Savannah, Georgia, 12, 16, 17–18
Savitt, Dick, 93
Schaffner, Joseph, 104, 113
Schayes, Danny, 90
Schayes, Dolph, 90
Schechter, Solomon, 119, 121
Schiff, Jacob, 73–76, 85, 103, 119, 120, 124, 195, 216
Schindler's List, 208
Schneerson, Menachem Mendel, 238–39
Schneiderman, Rose, 101
Schubert brothers, 77
Schuyler, Georgina, 70
Schwartz, Delmore, 203
Schwerner, Mickey, 196–97
Schwimmer, Adolf, 187–88
Scott, Sir Walter, 30–31
Sears, Roebuck, 147
Seattle, Washington, 153
Secret Relationship Between Blacks and Jews, The, 20

Seinfeld, Jerry, 158
Seixas, Gershom Mendes, 18, 160
Seligman, David, 58
Seligman, Fanny, 58
Seligman, James, 59, 61
Seligman, Jesse, 59, 60–61, 64
Seligman, Joseph, 58–63
Seligman and Company, J. & W., 58–61, 73
Senate, U.S., 52–53, 54, 218, 223
Sephardic Jews and Judaism, 4, 18, 51, 62–63, 153, 239
  see also names of individuals and congregations
Sermons, introduction of Sabbath, 38
Shahn, Ben, 87, 208
Shapiro, Irving, 215–16
Shapiro, Jacob ("Gurrah"), 143
Shearith Israel, see Spanish-Portuguese Synagogue (Shearith Israel) (New York City)
Sheftalls of Georgia, 20
Short story writers, 203
Siegel, Benjamin ("Bugsy"), 192
Sienkiewicz, Henryk, 126
Silver, Abba Hillel, 184–85
Simon, Neil, 204
Singer, Isaac Bashevis, 97, 202–203
Singer, Isidore, 128
Skullcap, wearing of, 232, 234, 237
Slavery, 50, 54
  abolitionists, 21, 50
  slave trade, 20–21
Smith, Al, 217
Socialist Labor party, 96, 101, 106
Socialist party, 88, 96–97, 105, 106, 107, 108–12, 216
Socialists and socialism, 88, 102, 105–12, 122, 140, 220
  democratic, 96–97, 98, 140
Solomon, Hannah G., 159
Sondheim, Stephen, 156
Songs of a Semite (Lazarus), 69
Sonneborn, Rudolf, 187
Sonneborn Institute, 187, 188
Soros, George, 210–11
South Carolina, 17
  Nullification Convention, 41
Southern Christian Leadership Conference, 197

Soviet Union:
  as Communist state, 82, 140, 224
  Jewish emigration from, 153–54
  the Rosenbergs and, 182–84
  see also Russia
Soyer, Isaac, 87
Soyer, Moses, 87, 208
Soyer, Raphael, 208
Spain, 3
  Inquisition in, 4–5
  see also Sephardic Jews
Spalding, Henry, 230
Spanish-Portuguese Synagogue (Shearith Israel) (New York City), 11, 17, 18, 39, 40, 63
Spielberg, Stephen, 207–208
Spies, 183–84, 206–207
Spirit of the Ghetto, The (Hapgood), 94, 96
Spitz, Mark, 93
Sports, 88–93
Sports broadcasters, 92–93
Sports journalists, 165
Springarn, Joel, 195
State Department, U.S., 26, 175, 218–19
Statue of Liberty, 67–70
Statutory Jurisdiction and Practice of the Supreme Court of the United States, The, 42
Steffens, Lincoln, 96
Steinem, Gloria, 201
Stern, Robert A. M., 214
Stewart and Company, A. T., 63–64
Stock traders, 130–31
Straus, Ida, 73
Straus, Isidor, 72–73
Straus, Lazarus, 147
Straus, Nathan, 72, 73
Straus, Oscar S., 72, 73
Strauss, Levi, 146
Strauss, Robert, 218
Strikes, see Unions, strikes
Stuyvesant, Peter, 10, 11
Suffrage, see Voting rights
Sullivan, "Big Tim," 142
Sunday school, 38
Supreme Court, U.S., 42, 54, 88, 118, 135, 210
  female justices, 209–10

justices, 67, 137, 144, 200, 201, 209–10, 217
    school desegregation and, 193, 196
Sutro, Adolph, 126–27
Sutro Tunnel, 126–27
Swimming, 93
Switzerland, U.S. treaty of 1855 with, 39, 40, 42
Szilard, Leo, 180, 181
Szold, Henrietta, 121, 138–40, 159

Tammany Hall, 96, 98, 106, 109, 110, 142, 216, 217
Taylor, Elizabeth, 158
Teachers, 115
    strikes of 1960s in New York City, 197–99
Television, growth of, 172–73
Tennis, 93
Theater, 158
    impresarios, 76–77
    Yiddish, 95
Theatrical Trust, 77
Theological seminary, first, 38
Tigerman, Stanley, 214
Touro, Judah, 24–26
Touro Synagogue (New Orleans), 25
Touro Synagogue (Newport), 68
Track and field, 92
Trade unions, See Unions
Trefa banquet, 65–67
Triangle Shirtwaist Company, fire at, 99–101
Trilling, Lionel, 229
Truman, Harry S, 105, 181, 219
    Zionists and, 185–86
Twain, Mark, 69
Tweed Ring, 63

Union League Club, 60–61, 64
Union of American Hebrew Congregations, 34, 40, 57–58, 65, 66
Unions, 71, 101–105, 108, 109–10, 122
    Communist alliances of, 140–42
    Cutters Local 4, 143
    elections and, 110
    preferential union shop, 103
    strikes, 82, 101–103, 104, 109, 136, 141, 142, 174, 197–99, 217
    see also names of individual unions
UNITE (Union of Needletrades, Industrial & Textile Employees), 105
United Air Lines, 216
United Brotherhood of Cloak Makers, 102
United Employee Acquisition Corporation, 216
United Garment Worker (UGW), 104
United Hebrew Trades, 101–102, 106
United Israel Appeal, 227
United Jewish Appeal (UJA), 193, 227–28
United Nations, 187, 197, 200
    Atomic Energy Commission, 132
    partition of Palestine and, 185
United Nations Relief and Rehabilitation Administration (UNRRA), 218
United Palestine Appeal, 227
U.S. Public Health Service, 191
Universal Studios, 166
Urban League, 195
Urban renewal, 143–44
Utah, 127

Van Buren, Abigail, 164
Versailles Peace Conference, 118, 131
Virginia, 14–15
Vorspan, Albert, 84, 125, 137
Voting rights:
    during Colonial period, 24
    for women, 162–63

Wald, Lillian, 83–86
Walker, Jimmy, 174
Wallace, Henry, 105
Wall Street scandals of 1980s, 204–205
Walt Disney studio, 169
Walters, Barbara, 164
Warburg, Felix, 74
Warburg, Paul, 74
Warburg bank, 74
Warburg family, 119
War Department, U.S., 55
Ward's Island, 68
War Industries Board, 131
Warner, Harry, 168, 169, 170
Warner, Jack, 168, 169–70

Warner, Sam, 170
Warner Brothers, 169–71
Washington, George, 13–14, 18
Wasserstein, Wendy, 204
Wealth and power, 223–25
Weil, Joseph "Yellow Kid," 145
Weinberg, Steven, 133
Weiss, Philip, 223–24
Weizmann, Chaim, 185–86
Welles, Orson, 223
West, Nathanael, 203
Western settlers, 126, 127, 146
Whitman, Walt, 69
Wiesel, Elie, 133, 205–206
Wigner, Eugene, 180
Williams, Roger, 12
Wilson, Woodrow, 107–108, 111, 131, 137, 174, 216–17
Winchell, Walter, 143
Wise, Isaac Mayer, 33–35, 39, 40, 65–66
Wise, Stephen, 135, 173–76, 184–85, 195
Wolf, Simon, 56, 57–58
Women:
    advancement of immigrant, 114–15
    education of, 114–15, 161, 162
    feminism, 158–60, 201, 233–34, 235–36
    Hasidic, 238
    Orthodox, 233–34
    as part of quorum for public prayer, 237
    as Prime Minister of Israel, 186–87, 188
    prominent, 138–40
    as rabbis, 202, 234, 236, 237
    seating in synagogue, 233, 234, 237
    Supreme Court justices, 209–10
    voting rights for, 162–63
Workmen's Circle, 220

World Jewish Congress, 175
World of Our Fathers (Howe), 6
World War I, 75, 122, 125
    opponents to U.S. entry into, 107, 111
World War II, 132, 166, 181, 218
    Japanese-Americans during, 56
Writers, 202–204
Written tradition, 239–40

Yalow, Rosalyn, 133
Yeshiva University, 83
Yeshuat Israel (Newport), 12–14, 17, 18, 24, 25
Yezierska, Anzia, 203
Yiddish, 3
Yiddish theater, 95
YMHAs, 123
Yom Kippur, 81, 130–31
Yom Kippur balls, 81
Young Israel (organization), 225
Young Israel synagogues, 225–26
Youngman, Henny, 158
Young Men's (and Young Women's) Hebrew Associations, 87, 123
Youth Aliyah, 140
Yulee, David Levy, 52–53
YWHAs, 87, 123

Zangwill, Israel, 124
Zhitlovsky, Hayim, 99
Zionism and Zionists, 27, 28, 111, 118, 121, 136–37, 138–40, 154, 174, 184–86, 220, 242
    see also Israel; Palestine; names of individuals and organizations
Zionist Organization of America, 137
Zorach, William, 87, 208
Zukor, Adolph, 166–68
Zworykin, Vladimir, 172